Bilingual Grammar

Does a bilingual person have two separate lexicons and two separate grammatical systems? Or should the bilingual linguistic competence be regarded as an integrated system? This book explores these questions, which are central to current debate in the study of bilingualism, and argues for an integrated hypothesis: the linguistic competence of an individual is a single cognitive module and the bilingual mind should not be regarded as fundamentally different from the monolingual one. This conclusion is supported with a variety of empirical data, in particular code-switching, drawn from a variety of bilingual pairs. López introduces key notions in minimalism and distributed morphology, making them accessible to readers with different scholarly foci. This book will be of interest to those working in linguistics and psycholinguistics, especially bilingualism, code-switching, and the lexicon.

LUIS LÓPEZ is a professor in the School of Literatures, Cultural Studies and Linguistics at the University of Illinois at Chicago. He has been the recipient of fellowships from the Alexander von Humboldt Foundation and the Fulbright Commission. He is the author of three books in theoretical linguistics and many articles.

Bilingual Grammar

Toward an Integrated Model

Luis López

University of Illinois at Chicago

CAMBRIDGE
UNIVERSITY PRESS

University Printing House, Cambridge CB2 8BS, United Kingdom

One Liberty Plaza, 20th Floor, New York, NY 10006, USA

477 Williamstown Road, Port Melbourne, VIC 3207, Australia

314-321, 3rd Floor, Plot 3, Splendor Forum, Jasola District Centre, New Delhi - 110025, India

103 Penang Road, #05-06/07, Visioncrest Commercial, Singapore 238467

Cambridge University Press is part of the University of Cambridge.

It furthers the University's mission by disseminating knowledge in the pursuit of education, learning and research at the highest international levels of excellence.

www.cambridge.org
Information on this title: www.cambridge.org/9781108706773
DOI: 10.1017/9781108756181

First published 2020
First paperback edition 2022

A catalogue record for this publication is available from the British Library

Library of Congress Cataloging in Publication data
Names: López, Luis, 1965– author.
Title: Bilingual grammar : toward an integrated model / Luis López, University of Illinois, Chicago.
Description: Cambridge, UK ; New York : Cambridge University Press, 2020. | Includes bibliographical references and index.
Identifiers: LCCN 2020004382 | ISBN 9781108485302 (hardback) | ISBN 9781108756181 (epub)
Subjects: LCSH: Bilingualism. | Code switching (Linguistics) | Minimalist theory (Linguistics) | Psycholinguistics.
Classification: LCC P115 .L67 2020 | DDC 404/.2–dc23
LC record available at https://lccn.loc.gov/2020004382

ISBN 978-1-108-48530-2 Hardback
ISBN 978-1-108-70677-3 Paperback

Contents

Figures

Acknowledgments

I would like to thank Kay González-Vilbazo and the members of the UIC Bilingualism Research Laboratory for constant inspiration through many years of research in code-switching and linguistics generally. I would also like to thank Carmen Parafita for numerous comments, discussion, and bibliographical pointers. Rodrigo Delgado, Margaret Deuchar, María José Ezeizabarrena, and Daniel Vergara also sent some crucial comments on an early version of this monograph. I would also like to thank the audiences that heard early versions of some of this material for their questions and comments: Western Ontario University; The Symposium on Bilingualism in the Hispanic and Lusophone World that was held at the Florida State University in Tallahasee; University of Utah; University of Minnesota; Southern Illinois University; the Workshop on Variation at the Interfaces that was held at the Universidad Autónoma de Madrid; Bergische Universität Wuppertal's workshop *The view from the bilingual child*; the Going Romance conference at Utrecht University. I would also like to acknowledge the generous support of the Humboldt Foundation for a summer fellowship, as well as the generosity of my host, the Zentrum für Allgemeine Sprachwissenschaft, as personified in Tonjes Veentra and Artemis Alexiadou. I would also like to thank the School of Literatures, Cultural Studies and Linguistics and the College of Liberal Arts and Sciences at the University of Illinois at Chicago for their support. I would also like to thank Helen Barton and Isabel Collins of Cambridge University Press for their guidance and good advice.

Finally, I thank Marina for being present in my life.

1 Introduction: Motivating a Unified Linguistic System

The literature on bilingualism takes it for granted that languages, grammars, and lexicons are countable entities; consequently, a bilingual is a person who has two languages, or two grammars, or two lexicons in their head.[1] This is why we can say things like: "Mary speaks three languages," "Joan speaks more languages than Chris does," etc. Moreover, languages are autonomous entities with clear boundaries. Let's call this the *separationist* framework or the *common-sense* view. According to this common-sense view, a bilingual has two grammatical systems in their head. This view is mainstream in linguistics and psycholinguistics. The quotation in (1) is an explicit statement of this assumption by a famous scholar of child bilingual acquisition.

(1) In acquiring two languages from birth, children are undergoing a sort of "double" acquisition process in which two morphosyntactic systems are acquired as fundamentally separate and closed systems.

(De Houwer 2005: 43)

However, it is worth pointing out that this view is often implicit precisely because it is so commonsensical.

Within separationism, code-switching is defined as a "going back-and-forth" from one language to the other or as an "insertion" of items from one language into a discourse constructed out of ingredients from a different language. Consider the example in (2), a sentence planted in my facebook feed by some marketer:

(2) *Antes de que se vaya*, thank President Obama for everything he's achieved. He's worked hard to protect and defend *nuestros terrenos, nuestro aire, nuestras aguas, nuestras comunidades, y nuestra madre tierra*. Add your name to our thank you letter today!
("antes de que se vaya" = "before he leaves")
("*nuestros terrenos, nuestro aire, nuestras aguas, nuestras comunidades, y nuestra madre tierra*" = our lands, our air, our waters, our communities and our mother earth")

For a separationist, this sentence follows the "back-and-forth" model: it is constructed by starting off in Spanish, switching then to English, going back to Spanish, and ending in English.

The following sentence exemplifies an "insertionist" style of code-switching:

(3) She brought the *manguera*.
hose

Herring et al. 2010 (from the Miami corpus, CSBTP, Bangor)

The Spanish word *manguera* is "inserted" in an otherwise English monolingual discourse.

I argue that the separationist perspective on the study of bilingualism is hindering progress and we should take a different path to conceptualizing bilingualism. This monograph is a first step in that direction. I believe our default assumption should be that a single linguistic competence grows out of the faculty of language on the basis of whatever ingredients the environment supplies. There are no two lexicons or two PFs. Bilinguals have two systems of exteriorization that link the linguistic competence to the articulatory/perceptual systems. The I-language of bilinguals is not substantially different from monolinguals.

A brief consideration of post-Creole continua will help us understand the futility of understanding 'languages' as countable, discrete entities. As is well known, many speakers of Creole languages possess a spectrum of linguistic ingredients that range from the *basilect* – a form of expression that is very distant from the lexifier language – to the *acrolect* – a form of expression that is very close, or identical, to the lexifier language.

Figure 1.1 is an example of Guyanese Creole from Bell (1976). Depending on environmental conditions, the same person might say the simple transitive sentence 'I gave him one' in a variety of ways, from the Standard English to the basilect form, which constructs the same proposition with a very distinct lexical and grammatical structure.

Let me now invite you to try a thought experiment. Let's imagine a remote country, that we may call Twin Guyana, in which only the varieties 1 and 18 were spoken and accepted – and some inhabitants of Twin Guyana would use both. The naïve linguist who would alight on this island would probably conclude that these speakers are bilingual – and the "separationist" scholar would say that these people have two distinct grammatical systems and two distinct lexicons in their head. But in real Guyana, we don't find this separation, rather, speakers can use a variety of forms distributed along a continuum. The existence of the continuum makes it apparent that a separationist understanding

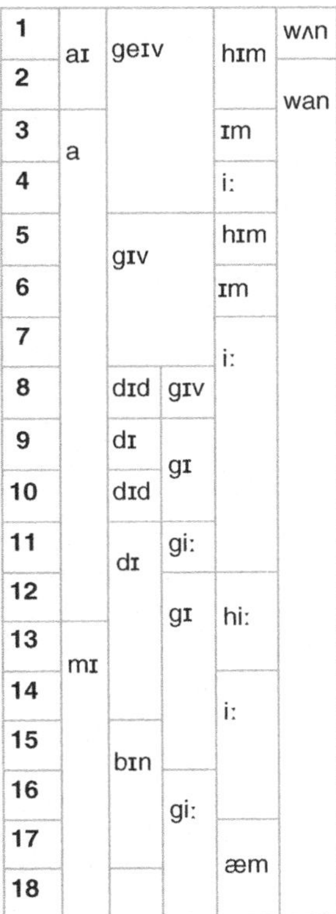

Figure 1.1 Guyanese post-Creole continuum

of human language is misguided. In particular, the staggered distribution of the different forms is very revealing. That is: it is not the case that the different subject pronouns /ai/, /a/ and /mi/ each trigger a verbal form in a one-to-one fashion; rather, each is compatible with a range of verbal forms that partially overlap.

I think that a separationist scholar would have to posit that speakers of Guyanese Creole could have eighteen languages in their head (or a subset of those eighteen languages, depending on the social milieu in which they grew up). But that would be patently absurd. Instead, we need to change our assumptions and stop thinking of languages as countable entities if we want to understand post-Creole continua. Arguably, the insight supplied by post-Creole continua should be fully incorporated into our theory of I-language in general and bilingualism in particular.

But, how about monolinguals? Could we say something like, "sure, a Creole speaker's I-language is a continuum, but one could not meaningfully say that a monolingual grammar is a continuum too"? I disagree. As Tom Roeper (1999) and others have shown, the grammar of English includes so many nooks and crannies that, Roeper claims, English speakers all have multiple grammars in their head. I think the right way to conceptualize this claim is not as "many" grammars, but as "one" linguistic system with a range of options. We should operate under the assumption of an integrated I-language.

The problem highlighted by post-Creole continua is a familiar one in the natural sciences. Everything in nature is a continuum. Biologists tell us that the barriers between species are often arbitrary and what they find is a continuum of finches or starlings or felines which are very similar in adjacent regions (or regions that were adjacent in the past) but become more distinctive as geographical distance increases. So, if we take our individual I-language, as any other phenomenon of the natural world, to be a continuum, the interesting part is how to study this continuum in a formal, explicit way. I think a first step in this direction entails abandoning the separation hypothesis and taking bilinguals to have a single system of linguistic competence.

In linguistics research, one commonly sees arguments structured in the following manner: "theory T claims that there is a categorical distinction between A and B, and this distinction gives rise to a set of predictions. However, this distinction is a figment of the linguist's imagination because what we have instead is a continuum of phenomena between A and B. That is the end of the analysis: theory T is bad. Therefore, we should give up on categorical distinctions and be satisfied with the description of continua." I don't agree with this reasoning. Everything we have in nature is continua, but sciences have advanced precisely when they are able to develop conceptual frameworks to study these continua rigorously. Identifying the continua is not the end but the beginning of the analysis.

Let's turn now to code-switching, which is the main empirical focus of this monograph. One important feature of code-switching by early or deep bilinguals is that the items used in a code-switched sentence enter in "mixed" dependencies. Let me explain this with three examples:

(4) *Basque*/Spanish

a. *Ez* *zen* nadie *etorri* *etxera*
NEG AUX.PAST anyone come home
'No one came home'

b. No vino *inor* a casa
NEG come. PAST anyone to home
'Nobody came home'

Vergara and López 2017: 270

(5) German/*Spanish*
Das Buch, Hans *lo* *hizo* verkaufen.
DEF.N book Hans CL.ACC.M did sell
'Hans sold the book'
González-Vilbazo: p.c.

(6) *Sranan*/Hindustani
a. *plafond boro* kare
ceiling bore.through do
'hit the ceiling' Muysken 2000: 254
Spanish/German
b. *hizo* nähen das Hemd
do.PAST sew the shirt
'She/he sewed the shirt'
González-Vilbazo and López 2012: 35

In example (4a), the Spanish word *nadie* is a negative polarity item, whose appearance in the sentence is licensed by the Basque sentential negation *ez*. These two words form a syntactic dependency even though they come from different languages. (4b) is the mirror image of (4a). (5) is an example of left dislocation in a Spanish/German code-switching variety. The dislocated constituent is the German *das Buch*, which is doubled by the Spanish clitic *lo*. They also form a ϕ-feature dependency, although German does not have an equivalent to Romance dislocations (it has some approximations with weak pronouns in lieu of clitics but the effects on the grammar are different). This dependency has consequences in semantic interpretation (*das Buch* is understood as a topic) and for phonetic representation (*das Buch* exhibits the peculiar intonation and caesura of dislocated constituents). Gender agreement between clitic and dislocate is particularly intriguing. German has a three-way gender system of masculine, feminine, and neuter, while Spanish only has masculine and feminine. Interestingly, the neuter DP *das Buch* is doubled with a Spanish clitic that is inflected for masculine gender – feminine would be unacceptable – which suggests that Spanish masculine and German neuter are somehow seen as having enough in common to establish a dependency.

Finally, consider now the examples in (6). They have in common that the predicate phrase consists of a light verb and a lexical verb as a complement. Example (6a) combines constituents from Sranan and Hindustani and (6b) combines Spanish and German. In (6a), the lexical verb and its complement are in Sranan and form a verb phrase with an idiomatic meaning. This verb phrase is the complement of the light verb *kare*, which is Hindustani. Interestingly, the verb and the object appear in OV order, which is the normative order in Hindustani, not in the VO order that is expected of Sranan. In this respect, (6a) contrasts with (6b). Although German normally requires OV when the VP is the complement of an auxiliary or modal, in this instance the order is obligatorily VO – and it is not chance that this is the obligatory word order in Spanish. Moreover, the intonational pattern and the expression of topicality also follow the Spanish mold. Although the constituents of the VP are "German," the VP itself is not; it is in fact a "Spanish" VP.

These examples are prime instances of one of the themes that run through this book: when bilinguals code-switch, they do not simply go "back and forth" from one language to another. Nor is code-switching about inserting words of one language into the other or alternating from one language to the other. These shallow descriptions do not provide us with insight into the properties of code-switching because code-switching involves establishing a network of dependencies among the disparate constituents that conform a sentence structure. When you take a syntactic object S (of language L1) and you merge it with constituent c (of language L2), both S and c are altered. Dependencies between S and c may be built, which affect the morphosyntactic composition of both as well as the spell-out of its morphemes and prosody. Even the word order of the constituents in S may undergo a full switch as a consequence of S merging with c (and vice versa). Unfortunately, the literature has rarely focused its attention on this fact, I surmise because the separationist perspective fogs the view. Let me exemplify this with two canonical examples.

In a celebrated series of articles and books, Carol Myers-Scotton and her collaborators (Myers-Scotton 1993, 2002, Myers-Scotton and Jake 2009) have put forward a view of code-switching based on the notion of the Matrix Language Frame. Very briefly, the idea is that code-switching always involves a language that provides the function morphemes (or a relevant subset of the function morphemes, the so-called "late outsider morphemes"), creating a spine into which the speaker can insert constituents from the other language. Thus, Myers-Scotton views code-switching as uniformly insertionist, as in (2). But this view of code-switching is extremely limiting. Take, for instance, example (4). Myers-Scotton would say that Basque is the matrix language in (4a) and Spanish is in (4b). But, how do we account for the "trans-linguistic" dependency? Is the concept of matrix language enough to account for it? Or take (5). Myers-Scotton could argue that in this sentence Spanish is the matrix language and this is the reason that the German object is dislocated rather than topicalized – so far so good. However, the matrix frame model has no insight on how the Spanish clitic pronoun is in a dependency with the German object or how the gender of the clitic is chosen. Myers-Scotton's theory presents code-switching as putting pieces from two puzzles together, with very little attention being paid to the dependencies among those pieces.

No less famous is the work of Pieter Muysken (in particular, Muysken 2000). He has developed a three/four-way typology of code-switching based on the notions of *insertion* and *alternation*, terms that mean approximately what they appear to mean. Insertionist code-switching consists of putting words or constituents of L1 into a discourse that is mostly structured as an L2 discourse, as in (3). Alternative code-switching swims between the two languages, as in (2). Again, this perspective on code-switching seems to hinder insight. To repeat: when two syntactic objects are merged together, each establishes syntactic dependencies with the other. Consider again example (5). Muysken would probably classify this example as alternational code-switching: the sentence begins in German, switches to Spanish and then back to German. Again, this gives us no insight on the appearance of the clitic, the fact that the clitic and the dislocated constituent agree in case, number, and person and, even more intriguingly, gender – the Spanish masculine is somehow able to match the neuter gender of the German constituent. Or consider example (6). Although Muysken himself provides us with (6a), he doesn't discuss why the VP has the peculiar word order that it has and how the presence of the light verb gives rise to it. I believe his separationist framework does not give him the analytical tools that would help him approach this datum.

To sum up: mainstream approaches to code-switching (and bilingual grammar in general) are fundamentally based on the idea that a bilingual has two discrete languages that are simply juxtaposed in discourse. This fundamental idea prevents scholars from training their lens on evidence that is crucial to understanding code-switching and bilingualism, including the possibility of building up dependencies in a cohesive structure.

It is not unrelated that a good chunk of bilingualism scholarship implicitly takes for granted that the notion of "grammatical system" is trivial and does not require definition or explication; it denotes the same thing for everyone and everybody recognizes what is meant when it is mentioned in an academic paper. I disagree: the notion "grammatical system" is in fact a loaded assumption, and different grammatical assumptions can lead to radically different interpretations of available data. Nonetheless, despite the lack of definition of the notion "grammatical system," it guides research questions, hypotheses, and explanations. The notion that bilinguals have "two lexicons" is also a common one and equally difficult, as will become clear throughout my discussion.

Thus, the goal of this monograph is to argue for a theory of bilingual grammar in which there is no such thing as distinct systems of linguistic competence within a person's I-language. The main data come from code-switching, but other types of data are discussed too. The focus of the analysis is the construction of linguistically cohesive language and the dependencies between the different components that constitute a sentence.

Before I start with the argument proper, I need to explain whose I-language I am actually trying to study and what data I am using. My main interest is the I-language of what I call *deep* bilinguals. Observationally speaking, deep bilinguals are people who learned two languages from birth or from a very early age (that is, they are early bilinguals) and were able to fully develop them into adulthood. Data from deep bilinguals is the focus of the discussions on code-switching in Chapters 5 and 6. The data in these chapters come mostly from acceptability judgments obtained via surveys or in-lab experimental settings carried out in the Bilingualism Research Laboratory (BRL) at UIC. These experiments have been described in detail in published work or in dissertations that are distributed through the BRL web page, and therefore I generally omit methodological descriptions in this monograph when citing work from the lab. I also liberally use data from González-Vilbazo (2005), which involves deep bilinguals and is extracted in an experimental setting. Occasionally, I use judgments obtained informally when it was not possible for me to gather them otherwise, as long as I could contrast them with more than two consultants (see Sprouse and Almeida, 2018, which summarizes a decade of research on the replicability of acceptability judgments). I also use a good helping of data borrowed from the literature: when I do so, I describe whatever information I have regarding subjects, sources, etc.

I do not try to make any claims on later bilinguals, L2 learners, or early bilinguals whose development of the heritage language is slowed down by environmental circumstances. I am fully aware that I am leaving out data that presents its own scientific interest and eventually needs to be integrated into any theory of I-language. The reason why I focus on deep bilinguals is methodological. In his study of German/Spanish code-switching, González-Vilbazo (2005) shows that his early bilingual subjects form a coherent speech community who report similar acceptability judgments. One can conclude that those judgments reflect some property of the consultants' I-language. On the other hand, the consultants who learned German starting at age 12, although they were fully proficient, did not report consistent judgments. Thus, if we have a community of speakers S1, S2, . . . Sn and each gives different acceptability judgments on a set of stimuli, we can't really conclude anything: the differences might be due to differences in their I-languages but there could be other reasons: maybe the constructions were beyond their linguistic development in the L2; there could be the effects of "shallow processing"; disparate results can even be due to their attention limitations, the task, etc.

This difference between deep bilinguals and other bilinguals has been discussed in the literature. Toribio (2001: 215–216) provides a thoughtful discussion on the issue, but also other linguists like Zentella (1997) and Poplack (1980) report that there are substantial differences in the way that deep bilinguals and other bilinguals code-switch; only the former are able to carry out the seamless assemblage of (what appear to the outside observer as) variegated elements in one sentence or sentence fragment. These observations confirm the methodological soundness of focusing on deep bilinguals, at least while we learn more about the differences among bilinguals.

I believe that a reasonable path (not the one and only path) to learn about a person's I-language is by obtaining acceptability judgments, either in the traditional way that has been used in linguistics since time immemorial or following formal experimental protocols (see Sprouse and Almeida 2018, for a summary of arguments pro and against acceptability judgments). Regarding code-switching, one can find occasional remarks in the bilingualism literature doubting that it is appropriate to use acceptability judgments with this type of data. For instance, Muysken (2000: 13) writes that "clearly it is difficult if not impossible to rely on judgment data." Likewise, Mahootian and Santorini (1996) reject acceptability judgments in code-switching research. It seems to me that this idea must be widespread, judging from the comments that I receive whenever I submit a manuscript for publication. However, I find it disturbing: essentially, we are being told that the speech of monolingual speakers as they use their linguistic resources is rule-governed, whereas the speech of bilingual people who are also using the entirety of their linguistic resources, is not. To my mind, this is an obvious example of the monoglossic linguistic ideology that pervades the Western World – including academic specialists in the language sciences within the Western World. This monoglossic ideology takes the monolingual speech as the norm and anything bilingual as marked. It is also a beautiful example of how the separationist assumption can lead you astray: The separationist believes that a speaker has two languages in their head, each with its own set of grammatical rules. Only from this point of view can one claim that the combination of two languages gives random results. On the other hand, an integrationist scholar takes for granted that the linguistic knowledge of a bilingual person is rule-governed *in toto* and this systematic character will be reflected in their judgments of sentences, regardless of the kinds of linguistic materials that go into those sentences.

One of my language consultants, a Turkish-German bilingual, wrote the following to me (certainly tongue-in-cheek because she knew that I couldn't understand it):

(7) Turkish/*German*
Ama lütfen *vergessen* yapma. Biz Almancılar hepimiz *verschieden* konuşuyoruz. Bu *Sprache* çok flexibel. Yani hangi *Wort*'u daha önce *erinnern* yapıyorsan. Bu *Sprache*' de bir *Regel* yok.
'But please don't forget. We *Almancılar* speak differently. This language is very flexible. Namely, the first word you remember. There are no rules in this language.'

While this consultant is telling me that *Almancılar* (Germans of Turkish background) play around with language in an apparent chaos, she is using a tightly constructed sentence to tell me so. In this insertionist code-switched utterance, the Turkish grammatical rules are carefully respected, including the appropriate case suffixes on the German nouns. As for the German verbs, they all appear in the appropriate German infinitival form as complements of a Turkish light verb.

Another argument that I have heard often in discussion is that since code-switched forms are stigmatized, speakers will simply give low ratings to any code-switched utterance that is presented to them (see Gullberg, Indefrey, and Muysken 2009 for discussion). I have three answers to this concern. The first is that, as Badiola, Delgado, Sande, and Stefanich (2018) show, it is indeed true that subjects with a negative attitude to code-switching give lower ratings to code-switched sentences than subjects with a positive attitude. But in the experiment that they reported, the distinctions *between* sentences were maintained proportionally regardless of attitude.[2]

A second answer to that concern is that there are methods to elicit judgments that circumvent this potential hurdle, such as two-alternative choices (Stadthagen et al. 2018). Finally, I would like to point out that if one should stop trying to access the I-language that underlies code-switching because of its marginality, then surely we should do the same to any marginalized and stigmatized language variety. I don't know any linguist who would like to walk down that path.

There are of course other linguists who cast doubt on acceptability judgments in monolingual work too, as a matter of principle (Silva-Corvalán 2001). I find this rejection surprising, since most of what we know about any human language – I would say, 99 percent – was learned by introspection and prodding the judgments of native speakers. I have yet to see a descriptive grammar of a language that is not entirely built on native speaker intuitions. The knowledge that we have been able to obtain in recent years via corpora studies or psycholinguistic work is very valuable and surely should be integrated into grammatical theory – but it is built on a foundation of native speaker judgments because only these judgments tell the researcher what to look for.

The data in Chapters 7 and 8 is exclusively based on the published literature and, as far as I can tell, it has been obtained through generally accepted protocols in psycholinguistic research. More often than not, it was impossible for me to see what kinds of bilinguals are discussed. As for Chapter 9, the data is also from published sources and obtained in a variety of ways.

The rest of this monograph is organized as follows. In Chapter 2, I continue the discussion of the separationist hypothesis and I present what is, in my view, the most formally rigorous model of separationist bilingual grammar: MacSwan's (1999, 2000) minimalist approach. This chapter also includes a brief discussion of Tom Roeper's Multiple Grammar Theory. In Chapter 3, I introduce some concepts of minimalism and distributed morphology that give theoretical shape to my proposals. This chapter also includes some contributions that code-switching has made to our understanding of these frameworks. In Chapter 4, I begin my argumentation that the I-language of a bilingual is fully integrated; in particular, I argue that the bilingual lexicon, understood in the realizational mode developed in distributed morphology, is not encapsulated in two systems. This chapter also includes a discussion of borrowing and other contact phenomena and shows how the framework presented here provides a fresh perspective on them. One conclusion of this section is that, from an I-language perspective, there is no difference between borrowing and code-switching.

Chapter 5 is dedicated to gender assignment and concord, an area that has attracted considerable attention among code-switching scholars and that I use as a playground to highlight the advantages of this approach. In Chapter 6, I extend the argumentation to PF. I develop empirical arguments that even PF is fully integrated in the bilingual and only the externalization systems are divided (although not necessarily along "language" lines). An extended discussion of MacSwan's PF-interface condition is included.

Chapters 7 and 8 switch gears toward topics in psycholinguistics that bear relation to the integrated hypothesis. In Chapter 7, I discuss psycholinguistic research that argues for separate lexicons and present alternative approaches to the empirical phenomena that they uncovered. In Chapter 8, I discuss the separationist hypothesis as developed in the bilingual acquisition literature. At this point, I am able to address the main argument in favor of functional separation: if bilinguals have an integrated system, how come they can speak "in a language" without mixing "the other language"? In the final section of Chapter 8, I discuss the findings of syntactic priming experiments.

In Chapter 9, I discuss other approaches that converge, in form or goals, to my own and I introduce the topic of *code-blending*, when one of the languages involved is a sign language. The monograph ends with some additional discussion and conclusions. Appendix A discusses a topic in the syntax of code-switching that has attracted considerable attention, namely, the restrictions on code-switching that make some code-switches grammatical and others unacceptable. In addition, Appendix B returns to the Creole continua briefly.

2 Remarks on Separationist Architectures

2.1 Two Grammars

As mentioned, the common-sense view on bilingualism holds that a polyglot individual is in possession of two separate grammatical systems. This is the import of the De Houwer quotation in Chapter 1, repeated here:

(1) In acquiring two languages from birth, children are undergoing a sort of "double" acquisition process in which two morphosyntactic systems are acquired as fundamentally separate and closed systems.

(De Houwer 2005: 43)

As far as I know, no one has presented such an assumption in an explicit model since Woolford (1983), couched within Extended Standard Theory (but see Paradis 2007 for another separationist model, from a different perspective). In contemporary terms, the resulting model should look as in (2):

(2)

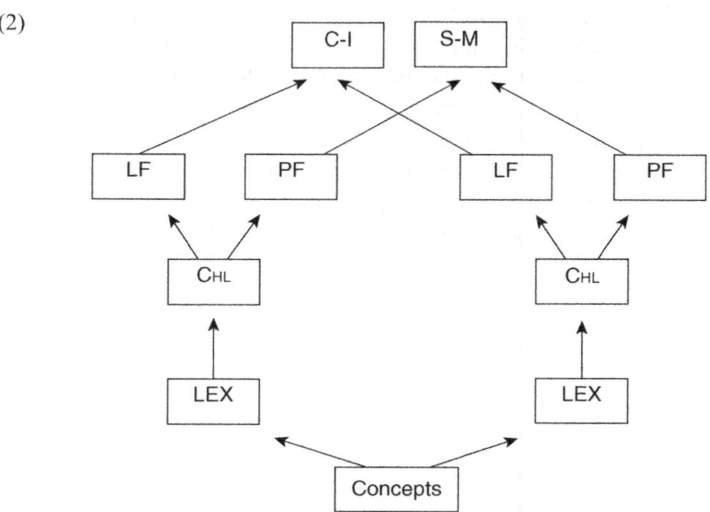

Assuming multiple complete grammatical systems inside one human's head, questions regarding the interfaces arise. Essentially, the question is whether each language should interface with "the other mind stuff" independently or not. If indeed a bilingual has two grammatical systems, then we should posit six interfaces for that person. This is shown in (2). The universal inventory of concepts maps onto two separate lexicons. There are two computational systems that yield two distinct PFs and LFs, which eventually map to one common cognitive-intentional system and one sensorimotor system. A person with three or four languages will have a system with nine or twelve separate interfaces with mind stuff. Is it reasonable that a polyglot's I-language should be organized this way?

Another feature worth noticing in this model is that if a person is bilingual in two typologically similar languages a lot of linguistic rules will have to be duplicated (this is a topic that has been pointed out many times). Again, questions arise as to why polyglots should have their linguistic competence organized in such an inefficient manner.

2.2 Two Lexicons, Two PFs, and the MDM Model

MacSwan (1999) shed some light on our understanding of code-switching by incorporating the view of language proposed in Chomsky (1995) and many of Chomsky's followers. Within this view – the so-called Minimalist Program – the computational system of human language consists of the operations *Merge*, which builds structure, and *Feature Checking*, which underlies displacement and dependencies. In work that appeared after MacSwan's contribution, the technical details of the minimalist program have changed. In Chomsky (2000), *Agree* becomes the engine of syntactic dependencies and in later work, he argues that movement is free and requires no motivation (Chomsky 2007, 2008). In any case, within minimalist assumptions, much of what constitutes the distinctive features of the grammar of a language – null subjects, scrambling of objects, presence or absence of wh-movement, dislocations and topicalization, etc. – is actually triggered by features or feature combinations present in the lexicon: the computational system itself is invariant in all humans. The computational system eventually maps onto two representational systems: semantics and phonetics, or LF and PF.

MacSwan incorporates the minimalist perspective on grammar (the 1995 version) into his research on bilingualism. MacSwan's theory of bilingual grammars includes one fundamental assumption: bilinguals have two lexicons and two PFs but the items from the two lexicons feed one computational system – thus giving rise to code-switching. Once the computational operations within a domain are finished, the resulting structure is fed to two independent PFs. PF is viewed as the repository of phonetic idiosyncrasies such as are described in traditional phonological textbooks. Presumably, the items from Lexicon 1 are processed by PF 1 and the items from Lexicon 2 are processed by PF2:

(3)

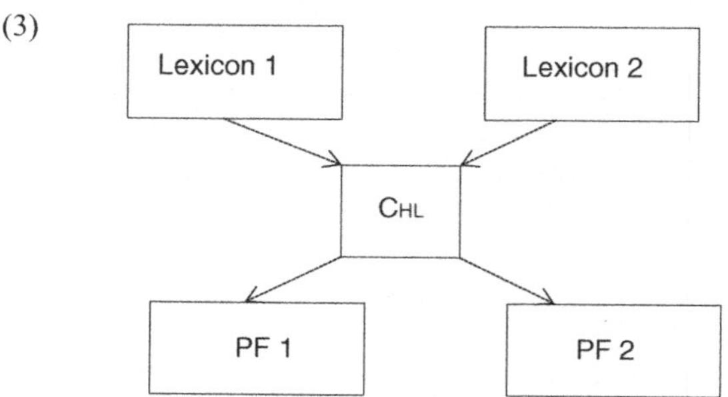

Let's call a model that posits two independent lexicons for bilinguals a *2Lex* model. Similarly, let's call a model with two separate PFs a *2PF* model.

MacSwan's framework provides a very elegant picture to understand code-switching: A bilingual person can draw items from the two lexicons in order to construct a sentence (see also: Sankoff and Poplack 1981, Poplack and Dion 2012). This is schematized in (4).

(4) Sample of a tree with code-switching. LIs from both lexicons are used to build one syntactic structure.

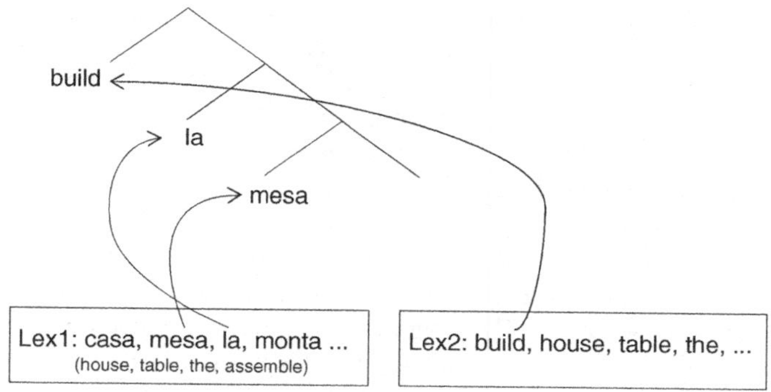

Some scholars have found it useful to posit a *Numeration* or *Lexical Array* that mediates between the lexicon proper and the computational system (Chomsky 1995). The Numeration or Lexical Array is a subset of items from the lexicon that is placed in a workspace and is accessed by the computational system. Within this view, MacSwan proposes that code-switching consists of constructing a Numeration with items from Lexicon 1 and Lexicon 2 and then the derivation proceeds normally.

MacSwan's model has been very influential within the community of code-switching scholars, and justly so, because it does provide a formal account of how code-switching happens, as well as making explicit what is meant with the notion of grammar. Notice that in MacSwan's system – or in any minimalist framework, for that matter – there is no room for an ill-defined notion of "grammatical system"; a good result, in my view. On the other hand, the assumption that bilingual linguistic competence consists of two separate systems is maintained, now displaced to the bookends of the computational system. Consequently, the polyglot person still has an I-language that has multiple interfaces with language-external modules.

The assumption of two lexicons is important for MacSwan to approach the distinction between code-switching and borrowing – a topic that is one of the leitmotifs of this work too. Within a 2Lex model, *borrowing* involves copying an item *i* from Lex1 into Lex2 and introducing *i* into the derivation as a Lex2 item. Formally, a borrowed lexical item assimilates to the properties of the receiving lexicon, while a code-switched word maintains the original properties.

(5) Sample of a tree with borrowing. LIs from Lex1 are borrowed into Lex2.

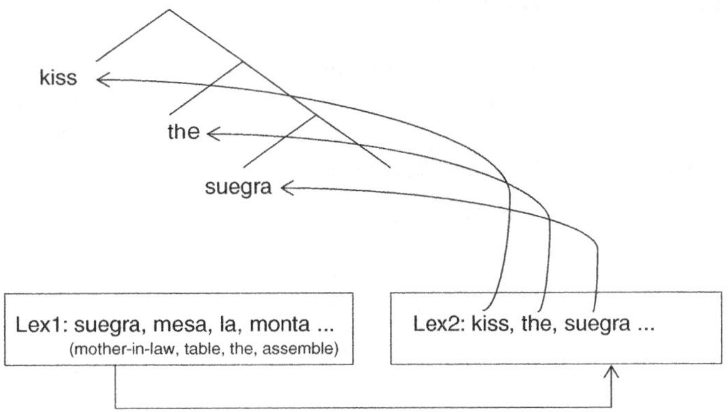

The distinction between code-switching and borrowing has figured prominently in work on contact linguistics since at least Poplack (1980), as I shall discuss later in this book. It is obvious that the integrated assumption that I argue for does not provide us with a formal way to tease borrowing and code-switching apart. This is, I argue in Section 4.4, a good thing, because the distinction is often used as a cop-out to dismiss counterexamples to one's theory. Instead, I will try to show that the code-switching–borrowing distinction is in fact empirically unnecessary.

Notice that the 2Lex approach does not assist us in understanding the Post-Creole continuum mentioned in Chapter 1. These are some of the questions one could ask: how many lexicons should a Guyanese speaker have? And how should they be organized? Or should we say that the Creole speaker has just one lexicon while the bilingual has two? And how would this division be implemented without falling into arbitrariness? Notice that we cannot simply say that MacSwan was only trying to provide a theory of code-switching, not a theory of the Creole continuum, which is a completely different phenomenon. Whatever we say about Creole is not orthogonal to MacSwan's proposals because MacSwan's overarching goal is to provide a contribution to our understanding of the faculty of language and therefore what he says has to be consistent with other forms that the faculty of language may have.

Thus, in these pages I develop an alternative to our understanding of code-switching (and bilingual grammar generally) that does not rely on any duplication of linguistic modules and that is therefore consistent with what we know of other linguistic phenomena. In order to flesh out my proposals, I adopt the general framework of assumptions common in minimalist work (as in Chomsky 2000), combined with the type of realizational morphology implemented by Distributed Morphology, which traces its roots to the work of Halle and Marantz (1993). Let's call this the MDM model, represented in (6). This model incorporates the theory of structure building and dependencies based on Merge and Agree with the assumption that there is no real lexicon as traditionally understood. Rather, within the MDM model, the lexicon is split in two lists, which we can call List 1 and List 2. List 1 consists of abstract roots as well as grammatical features. List 1 is what is fed to syntax. List 2 is a set of rules of *vocabulary insertion* (VIRs), which take care of assigning a phonetic shape to syntactic terminals.

(6) *Distributed Morphology framework* (see Harley and Noyer 2000 i.m.a.) (first pass)

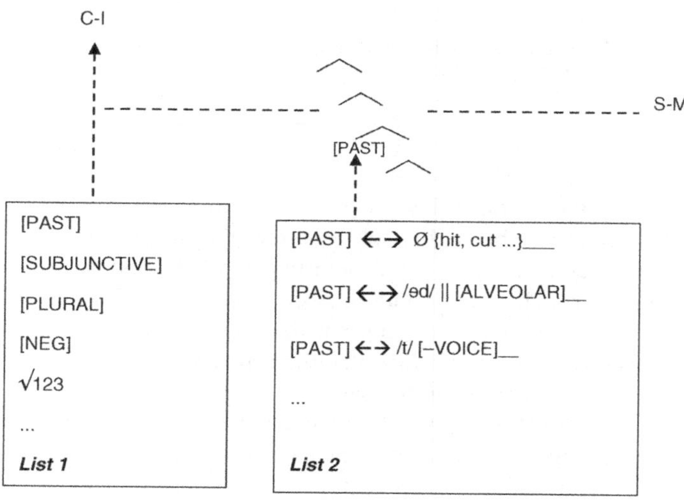

In this book, I assume the MDM linguistic architecture. Additionally, I argue that bilinguals have one linguistic competence: this means that any mature competence system has only one List 1, one List 2 as well as one set of VIRs. They are not separated into modules. Let's call these assumptions the *1Lex* assumption and the *1PF* assumption. This model is fleshed out in Chapter 3.

2.3 Empirical Difficulties of 2Lex Theory

In this section, I introduce two empirical problems for the 2Lex analysis of code-switching. Both of these problems eventually boil down to the same theme: code-switched constituents are not put together like Lego pieces but, rather, they are deeply imbricated in the structure of the clause that they form. This deep interweaving cannot be captured in a 2Lex theory. The issues discussed in this section are retaken in Section 4.1, where a solution based on the 1Lex hypothesis is presented.

2.3.1 Mixed Selection

Many code-switching varieties include structures in which a *light verb,* which can be glossed as 'do', takes as a complement a lexical verb in the citation form, which carries the lexical meaning. Descriptively speaking, the light verb and the heavy verb are drawn from different lexicons. We already saw example (6) in Chapter 1. The following is an additional English/Japanese example from Shim (2016):

(7) English/*Japanese*
one algebra question-*o* mark-*shite*.
ACC do
'(You) mark one algebra question.'

Shim 2016: 2

The light verbs that we see in code-switching varieties are often original creations, to the extent that none of the feeding languages has them (see González-Vilbazo and López 2011, 2012 and Veenstra and López 2016 for many examples in different code-switching varieties). Consider the Spanish verb *hacer* 'do'/'make'. I'm now describing the examples in (8). In monolingual Spanish, *hacer* has two uses: as a regular lexical verb of creation and as a causative verb. This is exemplified in (8a, b). In the German/Spanish code-switching variety usually referred to as *Esplugish* (González-Vilbazo 2005), it is also used as light verb – but only when it takes a German infinitive. The light verb usage is exemplified in (8c):

(8) Spanish/*German*

a. Juan hizo la cena.
Juan made the dinner.
'Juan made dinner.'

b. María hizo trabajar a Santiago.
Maria made work.INF DOM Santiago.
'Maria made Santiago work.'

c. Juan hizo *arbeiten*.
Juan made work.INF
'Juan worked.'

Let's focus now on the third usage. As I said, the light verb meaning for *hacer* only comes about if the complement is a German infinitive. This entails an interesting difference between the monolingual Spanish lexicon and the lexicon of Esplugish speakers. Esplugish speakers have an additional version of *hacer*, the light verb version, which selects for a German infinitive. This is shown in (9).

(9) Monolingual Spanish lexicon: *hacer*: 1. heavy verb
2. causative verb

Esplugisch lexicon: *hacer*: 1. heavy verb
2. causative verb
3. light verb (*selects only "German" verbs in citation form)

Here is the empirical problem for a 2Lex theory: if we have two independent lexicons, this restriction on *hacer* is not formulable. If we have *hacer* as part of the "Spanish lexicon," it cannot select for a German verb (or a lexical or functional item with German-like properties; this does not matter) because there are no "German words" or German features associated with a verb in the Spanish lexicon. The fact that one can see "mixed selection" is evidence that the mental lexicon of the bilingual person is fully integrated.

2.3.2 Noun Class in Swahili

English words can be integrated into Swahili sentences quite freely, particularly nouns.[1] Consider the following example:

(10) Swahili/*English*

Ø-saa hi-yo i-na-*depend* na certificate 10-zako 10-za
9-time 9-this 9-PRES-depend with 10-certificate 10-your 10-with
Ø-shule
10-school
'At this time, it depends on the school certificates.'

Myers-Scotton and Jake 2009: 339

Swahili classifies nouns into eighteen different classes – or genders – partially based on semantic criteria, partially on seemingly arbitrary grounds (see Carstens 1991, among many others). Classes 2, 4, 6, 8, 10 are the plural forms of classes 1, 3, 5, 7, 9. In example (10), the English noun *certificate* appears to have been classified in class 9/10, as revealed by concord on the possessor and the preposition. Although class 10 is a plural class, the noun appears without an English plural suffix – again, only the concord system allows us to detect that this is plural. The interesting datum is that seemingly every English noun can be used in a Swahili sentence with its corresponding noun class (Myers-Scotton 1993: 11–17), a situation that is not rare in bilingual communities.

The Swahili/English datum in (10) is a puzzle for 2Lex theories. If we have an "English" lexicon and a "Swahili" lexicon, how do Swahili speakers know the class of 'certificate'? Consider also the American Norwegian data unearthed by Grimstad, Lohndal, and Åfarli (2014):[2]

(11) Norwegian/*English*
den *field*-a
that field-DEF.F

Grimstad et al. 2014: 228

Grimstad et al. (2014) describe these data as English roots with Norwegian inflection. Interestingly, this inflection carries gender information, as shown in this example. Sometimes this gender information is created analogically with the equivalent Norwegian nouns, sometimes following phonetic criteria, sometimes apparently arbitrarily. As Grimstad et al. (2014) argue, examples such as (11) suggest that English and Norwegian roots are listed together (see Chapter 9 for details on their analysis). I agree. The problem is therefore a general one in code-switching and in our understanding of bilingualism.

In MacSwan's sort of model, we have two options to generate a sentence like (10). Option 1 is code-switching proper: the noun 'certificate' is an English noun that gets selected into the computational system together with some Swahili words to create a sentence like (10). But if so, where does the class feature come from? Do English words in an English lexicon have dormant class features? It does not seem very plausible.

Option 2 is to take (10) to instantiate borrowing: the noun 'certificate' that appears in the sentence is really an English word that has been borrowed into the Swahili lexicon. In support of this idea, one can point out that *certificate* does not inflect for plural, which suggests that it is not an "English word" in (10). However, it is worth pointing out that, as mentioned, many English nouns can generally be used as in (10) – in fact, there does not seem to be a formal limit. Thus, many English nouns will be represented twice in the minds of Swahili bilinguals, one in each lexicon. This solution is technically feasible but probably linguistic lexicons are organized in a more efficient manner.

Both Option 1 and Option 2 seem to me to miss the intuition underlying (10). I think *certificate* is just one root in the minds of Swahili/English bilinguals. What we see in (10) is that bilingual speakers can use it in two different morphosyntactic frames. This, I believe, is the intuition that we should try to capture.

I hope I have persuaded the reader that maintaining the assumption that bilinguals possess two separate lexicons leads to insurmountable problems. As the book progresses, the reader will find several other instances in which the 2Lex hypothesis is unable to cope with an empirical problem. I have hinted, but not yet shown formally, that a 1Lex alternative circumvents the problems I have just pointed out. I do this in Section 3.4.

2.4 Multiple Grammars Theory

I finish this chapter with a few words on Roeper's Multiple Grammars Theory (MGT). Roeper (1999) sketches a theory of optionality in grammar that later work (Amaral and Roeper 2014) extends to the interlanguage of L2 learners – and in this respect, their conclusions are relevant to the questions that occupy us here. The fundamental assumption of this approach is that the "human grammar readily accommodates sets of rules in sub-grammars that seem (apparently) contradictory." That is, it is not the case that grammars have optional rules; they have sub-grammars with alternative, apparently inconsistent rules. An example of what this approach is meant to deal with is quotative inversion in English, exemplified in (12). At an observational level, (12) seems to violate a rule of English grammar, which requires SV order in every other instance:

(12) "Nothing," said John.

Descriptively, it is generally the case that, in English, the verb never raises to T or C, and we can take this to be a true generalization of English grammar. But in quotative constructions like (12), the verb does appear to raise to C (Collins and Branigan 1997). The solution proposed within the MGT is that English speakers' I-language includes a general syntactic rule that leaves the verb *in situ* together with a lexical sub-grammar that allows movement of a particular set of verbs in a configuration that has the quotative property (possibly as a feature of C).

The same approach can be used to account for the presence of inconsistent rules in bilingual grammars. Take pro-drop. A Spanish-English bilingual will have a pro-drop rule and a non-pro-drop rule tagged for language (see Amaral and Roeper 2014: 13). Additionally, since English seems to allow pro-drop of expletive 'it', a separate sub-grammar of English will include a lexical rule of pro-drop.

Rather than a theory, I regard the MGT as an approach to reconceptualize a number of problems in the theory of grammar within an explicitly minimalist framework. It is open-ended and can be developed in many different ways. However, Amaral and Roeper discuss two alternative implementations of the MGT, both of which seem to me to presuppose a version of separationism, and therefore are incompatible with the framework laid out in this monograph. To quote: "the theory seems to presuppose the existence of a unique repository for all sub-grammars a learner possesses, which would have rules that belong to more than one language [...] the alternative view would be to have two independent storage spaces or completely separate grammars for the L1 and the L2" (Amaral and Roeper 2014: 15). Thus, either there is a common repository *for the rules common to the L1 and the L2* or we have separate (and therefore occasionally redundant) L1 or L2 grammars. At no point do they consider the possibility that two or more languages might be fully integrated within an individual I-language.

The MGT seeks to provide an account of apparent optionality in I-language, while my research is motivated by the observation that I-languages constitute continua, as shown by Creole languages, together with some phenomena in bilingualism – particularly code-switching – that lead to the conclusion that I-languages are not split in separate grammars.

Thus, the MGT and my integrated MDM model are two distinct contributions that respond to different research questions and seek to accomplish different goals. Having said this, I think the proposals of the MGT seem to be in harmony with the proposals in this monograph and there are indeed points of confluence. I could easily see how the two perspectives could enrich each other.

3 Phases, Distributed Morphology, and Some Contributions from Code-Switching

In this chapter, I present the MDM model, a label that intends to show that it incorporates the hypotheses developed in recent work in minimalism as well as Distributed Morphology (also often referred to as DM). I also discuss some findings from the code-switching literature that become relevant in subsequent sections. This section is divided into two subsections, dedicated to syntax and morphology respectively.

For the interested reader, Koeneman and Zeijlstra (2017) provide an excellent introduction to contemporary syntactic theory within the minimalist tradition. Embick (2015) can be used as an introduction to DM. In these pages, I limit myself to presenting and highlighting characteristics of these frameworks that I use in later analyses.

3.1 The MDM and Code-Switching: Syntax

The MDM model that I use is represented in Chapter 2, example (6). It assumes a classic Y-shaped theory of grammar in which a computational system inputs lexical items and outputs a syntactic structure that is fed into the conceptual-intentional systems as well as the sensorimotor systems. It is taken for granted that the system is built by means of the operation *Merge*, as defined in Chomsky (1995). Merge takes two constituents, a and b, and builds the set {a,b}. *External Merge* involves at least one constituent drawn from the lexicon while *Internal Merge* involves both constituents drawn from the work space (Chomsky 2007, 2008).

A second operation, *Agree*, establishes dependencies among constituents. Let's define Agree following the *valuation* mechanism proposed in Chomsky (2000). Take a category with unvalued features of a certain type, call it P (for *probe*). P looks for token values of the same type within its c-command domain. Let's call G (for *goal*) a category with valued features within the c-command domain of P. As a result of Agree, the token value of G is copied on the feature structure of P. This is expressed abstractly in (1):

(1) P[f:u] G[f:x] ➔ P[f:x] G[f:x]

The Agree model is used to formalize subject/object verb agreement as well as concord within the DP and even wh-dependencies.

Earlier minimalist approaches (Chomsky 1995) conceptualized agreement in terms of feature checking, so the two categories that participate in agreement enter the derivation with valued features and Agree is an operation that ensures that the features are compatible. If the features do not match, the derivation crashes. Note that under the feature valuation framework, it is not possible for a derivational output to yield non-matching features. Chomsky (2000) also claimed that when a probe does not find a goal to value its features, the derivation would crash. However, this assumption has been challenged, especially in López (2007) and Preminger (2014). In this book, I incorporate the assumption that when a probe does not find a goal, the unvalued feature remains so into the PF section of the grammar. This was found useful to account for the recurrence of third person singular forms in expletive and impersonal constructions (López 2007). I detail what happens to unvalued features after I have introduced some DM assumptions.

The basic syntactic structures for the clause and the noun phrase that I assume are the following:

(2) a. Clause: C [$_{TP}$ T [$_{VoiceP}$ Voice [$_{vP}$ v √R]]]
b. Noun phrase: K [$_{DP}$ D [$_{NumP}$ Num [$_{nP}$ n √R]]]

Thus, I take it that a root, represented by a √, may become the complement of a "nouny" or a "verby" categorizer, thus becoming a verb or a noun (as in Marantz 1997). A verb becomes the complement of a Voice head, which is itself selected by T. The head of the clause is C. A noun becomes the complement of a number head, which is itself the complement of D. Following numerous authors, harking back to proposals of Ken Hale in the 1990s (see Bittner and Hale 1996, among others), I take it that a head K (for case) heads every nominal.

Within this view, roots have no grammatical information. This is an innovation of DM, with interesting consequences: grammatical information such as gender, noun class, declension, or conjugation class cannot be inherent features of anything. In fact, these features must be syntactically emergent, the by-product of merging a particular root in a particular environment. For instance, I will assume throughout that gender is a feature on *n* that combines with a subset of nouns (see Acquaviva 2009, Kramer 2015, among many others). I develop this notion in Chapters 4 and 5. Further, I assume that the noun classes found in Bantu languages are essentially the same thing as gender features (Carstens 1991, Kihm 2005). These assumptions are represented in example (3). A root that eventually spells-out as /cas-/ is the complement of a little *n* that carries a feminine gender feature. This *n* spells-out as /-a/. Together they form the noun *casa* 'house'.

(3) *casa* 'house'

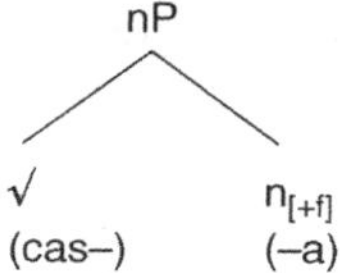

Roots can be merged with different types of categorizers. For instance, the Spanish root that spells-out as *estudi* 'study' can be the used to build a verb, an adjective, a masculine noun, and a feminine noun:

(4) √(estudi-) + v ➔ estudiar 'to study'
+ a ➔estudioso 'studious'
+ $n_{[+f]}$ ➔ estudiante 'female student'
+ $n_{[-f]}$ ➔ estudiante 'male student'

The categorizers themselves can be subcategorized or have *flavors*, in the felicitous expression of Arad (2003). We have seen that little *n* can appear in more than one version, which we refer to as *gender*. The Bantu languages have many *noun classes* that we can refer to as flavors of *n*, thus making explicit the long-standing intuition that Bantu noun classes and Indo-European genders are essentially the same grammatical property (Carstens 1991, Kihm 2005). Even more interestingly, a root may combine with different types of *n*, yielding forms like the following:

(5) Swahili

toto	'child'	
m-toto	'child'	m=class 1
ma-toto	'big child'	ma=class 5
ki-toto	'small child'	ki=class 7
u-toto	'childhood'	u=class 9

The conjugation classes of the Romance languages can be taken to be different flavors of little *v*. The classic study of Arad (2003) investigates how some psychological predicates fit in a nominative-accusative mold while others fit in a dative-nominative one; this alternation should probably be regarded as being based on Voice or an interaction of Voice and *v*. This separation of the root from the grammatical properties usually associated with it plays an important role in this monograph.

A third consequence of the assumption that roots have no grammatical properties is that roots do not have labels; since they do not have labels, they do not select complements or project phrases. A complement XP is really selected by the root in combination with the categorizing morpheme (Lohndal 2014). In the following diagram, y={n,v,a,p}:

(5)

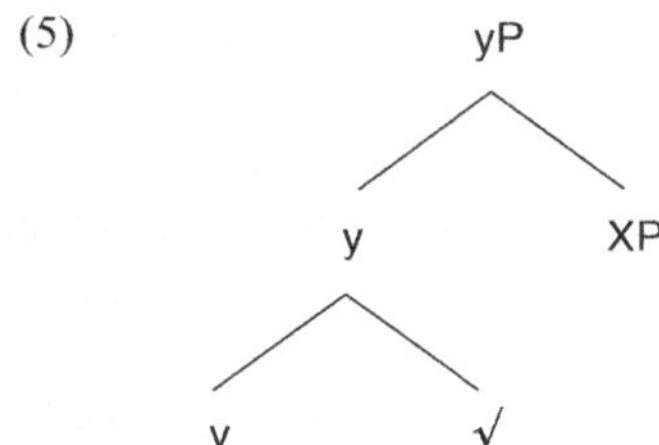

One advantage of taking selection as involving the root and the categorizer is that it allows us to understand certain selectional differences between nouns and verbs. For instance, the English noun 'talk' and the verb 'talk' grow out of the same root, but only the verb admits a complement headed by the preposition 'to'. This supports the conclusion that complement selection is an affair between a root and a category.

There are many functional categories not mentioned in this list: classifiers in the noun phrase, aspect and mood in the clause, etc.; I omit discussion of them for the purposes of this book.

Scholars' understanding of the lexicon-syntax interface has evolved considerably in recent years. In 1980s grammatical theory, it was understood that syntactic structures are the projection of properties of lexical items. Thus, the different predicate structures – transitive, intransitive, ditransitive – were constructed because these are the structures required by the head of the predicate: a transitive verb builds a transitive structure and so on. However, there are some obvious difficulties with this approach. Consider the following example (inspired by examples by Beth Levin):

(6)
a. John whistled a song.
b. The teakettle whistled.
c. A bullet whistled past him.
d. John whistled himself tired.

Example (6) shows that the same verb can be the lexical root for several types of predicate structure, a situation that is the rule rather than the exception. This suggests that the projectionist approach cannot be entirely right (see Levin and Rappaport-Hovav 2005 for detailed exposition). The so-called *exo-skeletal* or *neo-constructionist* models propose instead that a small set of basic structures provide frames within which lexical predicates can fit, with the only limitations being that a coherent meaning is available and idiosyncratic properties of the lexical roots are respected. For alternative exo-skeletal models, see Borer (2013) and Ramchand (2008), among others.

At specific points in the structure, called *phases*, the contents of the structure are *Transferred* to the interpretive modules: the intentional-cognitive one and the perceptual-articulatory one. As Chomsky (2000, 2001) describes it, when a phase head merges with a structure, the complement of the phase head is sent to the performance modules (see Citko 2014 for a thorough discussion of phase theory).

It is currently assumed that C and Voice are phase heads (on Voice being a phase head see Alexiadou and Lohndal 2017). This entails that v-√ are transferred in one shot when Voice merges with vP while T-Voice are transferred when C is merged with TP:

(7)

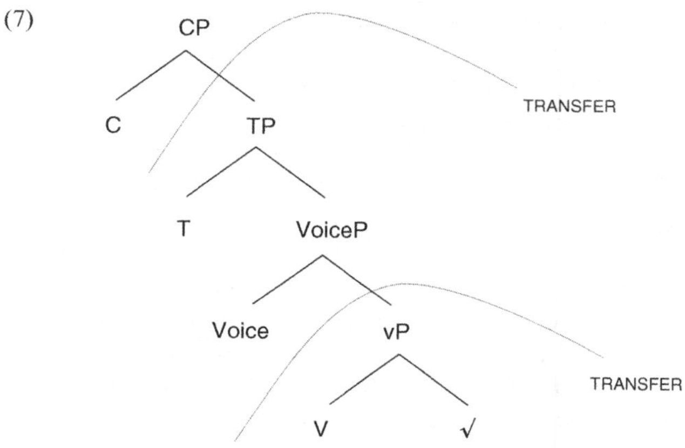

As for nominal phrases, I argue momentarily that K is also a phase head (remaining agnostic as to whether there are other phase heads within the nominal extended projection.) Finally, it has also been argued (most extensively by Embick 2010) that every categorizing morpheme is a phase head.

The notion of phase coupled with Transfer provides a very natural locality condition for Agree: once a structure has been Transferred, a probe cannot reach into it. Likewise, phases provide a clear motivation for successive cyclic movement (reconceptualized as successive cyclic internal merge). Take wh-movement of an object to Spec,C. At the point C enters the structure, the whole vP has already been transferred and therefore it is not possible for a direct object to move directly to Spec,C. It follows that a previous movement of the wh-phrase to Spec,Voice must have taken place.

Chomsky (2007, 2008) has enlarged the role of phase heads. In fact, he proposes the hypothesis that all syntactic dependencies ultimately originate in phase heads. How does T, which is not a phase head, initiate a dependency with the subject and exhibit agreement? He proposes a mechanism, which he calls *inheritance*, that allows the head of the phase to share its features with the head that it immediately c-commands. Thus, C and T would share the relevant features that trigger A-dependencies. The notion of inheritance has not been universally accepted among syntacticians (it would, among other problems, introduce an additional operation in the theory of syntax through the back door). However, code-switching may provide some empirical evidence in support of the idea that there is feature sharing between C and T. Consider Sande's (2018) investigation of pro-drop. Pro-drop theories have typically taken the ϕ-features of T to be the licensors of null subjects. An alternative is presented in Frascarelli (2007), in which it is really C that licenses null subjects. Sande tested both theories using code-switching as a database. Her rationale is as follows: take a language with null subjects (say, Spanish), and code-switch with a language that does not have null subjects (say, English). You can then code-switch between C and TP in two possible combinations: (i) $C_{[Eng]}$ + $T_{[spa]}$ or (ii) $C_{[spa]}$ + $T_{[eng]}$. If $C_{[spa]}$ licenses null subjects, then (ii) should allow null subjects while (i) should not. If $T_{[spa]}$ licenses null subjects, the opposite result should obtain. In fact, she finds that *both* C and T need to be Spanish in order for null subjects to be licensed:

(8) *English*/Spanish

a. * *I wonder what pro* vio.
saw

b. * Me pregunto qué *pro saw.*
Me.DAT wonder what

c. *I wonder* qué vio.
what saw

Sande 2018: 94–100

Ebert and Hoot (2018) reach the same conclusion in their discussion of that-trace effects. English has that-trace effects while Spanish does not, as shown in (9):

(9) a. ¿Quién dijo que traería el pan?
who said that bring.COND the bread

b. * Who said that would bring the bread?

There has been a long discussion as to what factors contribute to this cross-linguistic difference since Rizzi (1982) first asked the question. Ebert and Hoot (2018) ask whether the property that teases Spanish and English apart lies in C or in T. Code-switching again is very helpful: code-switching between C and T reveals what triggers or obviates the that-trace effect. It turns out that both C and T must be in Spanish to obviate the that-trace effect, as shown in the following examples:

(10) Spanish/*English*

a. * ¿Quién asumieron los maestros que *had read the text before the test?*
Who assumed.PL the teachers

b. * *Who did the teachers assume that* había leído el texto antes del examen?
had read the text before the exam

c. *Who did the teachers assume* que había leído el texto antes del examen?
d. * ¿Quién asumieron los maestros *that had read the text before the test?*

Ebert and Hoot 2018: 123

Sande's and Ebert and Hoot's results suggest that C and T do indeed participate in settling grammatical well-formedness, which provides additional support to the notion of feature inheritance.

González-Vilbazo and López (2012), another piece of code-switching work, has expanded our understanding of phases and the role they play in structuring the sentence. Consider constituent order. About half the languages of the world are VO while the other half is OV. How is this encoded in the grammar? The x-bar system of the 1980s presented it as a parameter: UG left the matter open and languages were then free to choose one or the other. Kayne (1993) claims that OV is derived from VO via movement while Fukui and Saito (1998) argue that order is imposed on the output of Merge. González-Vilbazo and López (2012) argue that a feature of the phase head decides if a language is OV or VO. Consider the following examples from the introduction:

(11) Spanish/*German*
Hizo *nähen* *das Hemd.*
do.PAST.3 sew.INF the shirt
'She/he sewed the shirt.' (Cf. 1.4b)

González-Vilbazo and López 2012: 35

(12) *Sranan*/Hindustani
plafond *boro* kare
ceiling bore.through do
'hit the ceiling' (Cf. 1.4a)

Muysken 2000: 254

Both (11) and (12) exemplify light verb constructions such that the light verb is in one language and the lexical verb, in its citation form, is in the other language. We are interested in the order of lexical verb and object in both examples. In German/Spanish code-switching, we have VO order, as shown in (11). This is unexpected: in a regular German sentence with an auxiliary or modal, the regular word order is OV. González-Vilbazo and López (2012) argue that the VO order is imposed by the Spanish light verb. In (12) we have the opposite situation. Sranan is a VO language, but in this example we have the OV order. This OV order has been imposed by the Hindustani light verb, Hindustani being an OV language. González-Vilbazo and López (2012) claim that the light verb in (11) is the spell-out of the phase head (in our terms, Voice). The phase head decides the order of the constituents within the phase and this is how we have the VO order instead of the expected OV. The same analysis can be extended to (12). Thus, it turns out that the VO/OV order depends on a feature of the phase head Voice.

(13)

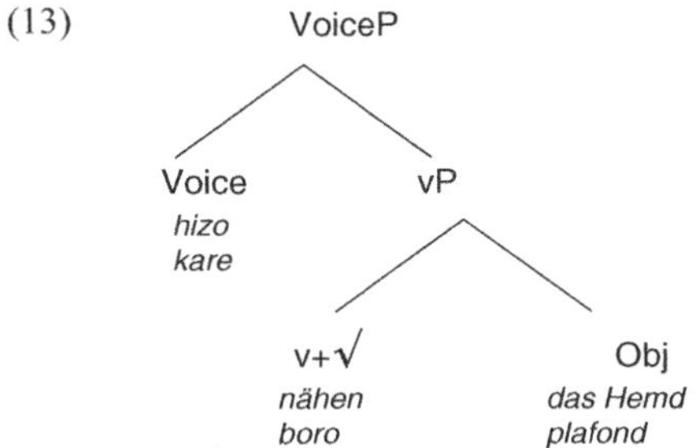

González-Vilbazo and López (2012) additionally argue that the expression of topic/comment structures (see example (5) in Chapter 1) and prosody also depend on the phase head Voice, thus building a complex picture of syntactic properties that turn out to be features of the phase head (more on this on Chapter 6).

This reasoning can be extended to the C phase. The previous discussion leads to the consequence that the relative order of T and VoiceP is a feature in C. González-Vilbazo and López (2013) argue that this is in fact the case,. The argument hinges on the following sentences:

(14) *Spanish*/German

a. *Puesto/ya* *que Juan* **ist** spät angekommen . . .
placed/already that Juan is late arrived
'Since Juan arrived late . . . '

b. * *Puesto/ya* *que Juan* spät angekommen **ist**.
placed/already that Juan late arrived is

c. * *Puesto/ya* *que Juan* **ist** angekommen **spät.**
placed/already that Juan is arrived late

González-Vilbazo and López 2013: 4

Sentence (14a) is an acceptable sentence for German/Spanish bilinguals. (15) shows the tree structure corresponding to (14a). The complementizer of the clause is Spanish, as shown by its spell-out *que*. Since C is Spanish, C is the phase head and Spanish is a head-complement language, the end result it that T precedes VoiceP – even though both T and VoiceP consist of German constituents. On the other hand, Voice is German, as shown by its spell-out in the form of the auxiliary *ist*. Consequently, the order of the constituents within the VoiceP follows the German pattern rather than the Spanish pattern, and so we have *spät angekommen* instead of **angekommen spät* .

(15)

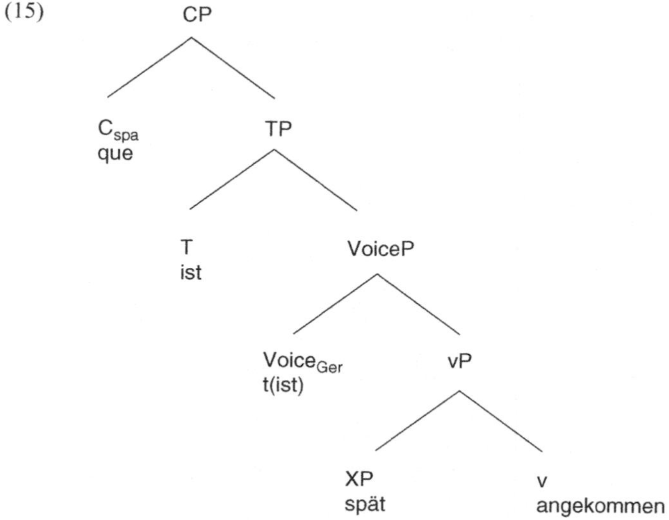

Sentence (14b) is ungrammatical because the Spanish complementizer *que* ensures that the TP complement has the order T + vP, not the head-final canonical order of German subordinate clauses. The unacceptability of (14 c) results from the Voice head. Notice that the lower VoiceP phase is headed by a German auxiliary: this forces the VoiceP phase to be verb final, and this accounts for the unacceptability of (14 c).

For more on the C phase, consider now the following example of Russian/ Kazakh code-switching:

(16) *Russian*/Kazakh
Chasten'ko poluchaetsya *shto* aralastïr-a-mïz
often occur-RFL-3SG that mix-PRES.1.PL
'It often occurs that we mix.'

Auer and Muhamedova 2005: 49

In this example, the complementizer *shto* is Russian while the subordinate clause is Kazakh. As Auer and Muhamedova (2005) explain, there is something odd with this sentence. Kazakh has very few subordinate clauses. Subordination is typically via nominalization, participles, or converbs. However, the subordinate Kazakh sentence in (16) is a regular finite clause that you don't expect to find in a subordination context. The reason for this unexpected appearance of a finite subordinate clause is the Russian complementizer. Russian subordinate clauses are regular finite clauses. In (16), the Russian complementizer determines that its complement will be a finite clause even if the actual exponents in the clause are Kazakh. Thus, it is indeed C that determines what grammatical shape the TP will take, regardless of how the linguistic material in TP spells-out.[1]

Along these lines, see also Cantone (2007: 192–193), who reaches the same conclusion on the basis of child code-switching data.

Finally, let's discuss the nominal realm. I would like to argue here that K is a phase head. The empirical evidence that K is a head comes again from code-switching: the case morphology that one chooses determines the grammatical structure of the selected DP in three varieties of code switching: Basque/Spanish, Turkish/German, and Russian/Kazakh (for a more detailed analysis, see López 2019). In Spanish, German, and Russian constituents within the KP exhibit concord but, interestingly, if the K head comes from a language without concord, concord disappears. Assuming that Concord is an instantiation of Agree, I take this as evidence that Agree dependencies within a KP depend on the properties of the head K.

We start with Basque/Spanish code-switching. Spanish exhibits number and gender concord in determiners, quantifiers, and adjectives. In Basque, there is residual gender morphology on nouns under the influence of Spanish but there is no number concord within the nominal phrase: number and case inflection always attach to the rightmost constituent of the nominal phrase leaving other constituents of the nominal phrase unchanged (Hualde and Ortiz de Urbina 2003: 113–114). In light of this information, consider the following Basque/Spanish code-switching examples (judgments by three deep bilingual speakers from Gernika, obtained informally):

(17) Spanish/*Basque*

a. Algún ancian-o maestr-o-*k* *fabrika-n* *bai* *barre egiten dut.*
Some old-M teacher-M-ERG factory-LOC indeed laugh do aux
'Some old teacher(m/f) laughs in the factory.'

b. Ancian-o maestr-o-*ek* fabrika-*n* *bai* *barre egiten dute*
old-M teacher-M-PL.ERG factory-LOC Indeed laugh do aux.PL
'Some old teachers(m/f) laugh in the factory

c. ? Algun-a ancian-a maestr-a-*k*
some-F old- F teacher-F-ERG

d. * Ancian-o-s maestro-*ek*
old-M-PL teacher-M-PL.ERG

e. * Ancian-a-s maestr-a-*ek*
old-F-PL teacher-F-PL.ERG

In (17a) we have a Spanish noun with a Basque case marker and the result is acceptable. Interestingly, although the nominal suffix is [-o], which in Spanish normally only marks masculine, here it is compatible with a masculine or feminine reading. (17b) shows the same thing in the plural. Example (17c) shows that gender concord on the quantifier and the adjective is largely acceptable. Examples (17d, e) show that any plural inflection on the noun or adjective is unacceptable – only the default masculine form is acceptable. I take this to mean that the Basque case marker forces the selected DP to have Basque properties even if the all the lexical roots are Spanish. I take this to be evidence that K triggers Concord within the nominal phrase and therefore that it is likely a phase head.

Consider now (18). This example was obtained with the help of two German/Turkish language consultants. In (18) we have an example with a German DP and a Turkish case marker. Turkish is a language without gender and concord while German has rich instances of both. But in the example in (18), the adjective is not inflected, resulting in a DP that follows the rules of Turkish and not German. Notice in particular that the corresponding (weak) inflection of the adjective in a regular German noun phrase would be *neuen*. The reason why concord has disappeared is the presence of the Turkish case marker:

(18) German/*Turkish*

Neu-e	Film-*i*	sehen	*yapıyor.*
new	film(m)-ACC	see	do.PROG

'Seeing a new film.'

These data parallel quite precisely the Spanish/Basque data in (17): the K head determines the properties of the complement DP.

The data in (19) present further evidence that K is the head of the nominal phase. Auer and Muhamedova (2005) show that Russian/Kazakh bilinguals can code-switch between a Kazakh case morpheme and a Russian DP. But when this happens, the Russian DP becomes almost unrecognizable because all its grammatical properties have to adapt to the Kazakh phase head K. In example (19), the Russian noun shkol 'school' should trigger feminine concord on the adjective vyssh 'high'. However, the adjective appears in a default, masculine form. We argue that the reason lies in the case morpheme: the case morpheme is Kazakh and Kazakh has no gender. Assume that concord, like other grammatical properties, is dependent on the phase head. Assume further that K is the phase head. If concord is triggered by K and K comes from Kazakh, concord is not possible. Crucially, the Russian noun, on its own, cannot trigger gender concord.

(19) Russian/*Kazakh*

Vyssh-*ij*	shkol-*dï*	*bıtır-d*	*osïnda.*
high-M.SG.NOM/ACC	school-ACC	finish-3.PAST	here

'He finished high school here.'

Auer and Muhamedova 2005: 43

To summarize: the presence of K determines fundamental grammatical properties of the DP that is selected by K. Evidence for this conclusion has been presented in Basque/Spanish, German/Turkish, and Russian/Kazakh code-switching. Since K plays such a clear role in DP structure, I suggest that K should be regarded as a phase head.

Many languages do not have overt case morphemes. Should we assume that they also have a K layer? Positing invisible categories in languages that do not provide any evidence that they possess them is a risky proposition. In all instances, our default assumption should be "what you see is what is, what you don't see is not." In the present case, however, the default assumption does not help with the analysis. Take Basque and Spanish as an example. The default assumption should lead us to conclude that the Spanish noun phrase does not include a K (in the general case, at least) and it consists only of a DP. Since there is only a DP, concord should be regulated by D or some other category within the DP. But then, why should placing this DP as complement of a Basque K affect the availability of concord? There is no answer to this question.

Let's assume, instead, that Spanish always has a K, even when we do not see it. Let's further assume that K triggers Concord. Then, when the Spanish K (a number concord K) is replaced by the Basque K (a non-number Concord K), number concord disappears. Assuming a silent K in Spanish does provide an analysis of the problem. We will have an opportunity to revisit this issue in Chapter 5, where concord becomes important, but for a detailed analysis see López (2019).

Thus, I conclude that the phase heads have a privileged role in the building of syntactic structures. Consequently, they also play a role in the construction of code-switched structures. And code-switching provides insight into the workings of phases that we would otherwise not have. For instance, code-switching has allowed us to clarify the phasal properties of K and C.

Let me now summarize the syntactic framework presented in Section 3.1. I assume the standard Y model traditional in generative grammar. Structures are built by means of Internal and External Merge. The operation Agree, based on the matching of unvalued and valued features, is the only tool built into the syntax to create dependencies. What we normally call nouns and verbs are emergent properties of specific structures, which consist of a feature-less root and a categorizing morpheme. The main source of locality in dependencies is the phase, which also determines the point of transfer as well as many (maybe all) the grammatical properties of its c-command domain up to the next phase boundary. In the clausal domain, Voice and C are phase heads. In the nominal domain, K is a phase head. It has been shown that code-switching offers important empirical support for many of these assumptions.

3.2 The MDM and Code-Switching: Morphology

Within DM, the traditional lexicon is now divided into two lists: see (20), repeated here from Chapter 2 for the reader's convenience. List 1 includes two types of items. The first type of item is lexical roots. Following Harley (2014), I take it that the lexical roots of List 1 are abstract indices that link a syntactic-semantic representation to a phonological realization rule. Thus, √123 in the picture represents a lexical root (from now on, I will keep referring to roots using arbitrary numbers). List 1 also includes a list of grammatical features, or feature bundles, such as [plural], [negation], [past], etc. It is reasonable to assume that these features constitute a Universal Feature Inventory (Embick 2015), from which languages choose a subset and assemble it in various feature bundles.

The items in List 1 can be fed into the computational system, which builds words and phrases with them, as detailed in Section 3.1. DM doesn't assume separate computational modules to build words and phrases.

List 2 consists of rules, called *Vocabulary Insertion Rules* (henceforth: VIRs), which bind phonological exponents to roots, features, and feature bundles. The VIRs are a stage in the process of taking the derivation toward the articulatory-perceptual systems. In this framework, exponents are often referred to as *vocabulary items*. Allomorphy is understood within the DM framework as the possibility of having several vocabulary items for the same syntactic terminal.

(20)

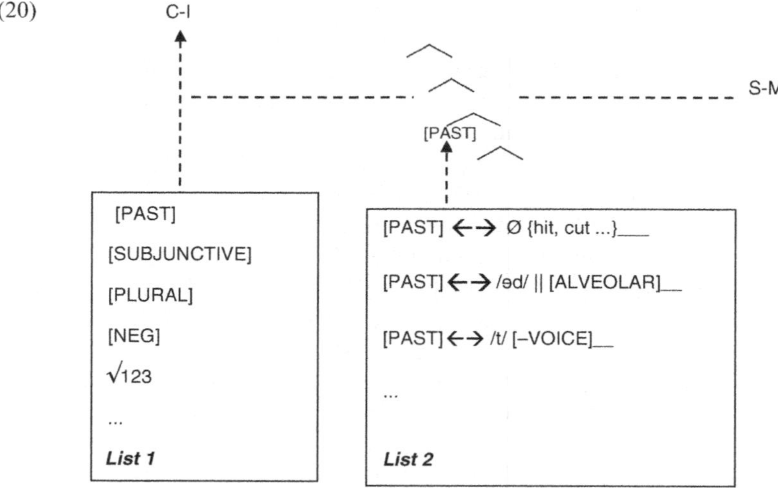

The rules in the box read as follows: [past] spells-out as [t] right after a voiceless segment, [past] spells-out as /əd/ after an alveolar stop, and so on. Some VIRs are amenable to an intensional definition, as in these examples. However, the context for some VIRs may consist of a simple list, as in "past tense spells-out as Ø when it is affixed to the verbs 'hit', 'cut', 'put' . . . "[2]

Another example of allomorphy based on a simple list is the thematic vowel of Spanish verbs. Spanish verbs are arbitrarily assigned to three conjugation classes. Each conjugation class is identified by a thematic vowel (TV), which follows the root and introduces the tense, mood, and aspect morphemes (although with some tense+ϕ-feature combinations the thematic vowel disappears). The morphology of the TMA morphemes depends on the conjugation class. This can be captured by means of rules like the following (the VIRs in (21) are only a first approximation for expository purposes):

(21) TV ⟷ /i/ || ______ {√herv- (boil), √viv- (live), √dorm- (sleep) . . .}
TV ⟷ /e/ || ______ {√com- (eat), √beb- (drink), √sorprend- (surprise) . . .}
TV ⟷ /a/

That is, the morpheme that we refer to as thematic vowel is a syntactic terminal that spells-out as /i/ when it governs one of the roots listed. /e/ spells-out the thematic vowel with a different set of roots. Otherwise, the thematic vowel spells-out as /a/, which is the only productive TV nowadays.

Many VIRs do not include a context in their definition: thus, [definite] spells-out as /ðə/ in English. The VIRs may be ordered, so the more specific ones apply before the more general ones. In the case of English past tense, applying the more specific rule first ensures that that the past tense of 'hit' is 'hit' and not '*hitted'.

One of DM's raisons d'être is syncretism. Morphological syncretism appears when an exponent seems to fit two possible feature bundles. In this situation, vocabulary insertion follows the subset principle (Halle 1997):

(22) Subset Principle: The phonological exponent of a vocabulary Item is inserted into a position if the item matches all or a subset of the features specified in that position. Insertion does not take place if the vocabulary item contains features not present in the morpheme. Where several vocabulary items meet the conditions of insertion, the item matching the greatest number of features specified in the terminal morpheme must be chosen.

In example (23), terminal T has the feature set {x,y}, vocabulary item I has the feature {x} and vocabulary item J has the feature set {x,y,z}. In this situation, I is inserted in T:

(23)

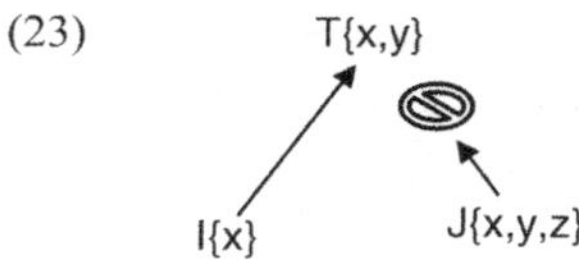

Let's consider an example. Verbs in Spanish conjugate in first, second, and third person in the singular but second and third person plural are conflated in Latin-American Spanish:

(24) *cantar* 'sing' (L.A. Spanish)

	SINGULAR	PLURAL
1	canto	cantamos
2	cantas	cantan
3	canta	cantan

Let's assume that Spanish verbs have the structure shown in (25a). When they are expressed in full, they consist of four syntactic terminals: a root, a thematic vowel, a morpheme that expresses tense, aspect, and mood, and a bundle of ϕ-features (active voice has no exponent in Spanish and I omit it from the following description). In the case of the root √cant, the thematic vowel spells-out as /a/. The ϕ-feature terminals may consist of feature bundles such as the ones in (25b). As is common practice, I decompose the feature person into the primitive features [±participant] and [±speaker]. First person has a positive value for both features while second person is solely [+participant]. Third person is regarded as having a negative value for [participant]. Likewise, I take number to consist of the binary features [±plural].

List 2 provides us with the vocabulary items in (25c). Notice that List 2 does not provide us with vocabulary items that match the second and third person plural bundles exactly – instead, we have the vocabulary item /n/, which is only specified as plural. Thus, if we have a terminal with the feature structure [+plural, +participant, –speaker] or [+plural, –participant] there is no vocabulary item that fits perfectly. Instead, the form /n/, may be inserted. Notice that the form /mos/, which has a [+speaker] feature, is too rich to fit into the terminal.

(25) a. √root + TV + TMA + ϕ

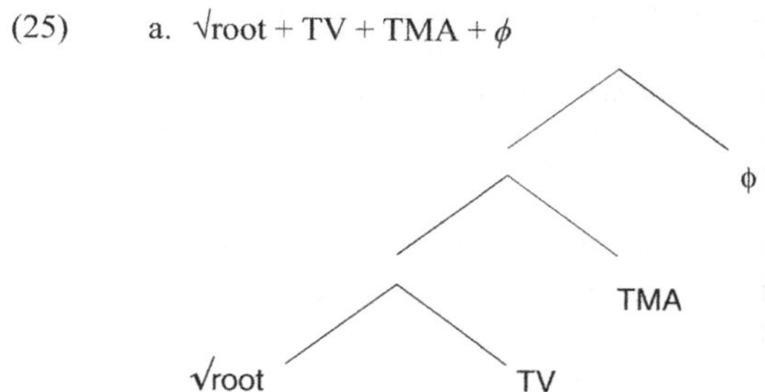

b. syntactic terminals for ϕ-features: [+plural, +participant, +speaker]
[+plural, +participant, −speaker]
[+plural, −participant]
[−plural, +participant, +speaker]
[−plural, +participant]
[−plural, −participant]

c. Vocabulary Items for ϕ-features:

/mos/:	[+plural, +participant, +speaker]
/n/ :	[+plural]
/o/ :	[−plural, +participant, +speaker]
/s/ :	[−plural, +participant, −speaker]
Ø :	[−plural, −participant]

Earlier, I mentioned that unvalued features on a syntactic terminal remain so into PF. Let's assume that unvalued features are indeed present in syntactic terminals at the point of vocabulary insertion. My hypothesis is that a terminal with an unvalued feature can be filled with a vocabulary item without the corresponding feature. This is shown in (26). The terminal T in (26) has the valued feature [G] and an unvalued feature [F]. The two exponents I and J have a matching feature [G], but J has a valued [+F]. This makes J too rich for T and I is inserted:

(26)

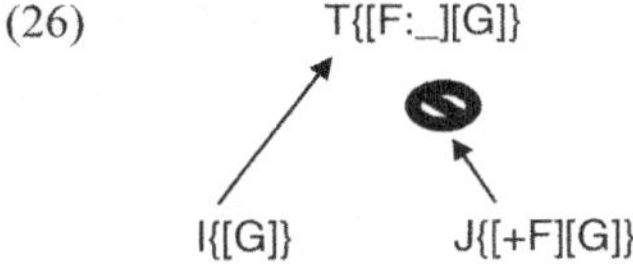

For instance, let's say a syntactic terminal has a valued feature [definite] and an unvalued gender feature [ugender]. A vocabulary item that has a valued [g] feature will be too specified to fit in the terminal. We will have to find a vocabulary item that has only the feature [definite] and no gender specification. In López (2007) this assumption was used to account for expletives and other default values. In this monograph, it will become useful to understand some code-switching patterns in Chapter 5.

Within the system of Embick (2015), VIRs are formalized as follows. Every syntactic terminal is a pair of bundles of features [F,Q]. F is a set of syntactic/semantic features. Q is a variable that stands for a phonological exponent for the terminal. At the point of vocabulary insertion, an exponent from List 2 targets Q and replaces it. I incorporate this understanding of vocabulary insertion, with the additional conception of roots in Harley (2014).

The tree in (27) fleshes out (25a). It adopts the common assumption that there is v-to-T in Spanish. Moreover, Tense acquires the value [present], which has no exponent in Spanish.

(27)

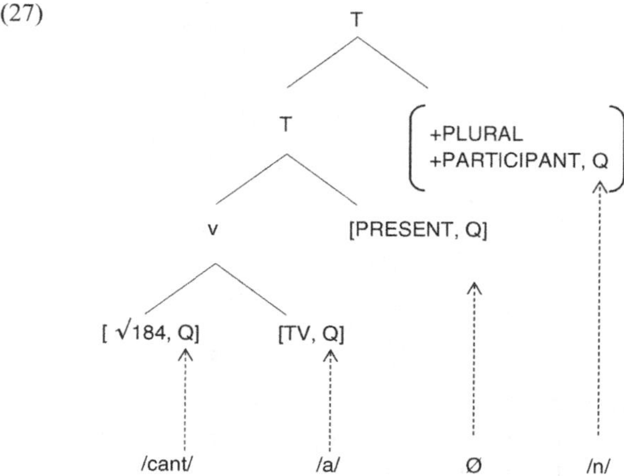

Within DM, the transfer of syntactic structures to the perceptual-articulatory systems is not trivial. Before the VIRs even get to apply, a number of *morphological* processes may alter the syntactic structure in noticeable ways (see Embick and Noyer 2001). I would just like to discuss two of the operations on terminal nodes that can optionally apply: *fusion* and *impoverishment*. Impoverishment plays a role in some of the analyses presented in Chapters 5 and 6 and fusion plays a role in Chapter 5. A third process, called *dissociation*, plays a more limited role in this monograph.

Let's start with impoverishment. Under certain contextual conditions, a terminal node might delink some of its features, therefore becoming available for vocabulary insertion by a simpler, less specified exponent. A classic example of impoverishment is the pronunciation of the Spanish third person dative clitic *le/les* as *se* instead of *le(s)* when in combination with the accusative clitic *lo/la*:

(28) * María **le** lo dijo ➔ √ María **se** lo dijo
Maria CL.DAT.3 CL.ACC.3 said
'Maria said it to him.'

The clitic *se* has always been understood among Spanish linguists to be an impoverished clitic, a clitic deprived of the features that make up the structure of the other clitics in Spanish: crucially, 'se' can be used in singular or plural and in dative as well as accusative and only in the third person – *se* is a pronominal clitic without extra features. Let's see how this impoverishment takes place adapting some ideas in Halle and Marantz (1994) (see also Bonet 1995).

These are the pronominal clitics in (Peninsular) Spanish, as they are normally presented in descriptive grammars:

(29)

me :	first person singular
te :	second person singular
le :	third person singular dative
la :	third person singular accusative feminine
lo :	third person singular accusative masculine
nos :	first person plural
(os) :	second person plural
les :	third person plural dative
las :	third person plural accusative feminine
los :	third person plural accusative masculine
se :	third person

We can posit that pronominal clitics in Spanish are feature bundles that fill a syntactic terminal with a person or a case feature. Plural, when present, is gathered in a separate terminal and spelled-out as /s/. It is also possible to have a clitic terminal without any features: that would eventually be spelled-out as *se*:

(30)

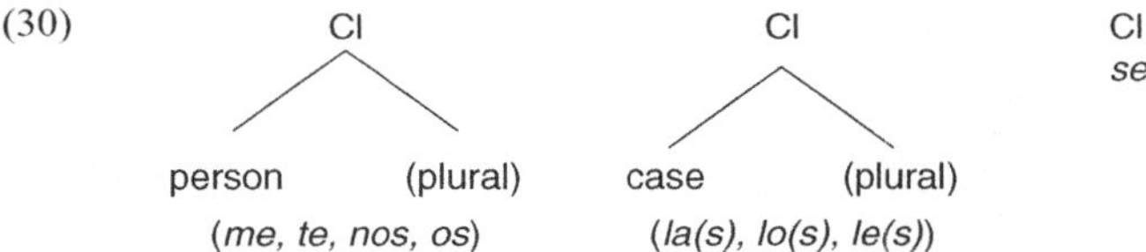

Halle and Marantz (1994) propose the rules in (31) to spell-out clitics in Peninsular Spanish (I alter the format for clarity and consistency, notice that I omit negative values in this list). The first rule says that a terminal with the features [+participant] and [+speaker] spells-out as /n/ when governed by a [+plural] feature. The other rules read similarly:

(31)

[+participant +speaker]	⟷	/n/	|| _____ [+plural]
[+participant]	⟷	/Ø/	|| _____ [+plural]
[+participant +speaker]	⟷	/m/	
[+participant]	⟷	/t/	
[case]	⟷	/l/	
Clitic	⟷	/s/	

As for the plural morpheme, the following rule suffices:

(32) [+plural] ⟷ /s/

They also add two redundancy rules: add vowel /e/ to clitic with dative case, /o/ or /a/ to clitic with accusative case (how these rules exactly work is not clear but does not need to detain us at this point).

We can now return to the rule that turns the sequence *le la/o* to the sequence *se la/o*, as exemplified in (28). (33) is the impoverishment rule that yields (28). It says that when two case clitics are adjacent in a structure, the dative clitic loses the case feature.

(33) CL[+dative] → CL || ____ [+accusative]

Since the resulting clitic terminal has no participant, number, or case feature, it can only spell-out as *se*.

Fusion is a process whereby two syntactic terminals merge into one, combining their respective feature bundles. The classic example of fusion is described in Embick and Noyer (2001). The French sequence *de le* (of the(m)) is obligatorily fused into one morpheme *du*. The following diagram shows a picture of this:

(34)

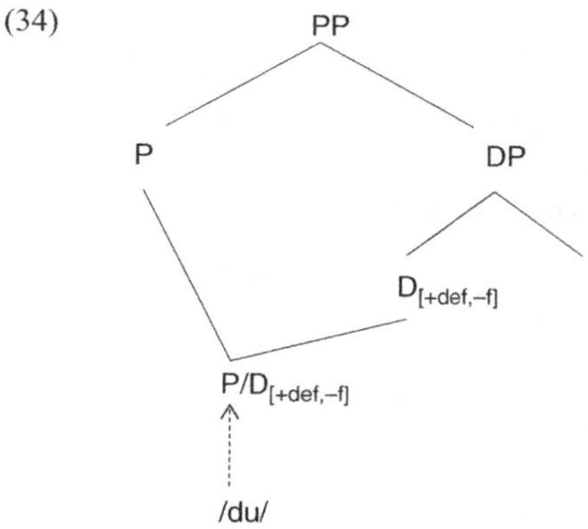

Also after transfer, a syntactic structure en route to PF may sprout additional morphemes, usually called *dissociated* morphemes. They are morphemes attached to a terminal post-syntax. Since they are not present in the computational system proper, dissociated morphemes play no role in semantic interpretation. Embick (2015) suggests that thematic vowels are dissociated morphemes.

After VIRs have applied and the syntactic terminals are enriched with exponents, there are still some operations that need to take place before a structure is sent to the S-M interface: the constituents in the tree structure need to be linearized and the suprasegmental phonology – in particular, nuclear stress and prosodic phrasing – needs to be set up. I take it that linearization and prosodification take place after vocabulary insertion (but see Richards 2016 for an alternative view). Regarding linear order, I take it as a given (see López 2009) that both syntax and prosodic phonology impose conditions on it. The syntactic condition is the Linear Correspondence Axiom of Kayne (1993). The prosodic condition is the wrap condition in López (2009). If González-Vilbazo and López (2012) are correct, a feature on the phase head determines the order of complements within that phase, as explained (see the discussion surrounding examples (11) and (12)). Additionally, there are some readjustment rules that take place after vocabulary insertion.

The picture of the MDM is completed with the *Encyclopedia*, also referred to as List 3. The Encyclopedia is the slice of conceptual structure that finds an index in List 1. It is a repository of non-compositional aspects of meaning. It is also the place where idioms are interpreted and connotations are processed as well as other aspects of meaning. (I discuss the Encyclopedia in some detail in Section 7.1.)

Here is a more complete picture of the MDM model:[3]

(35) *Distributed Morphology framework*

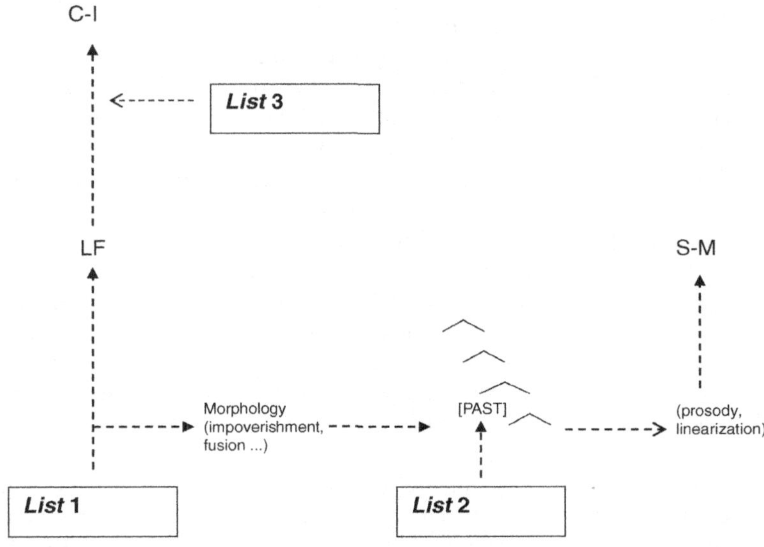

Let me now summarize the assumptions adopted in Section 3.2. The lexicon is divided into a List 1 and a List 2. The items in List 1 are roots and functional categories and make up the input to the computational system. List 2 consists of a list of VIRs for syntactic terminals. Competition among vocabulary items is regulated by the Subset Principle. Before the VIRs apply, some operations may affect the nature of syntactic terminals, among these operations, the most important are impoverishment and fusion. At this point, new nodes, so-called dissociated nodes, may be generated. After VIRs are applied, some further operations may apply: these are the operations that define constituent order as well as suprasegmental structure.

3.3 The Encyclopedia

The model that I have been developing can also be represented in compressed form in (36):

(36)

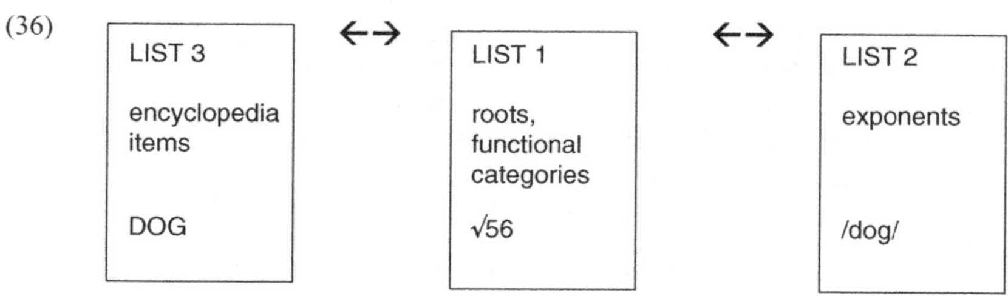

There is no theoretical primitive corresponding to the Saussurian notion of word, a mapping of a *signifiant* with a *signifié*. Instead, we have three separate lists linked by the computational system of human language, C_{HL}. List 1 consists of a set of roots and functional categories. The roots in this system are nothing but formal indices that help us link the items in List 3 and in List 2. These indices are devoid of any grammatical information; since they do not have a label, they cannot project onto fully fledged phrases. I also adopt the widespread assumption that functional categories are listed in List 1 (although, as far as I can tell, for my purposes they could also be listed as indices). Functional categories are drawn from a Universal Feature Inventory (Embick 2015). The idea is that a subset of items from the UFI are activated in a particular I-language and consequently are able to select roots or other functional categories and have an exponent. List 2 consists of a list of rules of exponence – called vocabulary insertion rules in DM – discussed in detail in Section 3.2.

The meanings of words are listed in List 3, what usually is referred to as Encyclopedia. I take it that the Encyclopedia is the set of slices of conceptual structure that find an indexed syntactic structure in List 1. I do not assume that there is a conceptual structure separate from the meanings of words. This assumption avoids a redundancy in many models of the lexicon, which have the meanings of words as copies of items in the conceptual structure. Within this model, this duplication is not necessary. From now on, I use the term "encyclopedia item" or "item in List 3" interchangeably to mean "slice of conceptual structure that is mapped onto an indexed syntactic structure."

Why do I say "indexed syntactic structure" rather than just "index"? Because the mapping to the Encyclopedia involves not a root but a bigger structure, including at least a categorizing morpheme. Consider the Spanish stem *manzan-*. This stem can be suffixed the word marker /a/, adopt feminine gender and mean 'apple'. Or it can take the word marker /o/, adopt masculine gender, and mean 'apple tree'. We can assume that *manzana* and *manzano* are derived from one root, say root √446. The root √446 maps onto the vocabulary item /manzan-/ in List 2. This root may be selected by a masculine *n* or a feminine *n*:

(37) $\sqrt{446} + n_{[-f]}$ → *manzano* = apple tree
$\sqrt{446} + n_{[+f]}$ → *manzana* = apple

The phenomenon that we see in (37) yields a number of pairs: *naranja/o* 'orange/orange tree', *ciruela/o* 'plum/plum tree', etc. (37) points to the following generalization: the root provides a conceptual basis for the meaning of the word but only after the word is categorized is a word meaning extracted. Or, to put it in the terms used in this chapter, only a categorized root can find a well-circumscribed item in List 3.

There are many examples in the world's languages that support this conclusion. If we stay within Spanish confines, we find other peculiar distinctions based on gender. The word *música* is feminine and means 'music', the word *músico* is masculine and means 'musician' (male or female). Less dramatically, we also see other differences in meaning between a noun and the corresponding verb: the verb *caminar* means 'walk' and the noun *camino* means 'path' or 'small road', not something that necessarily must be walked. The event of walking can be referred to with the noun *caminata.* In English, of course, the noun 'walk' means *caminata* and the verb 'walk' means *caminar.* English provides quite a number of examples of nouns and verbs that are based on the same root but one of the two has an idiosyncratic meaning: there are differences in meaning between the noun 'chair' and the corresponding verb, as well as other common words: 'book', 'fly', 'table'; in all of these words, the meaning of the noun and the verb is clearly related but this relation does not follow a predictable pattern.

Finally, consider the well-known semitic roots. These roots map onto very broad semantic fields. For instance, the Hebrew root √bxn may be used to construct many different words: exam, test-tube, diagnosis, etc. (Alexiadou and Lohndal 2017). It seems that the root directs the eye toward a broad, vague semantic field and it is only as a constituent of a categorized structure that it acquires a denotation (the categorial morphemes may come in different flavors, which accounts for the variety of meanings).

We want to maintain the idea that pairs of words like *manzana* and *manzano* are indeed derived from the same root while simultaneously finding a way to express that their meaning varies substantially and somewhat unpredictably. It seems that the mapping to List 3 should take place at the categorizing level at the earliest:

(38)

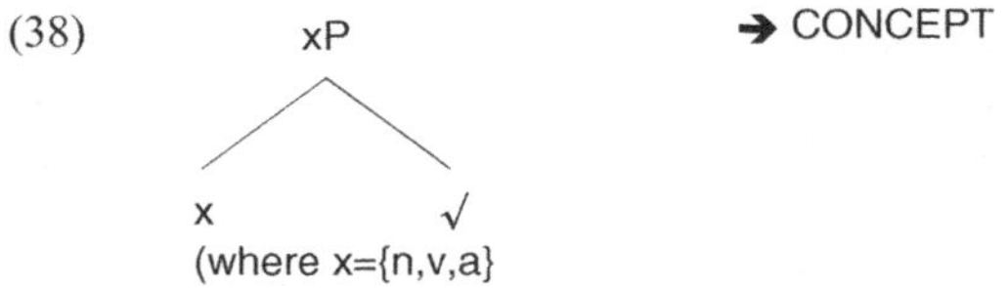

The following diagrams represent the *manzana/manzano* example:

(39)

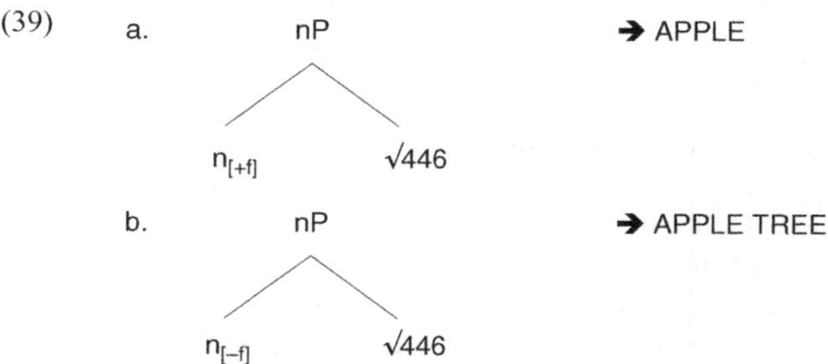

Thus, the mapping to List 3 involves items bigger than just the root. If we accept this conclusion, we may as well adopt it as a starting point to study idioms. We can take an idiom to be a syntactic structure that maps onto a concept:

(40)

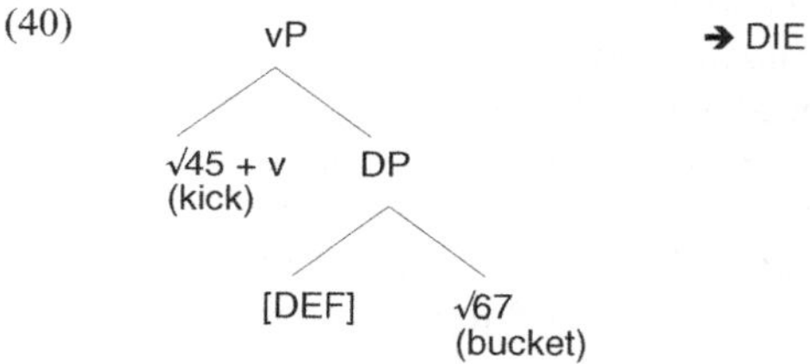

I don't know at this point if this approach to idioms can provide insight into the many puzzling properties of idioms (see, for instance, Siloni et al. 2018 for a recent contribution and references therein for the classic papers). In any case, it will prove very useful in our study of bilingual phenomena (in Chapter 4).

This sketch of the relationship between roots and the Encyclopedia is expanded in Section 4.2.1 and 7.1.

3.4 Language Differentiation

This model of linguistic competence can be used to understand the sources of language differentiation, a necessary step toward understanding bilingual grammars. I suggest there are four sources of language differentiation:

(i) List 1. Languages have different Lists 1. Although we can take it for granted that all languages draw the functional categories from the same Universal Feature Inventory (Embick 2015), languages make different selections from the inventory. In some languages one can find grammatical items in List 1 that are absent in others (tense, aspect, mood . . .). These features might also be bundled differently. For instance, both Spanish and English have a past tense, but in Spanish it is always bundled with (im)perfective aspect and with mood. One could hypothesize that some functional categories are always present in every human language: the structure of verbal predicates that Gillian Ramchand (2008) proposes is a good candidate.

There is of course also wide differentiation of roots and encyclopedia items. Any two languages have different lists of roots, in part because peoples living in different environments will parse the conceptual world in different slices, in part due to arbitrary variation, as I discuss in Chapter 4.

(ii) Before List 2. Some post-syntactic operations of local dislocation and impoverishment are strongly language specific and do not seem to derive from anything else, at least at our current level of understanding. Others reappear cross-linguistically often enough that we are bound to suspect that some deep design features are at play. The rules that simplify clitic clusters are a case in point: although the shape of the rule itself varies from language to language, clitic cluster simplification is very common cross-linguistically.

(iii) List 2. The VIRs are certainly different from language to language, not only with respect to the fact that 'survey' is pronounced *encuesta* in Spanish, but also because of the different allomorphic rules that apply in different languages.

(iv) After List 2. Languages also vary in relation to phenomena that take place after List 2. Best known of all, languages vary with respect to word order. Likewise, languages also vary with respect to the rules of nuclear stress assignment or the structure of prosodic phrases. Finally, readjustment rules are also very much language specific.

Therefore, we have multiple sources of language variation. As a consequence, multilingual individuals must navigate a linguistic input of considerable complexity and eventually build up a linguistic competence system in which the various features fit in their proper place. This monograph is a first approximation to understanding this.

4 1Lex in MDM

In this chapter, I discuss some issues that arise in an integrated theory of bilingual competence, in preparation for the full-blown empirical explorations in Chapters 5 and 6. Recall that my goal is to develop a model that adopts two sets of assumptions. First, as I suggested in Chapters 1 and 2, we should consider the linguistic competence of bilingual speakers as a single cognitive module. This assumption places stringent restrictions on the kinds of analyses that we can put forward.

Second, I am proposing that we explore the bilingual language competence within an MDM approach to the bilingual language faculty. The two sets of assumptions together entail that bilinguals have one List 1 and one List 2 of VIRs, which may therefore compete for insertion. One question that this chapter addresses is to what extent this competition actually takes place.

This chapter is organized as follows. Section 4.1 goes back to the empirical puzzles discussed in Section 2.2 and shows how they cease to be puzzles if we assume a 1Lex model within a MDM theory of I-language. Fortified with this encouraging result, I move on in Section 4.2 to discussing how the items from the two "languages" negotiate their place in the I-language of the bilinguals. This section is somewhat exploratory: it presents some puzzles, some possible answers and, in particular, what answers are not available to us if we adopt the assumptions of the 1Lex model. Section 4.3 discusses dependencies in code-switching. Section 4.4 discusses one direct consequence of this approach: the borrowing–code-switching distinction that has figured prominently in earlier research (see Chapter 1) is not formulable, which I take to be an advantage of this model. Loan translation and syntactic transfer/interference are also briefly discussed in light of the 1Lex MDM model. The chapter ends with a conclusion section.

4.1 Mixed Selection and Noun Class Revisited

Recall that in Section 2.3 we discussed two empirical challenges faced by the 2Lex theory: mixed selection and noun class/gender features.

Let's start with mixed selection. As shown in Section 2.3, many code-switching varieties have a light verb in one language that selects a verbal root or infinitive in the other language. In (1) is an example that, I believe, is already familiar to the reader at this point:

(1) Spanish/*German*
Hizo *nähen* *das Hemd.*
do.PAST.3 sew.INF the shirt
'She/he sewed the shirt.'
González-Vilbazo and López 2012: 35

That is, in Esplugish, *hacer* can function as a light verb only if it selects a German verb in citation form. I pointed out that the Esplugish light verb is a problem for the 2Lex theory because there is no clear mechanism that would allow a lexical item to recognize, let alone select, another lexical item that is a member of a different lexicon. But if all lexical items are represented within one lexicon, this problem does not arise. Let's see how this works. As I mentioned previously, I assume a universal clause structure in which a categorizer selects for a root and the output is selected by a *voice* head, as shown in (2):

(2) $[_{\text{voiceP}}$ Voice $[_{\text{vP}}$ v $\sqrt{}$R]]

Light verbs in code-switching are a spell out of *VOICE*. These light verbs spell out by means of a simple VIR. For concreteness, the VIR in (3) assumes a German/Spanish bilingual as in the Esplugisch variety where *hacer* can act as the light verb:

(3) VOICE ⟷ /aθer/ || ______ $v_{[ger]}$ *hacer* = /aθer/

This rule reads: "Spell out voice as *hacer* when it governs *v*[ger]." As mentioned, the sub-index [ger] should not be understood as a "language label," so thoroughly criticized in much work on code-switching (MacSwan 1999). This index is a convenient shorthand for the cluster of properties that define the German *v* as opposed to the Spanish *v*; for instance, Spanish *v* includes a family of conjugation classes absent from German *v*. The important thing to retain at this point is that the voice head can select for *v*[ger] because both are members of the same lexicon. Additionally, rule (3) needs to be modulated to capture the different tenses, aspects and moods of *hacer*.

Let's now look at the problem of mysterious class/gender assignments. As mentioned, English nouns can be used in English/Swahili code-switching and, when this happens, they always have a Swahili noun class feature. We can identify this feature because it triggers concord. In example (4), we know that *certificate* is class 9/10 because it triggers the corresponding concord on the possessor *-ako* and the preposition *-a*.[1]

(4) Swahili/*English*

Ø-saa	hi-yo	i-na-*depend*	na	***Ø-certificate***	z-ako	z-a
9-time	dem-9	9-pres-depend	with	10-certificate	10-your	10-with

Ø-shule.
10-school
'At this time, it depends on the school certificates.'

Myers-Scotton and Jake 2009: 339

Carol Myers-Scotton's discussion suggests that in the I-language of bilingual Swahili/English speakers, many English nouns can appear in two morphosyntactic environments: the regular English one and a Swahili one. I presented this as a problem for the 2Lex theory because the English nouns in the English lexicon could not possibly have an inherent class, and therefore all English nouns would have to be duplicated in the Swahili lexicon: we would have two nouns *certificate*, etc. The problem remains the same if we keep the 2Lex theory within contemporary MDM assumptions. As I mentioned in Section 3.2, within DM it has been argued that word class/gender is not an inherent feature of a noun but the result of putting a certain root in a certain structure (see, for instance, Kihm 2005, Picallo 2008, Kramer 2015). To make things more concrete, let's assume that gender/class is a feature of the Swahili *n* and that this class feature selects certain roots and not others in the semiconventional way in which noun classes are generally distributed in Bantu. This would still not solve our problem and, in fact, turns it into a version of the mixed selection problem: How could the Swahili *n* select for roots that are not part of the Swahili lexicon?

The only way to approach this problem is to adopt a 1Lex theory. Thus, I assume that the English *n,* the Swahili *n* and all the roots of the two languages are part of the same List 1. I further assume that the analysis of noun classes in Bantu should go parallel to the analysis of gender in Indo-European languages: it should be regarded as a feature of *n* (see Carstens 1991, Kihm 2005). Swahili *n* appears in many flavors, one for each noun class $n_{[1]}$ to $n_{[18]}$. Many roots can appear as members of different noun classes. In the following example, the root *toto* 'child' can appear as a member of classes 1, 5, and 7:

(5)

toto	'child'	
m-toto	'child'	m=class 1
ma-toto	'big child'	ma=class 5
ki-toto	'small child'	ki=class 7

Understanding that the same root can be selected by several different flavors of *n* is the foundation to understand how 'certificate' gets to have a Swahili noun class. I claim that in the mind of the English/Swahili bilingual, the noun 'certificate' may freely be selected by the English *n* or by the Swahili $n_{[9/10]}$ (i.e., noun of class 9/10). And this is how we obtain structures such as the one shown in (6).

(6)

The notion that the same root can be selected by two different types of *n* is not surprising. This is common in "monolingual grammars" as in Swahili, as shown in (5) or Spanish (Chapter 3 ex4). It is not surprising that "bilingual grammars" use the same resource.

Interestingly, this approach directly converges with Grimstad et al. (2014) and Alexiadou et al.'s (2015) DM analysis of noun phrases in English/Norwegian code-switching. Their focus is on examples such as the following:

(7) *English*/Norwegian
   a. den *field*-a
      that field.DEF.F
   b. den *track*-en
      that track.DEF.M

They point out that in English/Norwegian, English nouns are used in what is otherwise a Norwegian DP. When this happens, the English word noun has gender. They use these data as an argument for the claim that gender is not inherent to nouns but is assigned to a noun in a particular structure (more on American Norwegian in Chapter 9.)

4.2 Competitions

The assumption that bilinguals (or multilinguals) have only one List 1 and List 2 raises the possibility of all sorts of complex situations arising from competition among vocabulary items from the two languages. I discuss three possible situations:

1. Roots
2. Free Functional items
3. Inflectional functional items

The 2Lex model should lead to the conclusion that a Spanish/English bilingual has the word 'sock' as an item in the English lexicon and *calcetín* in the Spanish lexicon – although they denote exactly the same thing. The 1Lex assumption allows us to consider the possibility that two List 2 items spell out the same root (thus, a Spanish/English bilingual will have both 'sock' and *calcetín* as vocabulary items that spell out the same root.) It is even possible for one List 2 item to displace the other without altering the List 1 and I argue that this is what is involved in at least some instances of historical substitution via borrowing.

In the case of functional items, we have to consider both the features of the syntactic terminals and the features of the vocabulary items that would spell them out. The most common situation is that the vocabulary items have distinct bundles of features to which different vocabulary items can bond; in this scenario, there is no competition or free variation.

However, in the case of free functional items, I show that it is possible (although infrequent) for terminals from both "languages" to have the same feature bundles and for vocabulary items to have exactly the same structure, including their selectional requirements; when this is the case, items from either "language" can be inserted in the same syntactic terminal and therefore appear in free variation. The least frequent situation – the stars really need to line up for this to happen – is when vocabulary items from either "language" may compete for insertion in the same terminal. I discuss only one example from the history of Old English in which I believe this may have happened.

As for inflectional functional items, since they are bound to distinct morphosyntactic frames, I suggest that they are never in competition.

4.2.1 Roots and the Feminization of "Beer"

Figuring out what to do with roots presents additional complications, mostly because there is no clear agreement on what roots are but also because there is no empirical theory of how the conceptual systems map onto a List 1 and/or a List 3. Here I continue to assume a theory of roots inspired in Harley (2014), which proposes that List 1 is populated by referential indices – which bond to an exponent in PF and to an interpretation in the Encyclopedia – together with functional features or bundles. The roots themselves are atomic, and hence can be manipulated by the computational system as discrete items. There is no assumption in these pages that a root maps onto an atomic item in List 3: first, as discussed in Chapter 3, categorized structures, not roots, map onto Encyclopedia items; second, there is no reason to suppose that List 3 items are discrete: on the contrary, I find it likely that they overlap in multiple directions. Harley's indexed theory allows us to take the items that go into the computational system as atoms while maintaining that the concepts they denote are not; this is intuitively the correct result.

Let's start with an old discussion. Claude Levi-Strauss insisted that the American English term 'cheese' and the French *fromage* denote different entities. The English term denotes something that is low in fat and light, while *fromage* denotes something that is high in fat and heavy. Let's assume that this distinction is real and not a conceit of a French academic's petulance (see also Otheguy 2007 on the different connotations of apparently equivalent English and Spanish words in the lexicons of bilinguals; see also Pavlenko 2009 for some examples of Russian and English nouns and discussion; and De Houwer 2005 for discussion of the denotations of English 'bottle' and Dutch *fles*). We have now two options. We could assume that the bilingual French/English speaker should have two different roots, one that spells out as 'cheese' and another one that spells out as *fromage*. Alternatively, we could have just one root and let these matters of connotation be resolved by the interaction of Pragmatics and Encyclopedia (which entails some connection between the exponent of a root and its List 3 representation.) I adopt this second approach. My reason for adopting this approach is as follows: assume that Claude points at an object and says "that is cheese." If this is a true statement, I strongly suspect that the statement "that is *fromage*" is also a true statement when pointing at the same object. If my intuition is correct, this would suggest that 'cheese' and *fromage* do after all denote the same slice of conceptual structure, even if they each highlight some properties rather than others.[2]

I believe, in fact, that a great number of words in the bilingual lexicon can be subject to an analysis in which one root receives two spell-outs: *planeta* and 'planet', *drama* and 'drama', *renacimiento* and 'renaissance', *ácido* and 'acid' among many others, seem to denote the same concept in English and Spanish and therefore should be taken to involve the same root – they are what are usually referred to as *translation equivalents*. Moreover, an important empirical concept in the code-switching literature implicitly relies on this assumption, the so-called *analogical criterion* for gender assignment (discussed in more detail in Chapter 5). The analogical criterion is usually described as follows: a bilingual Spanish/English speaker who code-switches between an English noun and a Spanish determiner may assign the English noun the gender of the equivalent word in Spanish; thus, we have forms like '*la* house', '*la* table' etc., in which 'house' and 'table' are taken to be feminine because their equivalent words in Spanish, *casa* and *mesa* are feminine. The analogical criterion is an empirical fact that needs to be incorporated into any theory of code-switching or bilingualism generally. In our terms, it provides evidence that indeed many words of the bilingual lexicon should in fact be understood as alternative exponents of the same root.[3]

Let's assume that, in the mind of bilinguals, *planeta* and 'planet', *mesa* and 'table', *fromage* and 'cheese' do indeed expone the same root. Then we would have a clear example of a particular root with two exponents, as shown in (8).

(8) *fromage*, 'cheese'
List 1: √135
List 2: √135 ←→ {/ʧis/, /fromaʒ/}
List 3: CHEESE

Notice that, under this analysis, an apparent example of code-switching like the following could be, for many speakers, simply an alternative spell out for the same root:

(9) Let's have a piece of this delicious *fromage.*

In the previous example, we have assumed that the French and the English versions of 'cheese' have no distinct morphosyntactic features, an assumption that, depending on how we analyze masculine gender in French, may be unwarranted. Let's then introduce this factor into the analysis. The English word 'key' and the Spanish *llave* also seem to denote the same object in the world. However, *llave* is feminine, a feature that is kept in the lexicon of bilinguals (Delgado 2018). In this case, 'key' and *llave* will not be in competition. Rather, the root combines with two alternative flavors of *n* and each has its own spell-out. Example (10) exemplifies this hypothesis. The root √136 can be selected by a plain *n* and in this context it spells out as /ki/. But the same root can also be selected by the "Spanish" $n_{[+f]}$ and in this configuration it spells out as /jaβe/:

(10) *key,* 'llave'
List 1: √136
List 2: $[_n \; n \; \sqrt{136}]$ ↔ /ki/
$[_n \; n_{[+f]} \; \sqrt{136}]$ ↔ /jaβe/
List 3: KEY

There is no doubt that the phenomenon represented in (10) reflects a reality in the linguistic system of a bilingual, namely, that the same root can appear in two different morphosyntactic frames – recall our Swahili/English example in Section 4.1. For further evidence, consider the famous examples of US Spanish, where *troca* means 'truck' and *baica* means 'bike' (see Clegg 2006 for an extended study of morphologically adapted loan words into Spanish). The pairs *troca*/truck and *baica*/bike coexist in the linguistic systems of these bilinguals as exact synonyms. I suggest that for these speakers each pair of exponents spell out just one root in different morphosyntactic frames:

(11)

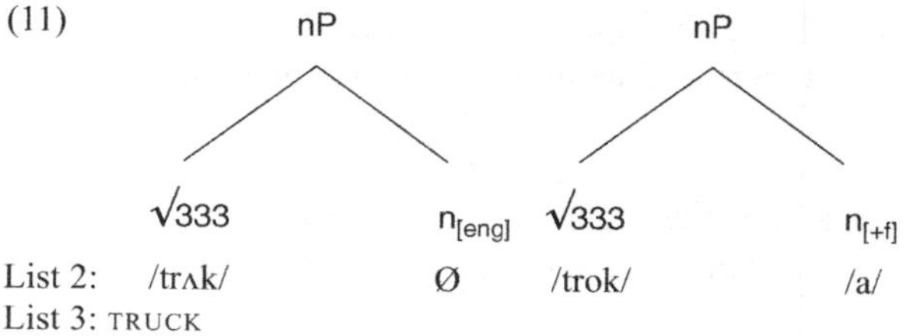

The "English frame" is headed by the "English" *n*, without a gender feature. The root ends up spelled out as /trʌk/. The "Spanish frame" is headed by the Spanish *n* with feminine gender. The root spells out as /trok/ and *n* spells out as /a/ (more on gender in Chapter 5).

Finally, let me briefly return to code-switching between determiner and noun phrase (*la* house, etc.). (10) gives us the tools to understand this phenomenon:

for bilingual speakers that code-switch, the vocabulary item /ki/ 'key' can also spell out the complement of $n_{[+f]}$. This is explored in depth in Chapter 5.

Other examples one can think of are not so simple. Consider now tools for sitting. There are several words for this in English and Spanish: 'chair', 'bench', 'sofa', etc. Interestingly for our purposes, they do not match exactly. In example (12) I use a feature system to show the differences: (I do not hereby endorse feature decomposition systems as an approach to the study of semantics, see Goddard and Wierzbicka 2014 for an account why they have fallen in disgrace; rather, I use a feature system as a descriptive tool to make a point about bilingual lexicons.) I use the features [back] (whether the seat has a back or not), [wide] (if it can accommodate more than one person) and [soft] (if it has a cushioned seat). This is the result:

(12) *Sitting tools in English and Spanish*

Spanish: Taburete: [-back]
Silla: [+back], [-soft]
Sillón: [+back] [+soft]
Sofá: [+wide] [+soft]
Banco: [+wide] [-soft]

English: Stool: [-back]
Chair: [+back]
Armchair: [+back] [+arms]
Sofa: [+wide] [+soft]
Bench: [+wide] [-soft]

Notice that 'stool' and *taburete* seem to mean the same thing. Consequently, they could be regarded as different spell-outs of the same root. The same assumption can be adopted for *sofá* and 'sofa' and *banco* and 'bench'. But notice that *silla* does not correspond exactly with *chair*, nor *sillón* with 'armchair'. My office chair could be a chair or an armchair in English; in Spanish, it could be a *silla* but not a *sillón* even though it has arms because it is not [soft] (in fact, it is not even comfortable). Let's assume a Spanish/English bilingual who has the same distinctions as I do. I surmise that this person has separate roots – indices – for 'chair' and *silla* in their List 1. In the Encyclopedia, their respective List 3 mappings will overlap substantially. Having said this, it is interesting to note the result of a typicality judgment task reported in Ameel, Malt, Storms, and Sloman (2005), which showed that French/Dutch bilinguals tended to categorize everyday objects such as jars, bottles, dishes, and cups in a manner that converged in a middle place, as compared to monolingual controls. In my view, this means that not only does a good chunk of the bilingual vocabulary consist of List 1/List 3 items with duplicated List 2 items (as 'key' and *llave* in (10)); but also, that bilinguals have a tendency to restructure semantic fields to make words fit into this sort of structure.

In any case, it seems that we should conclude that there is more than one way that morphemes in a bilingual lexicon (i.e., List 1 + List 2 + List 3) could be organized. This opens the door for a number of research questions that I hope will be addressed in future work.

Switching gears a bit, I would like to suggest at least two empirical applications of the model presented here. Here is the first one: It is well known that when a word is borrowed into another language, displacing the previous one, the new word often takes the gender of the displaced one. I refer to this as *gender transfer*. Gender transfer has been described countless times in the bilingualism literature as well as the historical linguistics literature. For example, the Old Germanic word for *beer* (OHG **bior*) was neuter (contemporary German: *das bier* (n)) but when it was imported into French and Italian it became feminine (*la bierre*, *la birra*). The reason for this gender change is because the Latin (really Celtic) word it replaced, *cervisia*, was feminine. Thus, **bior* became feminine because it replaced a word that was feminine.

There has never been an attempt at explaining formally how gender transfer takes place, as far as I know. In fact, under the traditional assumption that gender is an inherent feature of a noun, there could never be such an account, since it would require for an inherent feature of a noun to become attached to a different noun, while the old gender of the new noun disappears in the ether, unaccountably. Interestingly, a scenario can easily be assembled under the assumption that the syntactic/semantic features of a morpheme and its phonological features are separable representations. Let's see how.

Consider the *cervisia/birra* example. We can assume that Romance speakers in the galo-italic area started off with the List 1 items presented in (13a): a root, call it √123 and a little *n* with a feminine feature. These two items built the structure in (13b), consisting of the root √123 selected by the feminine little *n*. This structure mapped onto a List 3 item that we can paraphrase as BEER. The structure in (13b) spells out as in (13 c): *cervisia*. (13 c-e) represent successive diachronic stages in which *birra/bière* replaced *cervisia*. With the introduction of *birra* into the mental vocabulary of these speakers, the List 2 would be altered with the addition of a new spell-out for the old root, as shown in (13d). Eventually, the vocabulary item *cervisia* was displaced as shown in (13e):

(13) *Gender transfer*

a. List 1: $n_{[+f]}$
√123

b. $[_n\ n_{[+f]}\ \surd 123]$
List 3: BEER

c. List 2: $[_n\ n_{[+f]}\ \surd 123] \longleftrightarrow$ /kervisia/

d. List 2: $[_n\ n_{[+f]}\ \surd 123] \longleftrightarrow$ {/kervisia/, /bira/}

e. List 2: $[_n\ n_{[+f]}\ \surd 123] \longleftrightarrow$ /bira/

Notice that step (13d) is not obligatory. A word can also be imported with the original gender. If this had happened, a word like *bior*, which is neuter in the source language, could be imported into the default gender in the receiving language, probably masculine. In these cases, List 2 would have two VIRs. (14d') is an outcome alternative to (13d):

(14) *No gender transfer*
d'. List 2: $[_n\ n_{[+f]}\ \sqrt{123}]$←→ /kervisia/
$[_n\ n_{[-f]}\ \sqrt{123}]$←→ */biro/

Thus, we also have a scenario that shows how a new word may also bring its own gender with it, or find an appropriate gender in the receiving language.

Likewise, stage (13e) did not need to happen. The two vocabulary items could have stayed in the linguistic system of these speakers. Eventually, one of them might match to a different root and different List 3 item. You could end up with something like the English words 'beer' and 'ale'.

With a traditional lexicon no similar account of gender transfer can be presented. If gender is a feature inherent to a noun, the word *cervisia* would have an inherent feminine feature that should somehow transfer to the newly imported word and displace the old gender. But the mechanism by which a word can transfer an inherent feature to another would remain mysterious. In the present account, the feminine gender emerges from the syntactic structure and "gender transfer" is simply a question of accommodating a new spell out for the old root. Thus, gender transfer in vocabulary borrowing provides evidence that gender is a non-inherent feature of nouns.

Here is another application of the model: Pfau (2009, 2016) argues that speech errors show that exponents in List 2, even those that expone roots, are in competition for insertion. Consider examples like *shot* (chaude+hot) or *pinichon* (cornichon+pickle), both from Grosjean (1982). The people who produced these forms were bilingual French/English speakers. They blend vocabulary items from the two languages that mean the same: *chaude* (/ʃod/) means 'hot' and *cornichon* means 'pickle'. The person who produced the form "shot" must have had the following entries in their List 1 and List 2:

(15) List 1: √35 (√35=having a high temperature)
List 2: {/hot/, /ʃod/}

shot comes out of blending the two exponents for the root √35. This phenomenon cannot find an explanation within a 2Lex model, which does not predict any competition among roots in different lexicons.

4.2.2 Free Functional Items

A bilingual person may have free functional items in both languages. For instance, bilinguals in any two western European languages will have duplicated versions of the perfective auxiliary 'have'. Likewise, they may have duplicated complementizers and determiners. Questions then arise as to whether they could be in competition or free variation. Let's consider a few scenarios.

In order to observe free variation the following conditions must obtain. The grammars of both languages include free functional items with identical grammatical properties in the syntactic terminals as well as the vocabulary items. Bilinguals will then have one item *i* in List 1 and two spell outs of *i* in List 2. With this set up, the two spell outs should be freely exchangeable. I have found an example of this in the literature, involving code-switching between two Creole languages. Creole languages have TMA auxiliaries standing in a fixed position in the syntactic tree. According to many analyses, they tend to be semantically and grammatically equivalent across the Creole spectrum. Consequently, they allow us to make clear predictions. If speakers who are bilingual in two Creole languages code-switch, we should expect to find TMA items from the two languages in free variation. I have scanned some of the literature on Creole languages and have found a few examples that confirm this supposition. In Migge (2015) we find sentences such as the following:[4]

(16) Sranantongo/*Nengee*
I kan *taagi* en taki a tori dati *mu* skotu.
You can tell him say the story that must end
'You can tell him that issue must end.'

Migge 2015: 189

The two languages involved are Sranantongo and Nengee, two Creole languages spoken in roughly the same area of the French Guyana and Suriname. Both languages have a very similar Creole structure with order SauxVO, no ϕ-feature inflection, and so on. As can be evinced from Migge's descriptions, many speakers of Nengee engage in what Muysken (2000) would call "congruent lexicalization," a continuous, seamless code-switching with Sranantongo, which has the status of a lingua franca. In example (16) the speaker has used a modal verb from Sranantongo (*kan*) which selects for a Nengee verb (*taagi*) and vice-versa: a modal verb from Nengee (*mu*) selects for a Sranantongo verb (*skotu).*

Let's assume that the choice of one or another auxiliary involves allomorphy:

(17) List 1: √334
List 2: √334 ⟷ {mu, musu}
List 3: √334 ⟷ WEAK OBLIGATION

(*mu*: Neegan modal, *musu*: Sranantongo modal)

Let's further assume that appearances do not deceive and take it as a fact that the grammar of TMA is identical in both languages: TMA and verb have no inflection, word order is the same, and so on. If we assume that the feature structure of the auxiliaries in Nengee and Sranantongo must be very similar or identical, it comes as no surprise that auxiliaries from one language can take as a complement a vP in the other. We have what appears to be interweaving of free functional items from the two languages. However, the situation represented in (16) is probably infrequent outside Creole languages.[5]

For a different scenario, consider sentential negation. I believe that negation exists in every human language and therefore I think it is fair to assume that [negation] is a member of the Universal Feature Inventory (see Embick 2015 on the UFI) and it is always selected into a List 1. Negation is often a free-standing functional item, sometimes it is a clitic, sometimes it is a bound morpheme. With these considerations, one could regard it as very likely that a bilingual person has only one [negation] in List 1, rather than two copies of the same feature and a VIR provides two possible exponents for [negation], which could be found in free variation. In fact, this expectation is not fulfilled in the examples that I have looked at. Consider a bilingual Spanish/Basque speaker. *No* is the exponent of sentential negation in Spanish, *ez* is sentential negation in Basque. (18) represents the hypothesis just presented: only one [negation] in List 2 and two exponents in List 2:

(18) *Negation among Basque/Spanish bilinguals* (first pass)

List 1: [neg]
List 2: [neg] ←→ {/no/, /ez/}

With the set up as in (18), the two vocabulary items could be inserted in a [neg] terminal and therefore one would expect the free variation that we saw in the Creole example. This expectation is not confirmed. In fact, Basque negation does not go with Spanish T and vice-versa:

(19) Basque/*Spanish*

a. * Mutila ez *vino.*
boy NEG come.past

b. * *El chico no* zen etorri.
the boy NEG has arrived
'The boy didn't come.'

Vergara and López 2017: 277

Why should the sentences in (19) be ungrammatical? Most likely, because [negation] in Basque and Spanish is not merged in isolation into the structure but in combination with other features. In particular, Basque negation has a richer feature structure than Spanish negation. We know that Basque negation brings about a radical change in the word order of the clause, so that the auxiliary that normally appears at the end of the clause in a typical SOVAux configuration shows up on the left, adjacent to negation, giving rise to the order S[neg]AuxOV (Laka 1990). Thus, it could be that Basque negation heads a terminal that bears an additional feature "attract T." If this analysis is correct, /no/ and /ez/ are not in free variation because they have different feature structures.

(20) *Negation among Basque/Spanish bilinguals* (second pass)

List 1: [neg]
[neg, attract T]
List 2: [neg] ←→ /no/
[neg, attract T] ←→ /ez/

There is of course no way to know a priori what kind of analysis is best. One has to look at the data on a case-by-case basis. However, my impression is that competition among free functional items from different languages will be rare because the feature bundles associated with the syntactic terminals tend to be distinct, as we have just seen in the negation example.

Finally, here is an example in which true competition may have happened among free functional items leading to the disappearance of one form. Consider the replacement of the Old English plural pronouns with the Scandinavian ones in the XIIthC (for a thorough discussion of Middle English changes, see Campbell 1962). In old English we had the plural pronoun /hie/ for accusative and nominative and /him/ for dative. In the Scandinavian (and contemporary English) system, 'they' spells-out nominative while 'them' spells-out anything else. We can assume that the I-languages of Old English/Scandinavian bilinguals could generate syntactic terminals such as the ones in (21a). They would have two sets of vocabulary items to fill these terminals: the heritage Old English pronouns in (21b) and the new Scandinavian pronouns in (21c).

(21) a. 1. [pl, nom]
2. [pl, acc]
3. [pl, dat]

b. /hie/ ←→ [pl, +structural]
/him/ ←→ [−structural]

c. /they/ ←→ [pl, +nominative]
/them/ ←→ [pl, -nominative]

Let's look at the examples in (21) in detail. The feature [+structural] follows the ideas in Halle (1997) that suggest that morphological case can be broken down into binary features. In the case system of Old English, I suggest that the feature [+structural] unifies nominative and accusative together while [-structural] embraces dative (among others). Thus, *hie* spells out nominative and accusative plural terminals while *him* spells out dative singular and plural. The Scandinavian system had a pronoun /they/ for plural nominative and /them/ for non-nominative plural (i.e., the modern system).

Notice that if we have a terminal like (21a.1), 'they' beats 'hie' because the feature [nominative] is more specific than [+structural]. Likewise, if we have terminal (21a.2), 'them' beats 'him' because only the former has a [+plural] feature and [-nominative] is more specific than [-structural]. As for (21a.3), the plural feature carries the day again. I speculate this might be the reason why 'they' and 'them' replaced the Old English forms so fast.

4.2.3 *Bound Functional Items*

A bilingual person has drawn a variety of features from the Universal Feature Inventory with the result that their List 1 is a superset of the features of both languages. Their List 2 will also include exponents from both languages. Most likely, the exponents from one language will be more specified than the exponents of the other language. For instance, one language may have richer agreement or concord exponents than the other. Does the 1Lex hypothesis predict that the more specified affixes will always beat the less specified ones? The answer is yes and no. Maybe it could happen, but it seems to me that the likelihood is small because the environments that define the VIRs are, most likely, distinct. I explain why with an example.

Let's say a bilingual Spanish/English speaker has incorporated the root √165 (=switch) into their "Spanish" vocabulary, so now they can say *switchear* as easily as 'switching'. The question arises why both 'switching' and *switchear* coexist in the grammar of this speaker: shouldn't one of them be more specified than the other and therefore prevent its realization? the answer is no, and the reason is because the Spanish and English inflectional morphemes have different environments of exponence and therefore they will never be in competition. Let's see how.

The Spanish verb has exponents for all persons in the singular as well as a two-way distinction in the plural, while (standard) English only has the third person singular form in the present tense. The Spanish past tense is always amalgamated with perfective or imperfective aspect:

(22) a. Present

	Spanish	English
1	switcheo	switch
2	switcheas	switch
3	switchea	switches
1pl	swicheamos	switch
2pl	switchean	switch
3pl	switchean	switch

b.

	Past		
	Spanish		English
	Preterite/ indefinite	*imperfect*	
1	switcheé	switcheaba	switched
2	switcheaste	switcheabas	switched
3	switcheó	switcheaba	switched
1pl	switcheamos	switcheábamos	switched
2pl	switchearon	switcheaban	switched
3pl	switchearon	switcheaban	switched

Should the more specific Spanish exponents always beat the English ones? No. The syntactic environment of the Spanish and English inflectional morphemes are distinct enough that there will never be competition. As argued here, the appearance of *switchear* alongside 'switching' in the lexicon of a bilingual speaker means that the same root can appear in two different morphosyntactic frames. The structure of Spanish finite inflection before head-to-head movement is represented in (23). I take it that the agreement morphemes form a terminal merged with T. T itself consists of the bundle of features [±past] and [±perfect]. Additionally, *v* has a thematic vowel attached to it (see Chapter 3, example 25a):

(23)

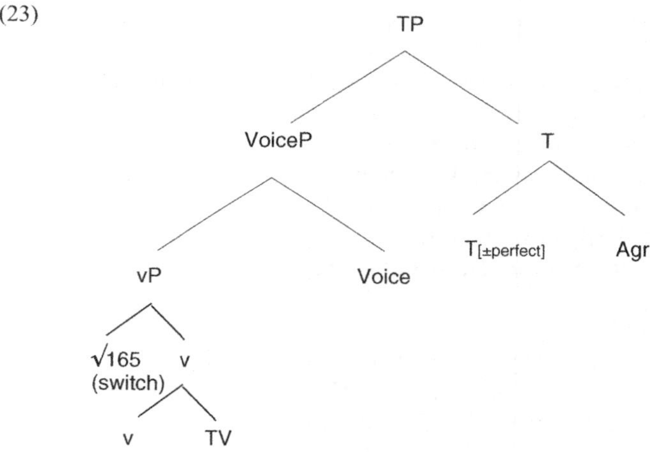

This structure forms a tightly knit framework. The exponents of agreement depend on the aspect features on tense. So, if tense is perfective, the third person of *switchear* is /o/, as in *switche-**ó***, a form that fuses tense and agreement in one morpheme; but if tense is imperfective the third person feature has no exponent (*switcheaba-**Ø***). The shape of T also depends on the thematic vowel, which defines the conjugation of the verb. Therefore, the VIRs will have to express all these factors in their formulation. On the other hand, the English agreement exponents (mostly Ø) are not sensitive to any of this information. The only one that requires a context for it is the present tense third person singular agreement. Finally, we have to take the syntactic terminals into consideration: the English-Spanish bilingual will have "Spanish" syntactic structures with terminals that include aspect as well as "English" syntactic terminals in which the past tense is featureless. Consequently, we have VIRs like the following:

(24) a. [3.singular.past.perfect] ←→ /o/ (switcheó)
[past]←→ /-ed/ (switched)
b. [3.singular] ←→ Ø || TV _______ (switchea)
[3.singular] ←→ /s/ (switches)

(24a) shows two options for a past tense syntactic terminal: a terminal may have aspect and a full battery of phi-features or it may be bare. In either case there is no competition: *switcheó* is too rich for the bare [past] terminal and 'switched' is always beaten by *switcheó* with the richer terminal.

(24b) shows the third person singular present tense, which has a Ø exponent in Spanish and a [-s] exponent in English. The Spanish exponent can only be chosen in the context of a thematic vowel, which ensures that it cannot compete with the English exponent. Thus, the different exponents never seem to compete for the same positions because their environments for insertion are different.

I suspect the following generalization holds: competition among inflectional items may rarely occur because the environments for the insertion of vocabulary items are distinct. I know only that this generalization is valid for the language pairs I am most familiar with (Spanish/English, Spanish/German, Spanish/Basque). As many other aspects in code-switching, decisions will have to be made on a case-by-case basis.

Finally, consider now a third example, the usage of plural markers among Spanish/Quechua bilinguals that Muysken (2012) discusses. Muysken shows how the Spanish grammatical exponent for plural on nouns was borrowed in some varieties of Quechua. This borrowing, however, did not lead to a disappearance of the Quechua plural morpheme. Rather, it yielded a range of results that involved a redistribution of real estate between the two morphemes. In some varieties, the Quechua morpheme is used only for animate beings. In other varieties, the Spanish plural exponent is reserved for Spanish-origin nouns. In a particularly extended variety of Bolivia Quechua, the Spanish morpheme is used after vowels and the Quechua one after consonants. This is shown in the following examples, where [-s] is the Spanish-origin plural morpheme and [-kuna] is the native Quechua:

(25)
a. warmi-s
woman-PL
b. algu-s
dog- PL
c. pay-kuna
3rd- PL
'they'
d. ñan-kuna
road- PL

Muysken 2012: 484

Thus, we can assume that the List 1 of these bilingual speakers has a unique [plural] feature which can be associated with other features (animacy, syllable structure) and various VIRs spell it out in two different forms. It looks like it is really difficult for an inflectional morpheme to displace another one – the new and the old seem to find ways to coexist.

To conclude Section 4.2: it is possible for the two languages of a bilingual to have roots that have two exponents, in which case free variation could happen – although, more often than not, the two exponents are associated with different connotations in the Encyclopedia. Likewise, it seems that, in most cases, exponents for free functional terminals of the two languages have different properties that prevent them from being insertable in the same environments, although there are some isolated examples in which the exponents are indeed in free variation. Finally, the possibility that the inflectional exponent of one language competes with the exponent of another is limited by the conditions that VIRs attach to the inflectional base.

4.3 Dependencies

In the introductory section, I pointed out that the ingredients that get combined in a code-switched sentence establish a net of dependencies across what we usually refer to as "languages." I also claimed that an "insertionist" or "alternationist" understanding of code-switching – really, offshoots of a separationist view of bilingualism – is delaying progress in our understanding of code-switching and bilingual grammar generally.

In code-switching, one can find any sort of dependency. There is subject-verb agreement, exemplified in (26) with an English subject and a Spanish verb. There is reflexive binding, as exemplified in (27), where a long-distance Korean reflexive finds an antecedent in the matrix English clause. There are also wh-dependencies, even between languages that express those dependencies differently. This is shown in (28), where the Korean wh-phrase stays in situ although the rest of the sentence is in English. Finally, there is also NPI licensing, as shown in (29), an example of Spanish/Basque code-switching. We can see that negation is in one language and the NPI is in a different language:

(26) English/Spanish
That goblin lucha todo el tiempo.
fights all the time.

Koronkiewicz 2014: 71

(27) English/*Korean*
Tom$_i$ believes that Bill likes *caki$_i$*
REFL

Finer 2014: 53

(28) English/*Korean*
I wonder he bought *muet* yesterday.
what

Finer 2014: 55

(29) *Basque*/Spanish
a. *Ez zen* nadie *etorri etxera*
NEG aux.PAST anyone come home
'No one came home'
b. No vino *inor* a casa
NEG come.PAST anyone home
'No one came home'

Vergara and López 2017: 270

The MDM model that I am developing in this monograph is ideally suited to understand these switched dependencies. That is because, at the point when the dependency is established, the different probes and goals are only bundles of features that do not belong to a "language," rather, they are part of the unified linguistic competence of the speaker. Notice also that the code-switching data can be very useful in theoretical debates. For instance, notice that the Korean wh-phrase stays in situ, even if C is English, which provides support to the family of movement theories that attribute the trigger of movement to a feature of the moving item, as in Chomsky (1995, ch3) – while suggesting that those analyses that attribute movement to a feature of the probe (Chomsky 2000) might be wrong.

Let me now retake example (5) from Chapter 1, which I presented as an unexamined puzzle in the introduction. I repeat it here for the reader's convenience as (28):

(30) Spanish/*German*
Das Buch, Hans lo hizo *verkaufen*.
DEF.N book Hans CL.ACC.M did sell
'Hans sold the book.'

González-Vilbazo (p.c.)

The direct object *das Buch* 'the book' has been clitic-left dislocated in the Romance manner. This direct object is in a dependency with the clitic, agreeing in number and case. Let's assume that this clitic is the spell out of a definiteness feature that includes a probe with unvalued number, gender, and case features.

As a result of Agree(p,g), the clitic copies the case and number features of the DP. As for gender, we leave it as a question mark in (31):

(31) CL [uc],[u#],[ug] DP[acc],[-pl],[n] → CL [acc],[-pl],**[?]** DP[acc],[-pl],[n]

The fact that a dependency is established is in itself quite an interesting datum. Let's look at this from a 2Lex perspective: an item from one lexicon is able to probe and value features with an item from a different lexicon. Even the fact that the probe can recognize the ϕ-features of *das* is already intriguing. However, the feature that we are interested in here is gender: the German noun phrase *das Buch* is neuter in a three-way system – feminine, masculine, neuter. The Spanish clitic is masculine in a two-way system. The dependency works just fine, which entails that the German neuter and the Spanish masculine must be perceived as somehow equivalent. Let's look at this in more detail.

Following many authors (González-Vilbazo 2005, and so on), let's assume that the German gender can be described using the binary features [±f] and [±m]. Feminine is [+f], neuter is [−f,−m] and masculine is [−f,+m]. German gender can be expressed with the help of the following diagram:

(32)

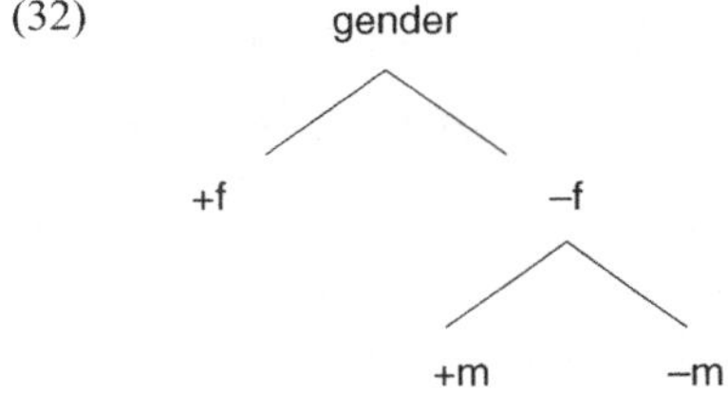

The Spanish gender system could be taken to be a [±f] system:[6]

(33)

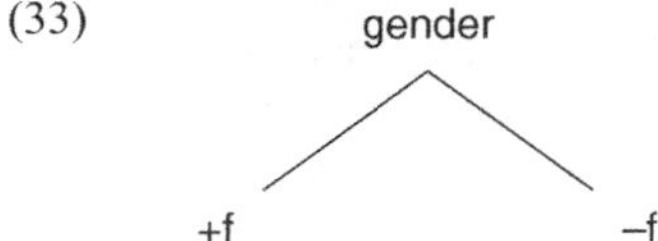

Let's then assume that as a result of the dependency between the clitic and the DP, the clitic ends up with the following feature structure:

(34) CL[uc],[u#],[ug] DP[acc],[-pl],[−f−m] → CL[acc],[-pl],**[−f,−m]** DP[acc],[−pl],[−f−m]

Now the clitic has the feature bundle [−f,−m] as the result of having probed the German determiner *das*, which is neuter. The I-language of this bilingual has two exponents with the label CL: one of them, /lo/, has the feature [−f], the other one, /la/ is [+f]. The subset principle tells us that the exponent with [−f] can fit in the structure, while the exponent with [+f] is incompatible with it. This is how *lo* can double *das Buch*.

Two things to note of this analysis. First, notice that it requires a realizational morphology, including Halle's subset principle. Second, it is a clear example that the "insertion" or "alternation" / "back and forth" concepts do not provide us with the proper framework to approach code-switching. A constituent *das Buch* is not simply "inserted" into the structure but rather, once it is merged, it enters into a web of relations with other constituents, sometimes in long-distance dependencies.

4.4 Other Contact Phenomena

In this section we train our lenses on other contact phenomena with the aim of looking at the possibility of expanding the 1Lex MDM framework to broader empirical areas. We are going to find that the 1Lex MDM framework allows us to cast a new eye on them and we are going to find even new evidence for it.

4.4.1 Code-Switching and Borrowing

The model presented in these pages bears on a lively debate in the bilingualism literature: the distinction between borrowing and code-switching. Here borrowing does not refer to the E-language phenomenon that words used in a language community become words of a different language community. Rather, the question is whether borrowing and code-switching are two different processes in the I-languages of bilingual speakers. Within a 2Lex model like MacSwan's (1999) it is possible to formalize such a distinction. Code-switching involves using lexical items from two lexicons in one numeration (and therefore one derivation) while borrowing involves copying a lexical item (call it LI1) from one of the lexicons (call it Lex1) into the other lexicon (call it Lex2). Borrowing entails creating a new lexical item LI2 with the morphophonological properties related to the language of Lex2. Then LI2 can be drawn to a numeration. I copy here two trees from the introductory section for the reader's convenience. The first tree exemplifies the derivation of code-switching:

(35) Sample of a tree with code-switching. LIs from both lexicons are used to build one syntactic structure.

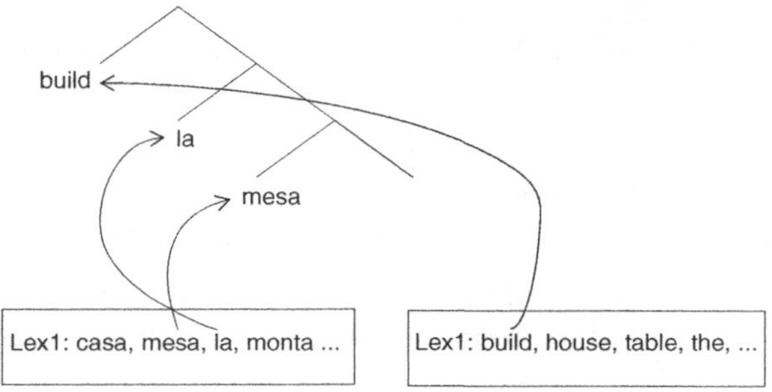

The output of this derivation is a structure that includes items from two lexicons. Since the English word 'build' remains an English word – an item of Lex2 – 'build' retains its English phonology and phonetics.

The following tree exemplifies a derivation in which an item has been borrowed:

(36) Sample of a tree with borrowing. LIs from Lex1 are borrowed into Lex2.

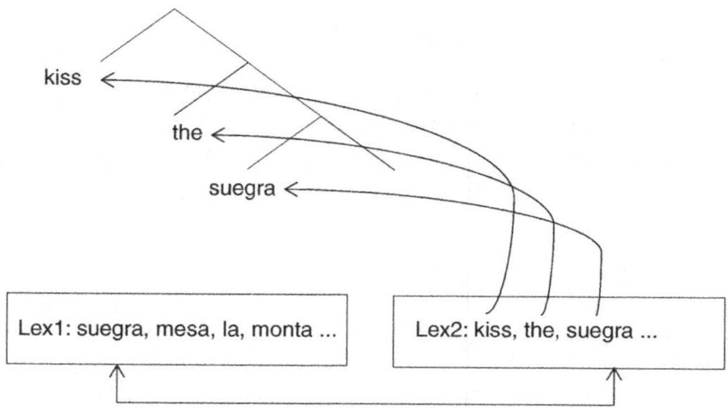

We can see that the word *suegra* 'mother-in-law' has become a member of the English lexicon. Therefore, there are two words 'suegra' in this bilingual person's I-language. The 'suegra' that is housed in the English lexicon – the Lex2 – is fully adapted as an English word, including its phonology and phonetics.

The hypothesis that both borrowing and code-switching exist is actually used in MacSwan (1999, 2000) to account for the prohibition against code-switching within the word (discussed in detail in Section 6.5). It is obvious that this analytical option is not open for me: if my assumptions are right, there is no borrowing in I-language. (Moreover, in Section 5.3, I argue that the borrowing assumption predicts that a number of impossible code-switching combinations should in fact be possible. Thus, there are empirical reasons why I-language borrowing should not exist.)

It is the case that indeed sometimes lexical items seem to preserve grammatical properties of the original and sometimes not. So, let's then consider two possibilities:

(37) a. kiss the suegra [swegrə] (English)
mother-in-law

b. kiss the suegra [sweɣra] (Spanish)

As mentioned, MacSwan would say that (37a) is the output of borrowing because the Spanish word has been fully adapted to English phonetics, while

(37b) is true code-switching. In my framework there is no I-language difference between the two. The derivation of (37a) and (37b) is identical and follows one single channel, including the PF derivation. The only difference is the features that enter the derivation, which themselves provide instructions to the external interfaces. But there is no reason to assume that these features belong in separate compartments (and, as I hope I shall show, good reasons that they do not belong in different compartments).

As far as I can tell, there is really no debate among practitioners as to whether borrowing exists as separate from code-switching: they all agree it does. The debate is whether the borrowing/code-switching distinction affects only the lexicon or the grammatical system as well. MacSwan, as we have seen, argues that borrowing is something that involves only the lexicon. The grammatical system, to the extent that it consists exclusively of the operations Merge and Agree, is indifferent to the origin of the word itself. Myers-Scotton (1993, 2002) is approximately in the same camp: she claims that lemmas involved in code-switching are tagged for one language (the embedded language, in her system) whereas those involved in borrowing are tagged for both languages (the embedded and the matrix) (Myers-Scotton 2002: 153). Having lemmas tagged for one language or the other is formally equivalent to having two lexicons and so I take it that Myers-Scotton and MacSwan agree on this point.

On the other hand, Shana Poplack and collaborators (see Poplack and Meechan 1998 and Poplack and Dion 2012) argue that code-switching and borrowing are distinct linguistic processes, more or less along the lines described: code-switching is about the alternation of two linguistic systems (in which all the participating constituents retain their grammatical properties) while borrowing entails only bringing a foreign element to what is an expression in one linguistic system (therefore adapting the foreign element to the grammatical properties of the host language). This difference can be detected superficially by looking at the morphophonological structure of the word (see also MacSwan 2005). Consider the following examples:[7]

(38) French/*English*
J'ai pas lavé de *shorts* /ʃor/
'I haven't washed any shorts.'

(39) French/*English*
Cinq-cents piasses par trois jours, avec tes *tips* /tɪps/
'Five hundred bucks every three days, with your tips.'

Poplack and Dion 2012: 300–301

In the first example, the English word 'shorts' is pronounced without a /s/ – that is, the plural feature has no exponent, as is the rule in French. This word is therefore a true borrowing (according to Poplack and Dion), because the word has been fully adapted to the French grammar. In the second example, the word 'tips' maintains the plural form of English: it is an example of code-switching. Notice that this analysis includes an implicit separationist assumption: bilingual French/English speakers are in possession of two distinct lexicons and two distinct grammars. Poplack and Dion do not explain what a grammar is, but they seem to assume that it consists of a set of rules like "plural in English is formed by adding [s] at the end of a noun"; "plural in French does not add an exponent at the end of a noun."

These data are interesting and need to figure in any discussion on contact linguistics. However, I argue they do not require the assumption that there are distinct borrowing and code-switching processes. Within the MDM model I have presented, the difference between (38) and (39) can be accounted for without extra assumptions. Let's see how.

As I discussed earlier in this chapter, lexical roots may be available in more than one morphosyntactic frame. For instance, in Romanian many nouns change gender in the plural, in Swahili many nouns belong in more than one noun class. This flexibility is exploited systematically in the I-languages of bilinguals: for instance, for bilingual Swahili speakers, an English noun can appear in two morphosyntactic frames headed by two variants of *n* and this is how the root *certificate* can be the complement of a plain English *n* but also the complement of Swahili $n_{[9/10]}$. And this is all we need to account for the data presented by Poplack and Dion (2012).

Let's assume that the French/English bilingual has two flavors of n, let's call them $n_{[fr]}$ and $n_{[eng]}$. As usual, the sub-indices "fr" and "eng" are only a short cut to the bundle of properties that differentiate an English *n* and a French *n* – including, for instance, gender in the French noun. This bilingual also has two rules to spell out plural: one that spells it out as silent and another one that spells it out as /s/. These two rules are keyed to the type of *n* that they collocate with: silent plural collocates with $n_{[fr]}$ and /s/ plural collocates with $n_{[eng]}$. Finally, a "borrowed" noun is an "English" word that can be selected by a $n_{[fr]}$. Thus, the word *short* in the I-language of the person who produced (38) can be inserted in the morphosyntactic frame of a French noun:

(40) [[[√short] $n_{[fr]}$ PL]
List 2:pl ←→ Ø || $n_{[fr]}$ ______

Since the structure is French, the plural acquires the French exponent (which happens to be Ø). On the other hand, 'tips' is inserted in an English frame:

(41) [[[√tip] $n_{[eng]}$ PL]
List 2: pl ←→ /s/ || $n_{[eng]}$ ______

Consequently, the plural morpheme spells-out as /s/. (In fact the VIR in (41) can be simplified if we take it to be the elsewhere rule.)

Notice that this analysis does not require the assumption that borrowing and code-switching are distinct processes that engage distinct theoretical primitives – in fact, neither code-switching or borrowing *is* a theoretical term, they are simply descriptive labels for what is always the output of the same Merge operation. To sum up: the 1Lex model that I propose does not allow us to make a distinction between code-switching and borrowing as I-language processes: I take this as a feature and not a bug of the system, which allows us to provide an elegant description of the phenomenon that is usually referred to as borrowing.

Before I move on, I would like to discuss Deuchar and Stammer (2016). In this article they inspect a corpus study of English verbs extracted from a Welsh corpus and find that they are not all adapted in the same way. Thus, they find that the English verbs take on Welsh morphology quite readily but in two other respects they behave somewhat differently. First, although Welsh verbs may appear in analytical structures (with a dummy auxiliary that carries inflection) and synthetic structures (without an auxiliary, inflection attaches to the main verb), English verbs have a strong preference for the analytical structure. Second, loan English words tend to mutate a lot less often (mutation is a phonological process that affects word-initial consonants in certain syntactic environments, more on this in Section 6.3), and this preference correlates with frequency in the corpus. This would seem to lead to two conclusions: (i) the divide code-switching /borrowing is not categorical but a cline and, consequently, (ii) "English" words may maintain their Englishness in some respects but not others when used in a Welsh discourse.

However, it is important to emphasize that "native Welsh" verbs are perfectly comfortable in an analytical structure and that mutation is not an obligatory rule – Welsh verbs mutate only 76 percent of the time in their corpus. So, from the point of view of the grammatical structure, there is nothing categorical that separates the English origin words from the "native Welsh" words. Thus, I believe the results of Deuchar and Stammer (2016) are consistent with the 1Lex framework. What we see here is that English words can be integrated into a Welsh discourse, which entails becoming constituents in a Welsh morphosyntactic structure. This is a process that, as I argued in Section 4.1 in the context of Swahili/English code-switching, argues for a 1Lex system. Interestingly, it looks like in order for these words to fully participate in optional grammatical features such as synthetic structures and mutation, a certain degree of familiarity is necessary. This is an interesting fact in need of investigation but does not, as far as I can tell, impinge on my proposals.

4.4.2 Loan Translation

Backus and Dorleijn (2009) define loan translation as "the result of literal translation [in Language A] of one or more elements in a semantically equivalent expression in Language B" (p. 77). Consider the following example:

(42) Turkish
bugün çok kalabalığım
today very crowded.COP.1.SG
'I am very busy today.'

Backus and Dorleijn 2009: 83

The Turkish word *kalabalığım* is not used in regular standard Turkish to express the meaning of being very busy, however, this meaning is common among Turkish/Dutch bilinguals. As Backus and Dorleijn explain, this expansion of meaning is modelled after the Dutch *druk* which does mean both crowded and busy. Loan translation is therefore different from lexical borrowing, because the latter involves both the phonological form and semantic interpretation of a word from Language A into a speech act in Language B while the latter imposes a semantic interpretation extracted from a word of Language B onto a phonological form in Language A.

Notice that the process that yields loan translation is easy to represent within the 1Lex model developed in these pages. Take root √23, a component of List 1 of Dutch speakers. It carries the meanings 'crowded' and 'busy' and it is spelled out as /druk/. Among bilingual Turkish/Dutch speakers, the root √23 has a new vocabulary item: *kalabalık*. This is what we call loan translation:

(43)

List 3		List 1		List 2
DRUK	←→	√23	←→	{/druk/, / *kalabalık/*}

Sometimes the loan translation involves idiomatic meanings involving more than one lexical item. The model presented in these pages is helpful also for these. Consider the following example:

(44) Turkish

a. piano çalmak
piano sound.INF
'play the piano'

b. piano oynamak
piano play.INF
'play the piano'

Backus and Dorleijn 2009: 77

Both verb phrases mean 'play the piano'. (44a) is used in ordinary Turkish. The verb phrase in (44b) is found among Turkish/Dutch bilinguals. *oynamak* means to play and it is probably used in this construction as a calque from Dutch *piano spelen* 'play the piano'. Notice that the calque does not involve the words *spelen* and *oynamak* in all their uses, it involves these words only in the context of playing a musical instrument. This can be analyzed using the assumptions presented in Section 3.3, particularly my suggestion concerning idioms. The idea is the following: take the root √44, a component of the List 1 of Dutch/Turkish bilinguals. The verb that includes this root may spell out as /spelen/ or /oynamak/. The meaning 'play (an instrument)' comes about when the root takes a complement of a certain type, which the Encyclopedia specifies as being a musical instrument.

(45)

For monolingual Turkish speakers, on the other hand, /oynamak/ can only spell out a different root but the List 3 rule should be very similar.

The contact situation may affect a functional item and, as a consequence, there are several possible outputs. There can be plain code-switching or borrowing, as documented in previous sections. There can also be loan translation. Backus and Dorlejin (2009: 90) show some examples of using conjunctions in a monolingual Turkish speech in a manner that the Turkish conjunctions have become a calque of Dutch conjunctions in the minds of Turkish/Dutch bilinguals. This phenomenon can also be approached within the model presented here, as having the Dutch and the Turkish conjunctions as alternative spell-outs of the same functional category.

Consider now the famous examples *llamar para atrás* 'call back' and *dar para atrás* 'give back' (Otheguy 1993):

(46) Spanish

a. llamar para atrás.
   call toward behind
   'call back'

b. dar para atrás
   give toward behind
   'give back'

These examples are usually studied under the rubric "loan translation," although in fact they should be regarded as the creation of a new idiom since there is no formal equivalence between the English and Spanish constructions. The Spanish word *atrás* is formally distinct from 'back': *atrás* behaves like an ordinary adverb in Spanish and it can collocate with the intensifier *muy* 'very' or with the comparative and superlative *más* 'more'. *atrás* does not by itself carry a directional meaning, hence the need of the preposition *para*. The English 'back' is a particle and not an adverb – it does not collocate with an intensifier like *very* nor can it be the head of a comparative construction. The difference between the English and Spanish idioms can be highlighted in our model. Loan translation in our model involves adding an additional spell-out for what remains the same List 1 and List 3 item. But notice we cannot extend this analysis to the examples at hand: it is not the case that *atrás* is an alternative spell out of 'back'. The whole expression *para atrás* carries the meaning that in English is carried by 'back' but it is a full PP.

(47)

The creation of the *para atrás* structure is, no doubt, a result of contact with English, but it is not a phenomenon that can be classified easily within any of the labels that we have available. It is a novel creation.

4.4.3 Syntactic Transfer

Finally, the contact situation may lead to *interference/transference*, which is usually defined as a phenomenon in which a formal structure of one language impinges on a parallel structure in the other language. However, the current model leads to a reconsideration of the data. Consider the possibility that a Turkish speaker learning English produces forms such as the ones in (48) (from White 2003: 62):

(48) I something eating.

Since Turkish is an SOV language, this sentence can be taken to exemplify syntactic transfer, that is, the interlanguage of the Turkish speaker takes his L1 as the starting point for L2 acquisition (the *Full Transfer Hypothesis*). However, within the integrated MDM model that I am presenting in these pages, this example should be analyzed somewhat differently. The sentence in (48) involves nothing syntactic, rather, it shows the addition of new exponents for roots that already existed in the lexicon of the Turkish speaker. But the L1 syntax has not been altered.

Consider the following more complex example:

(49) Turkish

birin-i	sorumluluk-la	yükledi
somebody-ACC	responsibility-COM	burden.PAST.3.SG

'He burdened someone with the responsibility.'

Backus and Dorleijn 2009: 88

The verb *yükledi (yüklemek* in citation form) in regular standard Turkish governs accusative on the direct object and dative on the indirect object. In this example, pronounced by a Dutch/Turkish bilingual, the indirect object receives accusative case while the direct object appears in a prepositional phrase. This happens to be the case distribution of the Dutch verb *opzadelen* 'to burden'.[8] As Backus and Dorleijn argue, Turkish/Dutch bilinguals seem to have imposed the case distribution of the Dutch verb onto the Turkish one. Backus and Dorleijn classify this sentence as an example of loan translation. From the perspective of our model, this sort of example is not substantially different from others we have seen, like the *shorts* example in Canadian French or the *cervisia/birra* example. For instance, in the *shorts* example we saw that the root 'short', which is normally the complement of an English *n*, may appear as the complement of a French *n*, with the result that the plural morpheme has no exponent, following the French rule. In the Turkish example in (49), we see that the verb *yükledi* is now integrated into a (particular flavor of) Dutch verb phrase structure, with the result that the case distribution is as in Dutch. This is shown in (50). The root √866 merges with a verbal head that has the property of selecting an accusative beneficiary and a prepositional theme. This option can receive two spell outs in the List 2 of Turkish/Dutch bilinguals:

(50)

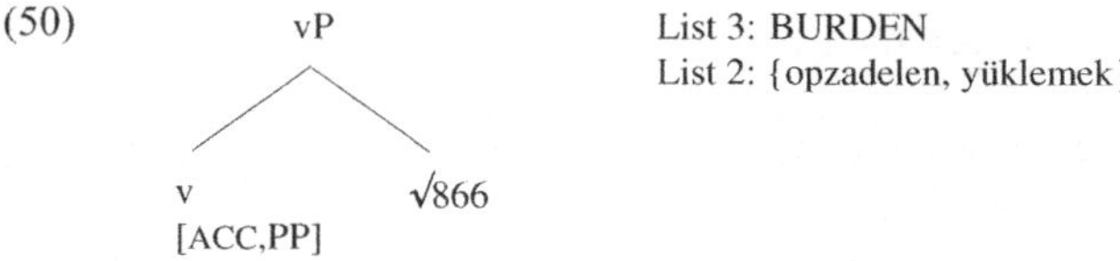

Interestingly, the Dutch functional categories find Turkish exponents in List 2 – further confirming our 1Lex hypothesis.

In the previous examples, I showed that contact phenomena could be reanalyzed in the integrated MDM model. But, could we find actual empirical support for it? I think there is. Consider example (51):

(51) I already give the mosquito to bite.
'I have been bitten by a mosquito.'

Yip and Matthews 2009: 385

This sentence was uttered by a Cantonese/English bilingual child. In Cantonese, the verb *hor,* glossed as 'give' does double duty as the auxiliary used in passive sentences. We can assume the lexical entries for these words in monolingual English and Cantonese are as shown in (52) (we take √55 to be the root that lexicalizes the meaning of transfer of possession, or "give"):

(52) √55 = TRANSFER OF POSSESSION

Cantonese	√55	←→	/hor/
	Voice[pass]	←→	/hor/
English	√55	←→	/give/
	Voice[pass]	←→	/be/

That is, in Cantonese the vocabulary items that spell out √55 and passive voice are the same. In English, the equivalent morphemes are spelled out by different vocabulary items.

In the MDM 1Lex framework, we can posit that (51) is due to an application of analogical process in the mind of the bilingual child: since both 'give' and *hor* can spell out the root √55, then they should also both spell out Voice[pass]. The process is no different from how *birra* displaced *cervisia*.

(53) Cantonese/English bilingual child

√55	←→	{/hor/, /give/}
voice[pass]	←→	{/hor/, /give/}

But I think that a separationist would have trouble providing an account of this. The separationist has to assume that the bilingual Cantonese/English child assigns an extra meaning to the English lexical item 'give' because of the influence of the Cantonese *hor* but, beyond some intuitive reasoning, there is no formal account of how this would be done. The separationist account should cross the boundaries between the two lexicons, destroying the raison d'être of the approach.

To conclude Section 4.4, I have shown that the code-switching–borrowing distinction is not necessary to account for phenomena like the Canadian French borrowings that Poplack and Dion (2012) discuss. Moreover, I have also shown that our system provides insight into the properties of other contact phenomena like loan translation and syntactic transfer/ interference

4.5 Conclusions

With this I conclude Chapter 4. This chapter has developed the 1Lex MDM model sketched in Chapter 3, explored some consequences of adopting it and provided responses to some potential objections. I have shown that the empirical problems that plague any 2Lex models are easily obviated in a 1Lex model while gaining insight into old problems. I have discussed a potential objection to my model: the possibility of competition between vocabulary items that are usually regarded as belonging in two different languages. I have shown that this model is particularly well-suited to analyzing dependencies in code-switching contexts. I have shown preliminary evidence that the distinction between borrowing and code-switching, which is implicit or explicit in all 2Lex theories, is unnecessary and therefore spurious. Finally, I have shown how this model may shed new light on well-known contact phenomena. The following chapter pursues this project with an in-depth analysis of gender.

5 Building the Case for 1Lex: Gender in Code-Switching

This chapter focuses on gender assignment and concord to further explore the empirical consequences of the 1Lex approach to code-switching and the MDM model. Why gender? Bilinguals code-switch between the determiner and the noun – in fact, it is one of the most frequent forms of code-switching there is. Moreover, it is very likely that the two grammars involved in code-switching have different requirements regarding gender assignment and concord. Consequently, there is going to be some possible and impossible code-switches that have the potential to illuminate both code-switching and linguistic theory in general.

The model presented– particularly in Sections 4.1 and 4.2.2 – would seem to predict that all kinds of combinations should be possible (as Pierantozzi 2008 points out in a different context). For instance, I have argued that it is possible for a root – √455 (=certificate) – to be merged in the structure in two different morphosyntactic frames, the Swahili one with a class feature and an English one without it. If we take this argument to its logical conclusion, one should expect that a L1/L2 bilingual can insert any noun of L1 in the frame provided by L2 and vice-versa. For instance, a Spanish/English bilingual should accept either of the following:

(1) Spanish/*English*
  a. la *key*
  b. *the* llave

The data do not (always) confirm this expectation and some D+N combinations are rejected. In exploring these rejections, we will have a chance to explore our model and show that it does in fact make a number of intricate correct predictions.

The problem can be broken down into two parts. First, as pointed out, not every code-switching between a determiner and a noun is acceptable. For instance, González-Vilbazo (2005) reports that while (2a) is acceptable among the community of Esplugisch speakers that he carried out his fieldwork with, (2b) is not. In (2a) we have a Spanish feminine noun with a German feminine determiner, a combination that is always acceptable. In (2b) the

Spanish noun is masculine and the German determiner is also masculine, with further inflection for nominative case. In fact, no combination between a German definite nominative determiner and a Spanish masculine noun is acceptable:

(2) German/*Spanish*

a.	die	*torre*
	DEF.F.NOM/ACC	tower(f)
b.	??der	*cuaderno*
	DEF.M.NOM	notebook(m)

González-Vilbazo 2005: 162

On the other hand, a combination of a German dative determiner and a Spanish noun is grammatical, even if the noun is masculine:

(3)

a.	dem	*interruptor*
	DEF.M/N.DAT	switch(m)
b.	der	*torre*
	DEF.F.DAT	tower(f)

González-Vilbazo 2005: 162

The difference between (2) and (3) falls out of the feature structure of the determiner, as I show in a minute.

Second, even in the contexts in which code-switching is possible, code-switchers have to make a choice concerning the morphological form of the determiner. Consider Spanish/English code-switching. Determiners in Spanish must bear masculine or feminine gender in concord with the noun but English nouns have no gender. Thus, code-switchers who use a Spanish determiner and an English noun have to make a choice: sometimes they choose feminine for the determiner, sometimes masculine. To make this decision, they use two possible strategies. One strategy is the *analogical gender* strategy, which consists of transferring the gender of the Spanish noun onto the English translational equivalent noun. We are already familiar with this phenomenon because we were able to inspect a variant of it in our discussion of the feminization of beer in Section 4.2.1. The analogical gender strategy is shown in (4): since the Spanish word *fiesta* is feminine, the code-switched 'party' is selected by a feminine determiner.

(4) Spanish/*English*

la	*party*	(Spanish: *fiesta*(f))
DEF.F		
the		

Recent neurolinguistic work has shown that analogical gender is not just an on-the-fly strategy to assign gender to new nouns but it is rooted in our linguistic competence system. Boutonnet, Athanasopoulos, and Thierry (2012) asked a group of Spanish/English bilinguals if the third picture was the same as or different than the previous two. Although the task was carried out entirely in English, ERPs showed a brain wave pattern modulated by gender inconsistency. This result suggests that the hypotheses put forward in this monograph must be right: the lexicon of the bilingual is not split in two, grammatical features such as gender are not inherent on the nouns but rather are features associated with subsets of roots.

An alternative strategy is to take one gender – say, masculine –as the *default gender*, as shown in (5):

(5) el survey (Spanish: *encuesta*(f))
DEF.M
the

We can tell that masculine is default because in corpora the masculine determiner is used much more frequently than the feminine determiner (Valdés-Kroff 2016) and the masculine determiner is used even for nouns whose Spanish equivalent is feminine, as in (5).

Liceras, Fernández Fuertes, and Klassen's (2016) survey article finds that both strategies – analogic replacement and masculine default – are available to bilinguals as reported in various studies, although the type of bilingualism seems to play a role in how much they use one or the other. What influences the choice between the two strategies? One factor that has been identified is language dominance: if your dominant language is Spanish, you are more likely to choose the analogical gender (Otheguy and Lapidus 2003, Liceras, Fernández Fuertes, Perales, and Spradlin 2008). Similarly, early simultaneous bilingual adults are reported to prefer masculine as default while those who learned Spanish first and English later might be inclined to use the analogical criterion more often. An additional factor is semantic field: if the noun comes from the familial environment, analogical gender becomes the chosen strategy (Delgado 2018). As Delgado (2018) argues, the usage of feminine determiner among code-switching bilinguals may reflect the way the word was learned from their parents and caretakers if they are L2 speakers of English.

What happens when the determiner is English and the noun Spanish, as in (1b) *the llave*? What we find is even more interesting: we find that the noun influences the pronunciation of the determiner, which acquires a distinctly Spanish phonetics.

Given the wealth of data and its intriguing properties, it is not surprising that there is a considerable pile of literature on the topic. We find papers that use corpora data as well as experimental data (and the experiments can be designed in several different ways, from AJTs to completion tasks). We also find data from different types of bilinguals: early adult bilinguals, child bilinguals, and advanced L2 learners. We also have studies of different code-switching pairs: Spanish/English, Basque/Spanish, Spanish-French-Italian/German, Welsh/

English, Arabic/French, Arabic/Dutch. See in particular: Badiola and Sande 2018, Cantone and Müller 2008, Delgado 2018, Eichler, Janssen, and Müller 2013, González-Vilbazo 2005, Herring et al. 2010, Jake et al. 2002, Klassen and Liceras 2017, Liceras et al. 2008, 2016, Moro 2014, Myers-Scotton 2002, Parafita Couto et al. 2015, Parafita and Gullberg 2017, Pierantozzi 2012, Radford et al. 2007.

In this section, I present four case studies that are representative of the range of problems and show how in every case the data presents further support for the MDM+1Lex model. Section 5.2 discusses Spanish-Basque code-switching, Section 5.3 moves on to Spanish-English code-switching, Section 5.4 briefly approaches MacSwan's (1999) data on Nahuatl, and Section 5.5 is dedicated to Spanish-German bilinguals. But before we begin with the analyses, Section 5.1 discusses the grammar of gender in general and – given the centrality of Spanish in the discussion – of Spanish gender in particular.

5.1 Remarks on Gender Assignment and Concord

Traditionally, gender – and more generally, noun classification systems – has been understood as a feature inherent to the noun itself. For instance, *puente* 'bridge' is masculine while *fuente* 'spring' is feminine – for no reason at all. In Section 3.1 we briefly mentioned that this assumption has been challenged in recent work. In fact, the assumption of inherence presents empirical problems that have been recently brought to the fore. Take, for instance, gender in Romanian. There is a large class of nouns in Romanian that are masculine in the singular and feminine in the plural. Recall also the fluidity of noun classes in the Bantu languages mentioned in Section 3.1. This is not possible if gender is inherent to the noun. Rather, it seems that gender is an emergent feature that arises out of the interaction of a root with the *n* head and even other constituents in the noun phrase such as number (see Kihm 2005, Saab 2008, Acquaviva 2009, Kramer 2015, Estomba 2016, among others).

For our purposes, we assume that gender is a feature bundled with *n*, which therefore may come in different flavors in a gender language. Spanish is a two-gender language, and therefore we can distinguish $n_{[-f]}$ and $n_{[+f]}$. Languages without gender then have an *n* devoid of any features.

(6)

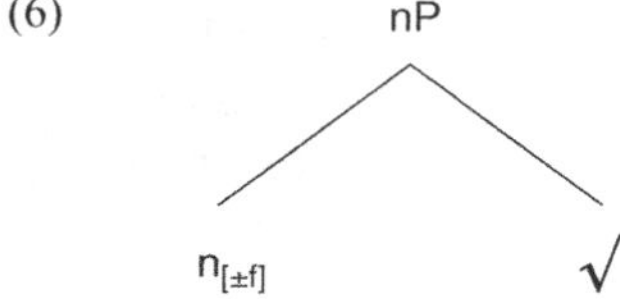

Each of the gender morphemes can be spelled out in a number of ways. The general rule in Spanish is that [+f] is spelled out as /a/ and [−f] as /o/. But there are other possibilities: a few feminine words actually spell out as /o/ and some masculine nouns spell out as /a/. Nouns that end in a consonant or any of the other vowels can go either way. Derivational affixes carry their own gender. For this reason, Harris (1991) made a distinction between the gender feature and the word marker (or desinence). The suffixes [-a] and [-o] are regarded as word markers whose relationship with the grammatical feature gender may be complicated. In my view, a word marker is the particular spell-out that a noun+gender combination may exhibit.

Thus, every root that becomes a noun has to become a noun of the right gender. The root √mes has to merge with an $n_{[+f]}$ and spell out as *mesa* 'table' and the root √fuent has to merge with $n_{[+f]}$ and the latter has to spell out as [e]. Thus, I propose that in order to describe Spanish gender within a DM framework, we need a set of rules that simultaneously ensure that nouns get the right gender and the right spell out for *n*. The rules have the form: "spell out $n_{[\alpha g]}$ as /x/ in the context of / . . . /," where / . . . / is the spell out of a root. Here is a partial (and somewhat informal) picture of gender in Spanish.

(7) *Partial set of rules that spell-out Spanish gender on nouns*

R1: $n_{[+f]}$ ⟷ /o/ || _____ {man– (hand), mot– (motorbike), fot– (photo), . . .}
R2: $n_{[-f]}$ ⟷ /a/ || _____ {poet– (poet), tem– (theme), di– (day), . . .}
R3: $n_{[\pm f]}$ ⟷ /e/ || _____ {estudiant– (student), representant– (representative), . . .}
R4: $n_{[-f]}$ ⟷ /e/ || _____ {(rebot– (bounce), sirvient– (servant), . . .}
R5: $n_{[+f]}$ ⟷ Ø || _____ {luz– (light), . . .}
R6: $n_{[-f]}$ ⟷ Ø || _____ {camión– (truck), pez– (fish), . . .}
R7: $n_{[+f]}$ ⟷ /a/
R8: $n_{[-f]}$ ⟷ /o/

These rules read as follows. R1 says: a feminine *n* spells out as [o] in the context of the vocabulary items √man-, √mot-, √fot- (and a couple others). R2 says: a masculine *n* spells out as /a/ in the context of the vocabulary items √poet–, √tem–, √di–, etc. The rules are ordered from more specific to more general. At the bottom, the most general rules for Spanish gender are the ones here listed as R7 and R8: /o/ is linked to masculine gender, /a/ is linked to feminine. R7 and R8 are in fact the only rules that will be relevant in the ensuing discussion. To sum up, I take it that a Spanish noun is a syntactic structure consisting of a root and a functional category *n* that comes in two flavors $n_{[+f]}$ and $n_{[-f]}$. Both the root and the functional category include a variable Q that is eventually replaced with a vocabulary item.

I take it that the application of VIRs works from the bottom up (Embick 2015). This is shown explicity in (8)

(8)

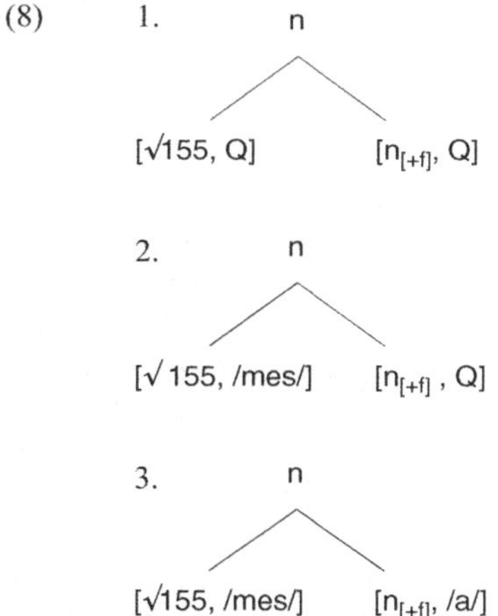

(8.1.) shows the structure generated by the computational system. At this point, [√155, Q] is targeted by a VIR with the result that √155 receives the spell-out /mes-/, as shown in (8.2). After that, [$n_{[+f]}$, Q] is targeted by the VIRs, yielding [$n_{[+f]}$, /a/], as shown in (8.3). Notice that the rules in (7) make the spell out of *n* dependent on the exponent of the root, rather than the root itself. This technical detail becomes important when we discuss bilingual speakers, whose I-language may include two vocabulary items for the same root – say, *llave* and 'key' – and one of them has gender and the other does not. To the extent that this situation exists, it suggests that gender assignment is keyed to the exponent of the root rather than the root itself.

The set of rules listed in (7) is meant to be a tool for the description of Spanish gender, not a fully fledged theoretical proposal. For instance, the /e/ that ends many nouns is usually an epenthetic vowel rather than a declension class and so rules R3 and R4 would probably be eliminated in a more sophisticated analysis. Another feature absent from table (7) is that nominalizing suffixes carry their own gender feature: thus, nouns that end in the suffixes /ion/ (*revolution* 'revolución'), /ura/ (*licenciatura* 'college degree') or /dad/ (*caridad* 'charity') are feminine while /ento/ (*entretenimiento* 'entertainment') is masculine. Natural gender is also not included in (7). Rules that generate these facts should be included in a more complete picture of Spanish gender (see Kučerová 2018 for a recent contribution).

As Roca (1989) and Harris (1991) point out, masculine in Spanish seems to be working as a form of default gender, assigned to items that do not normally have any gender. In example (9), a conjunction is used as a nominal and it automatically triggers masculine concord:

(9) No quiero ningún pero.
NEG want.1 no.M but
'I don't want any buts.'

Harris concludes that what we call masculine is the absence of any gender feature – Spanish gender system would be a privative system. I would rather say that Spanish does have a binary [±feminine] feature choice and that roots can be selected by [–feminine] or [+feminine] *n*. Examples such as the one in (9) can be accounted for under the assumption that $n_{[-f]}$ is the default nominal-making strategy. Thus, as the root √pero is inserted in a nominal morphosyntactic frame, it is selected by $n_{[-f]}$. The advantage of assuming a [−f] feature instead of adopting a privative system will become clear when we study German/Spanish code-switching. In a nutshell: German is a three-way masculine, feminine, neuter system, and we find that Spanish masculine nouns are compatible with masculine and neuter determiners in German; this is only possible if the masculine/neuter determiners in German and the Spanish masculine nouns have some feature in common; I take this feature to be [−f] (see also the discussion in p64).

DM approaches to Spanish gender are typically different. Saab (2008), Embick (2015), Kramer (2015), and Estomba (2016) assume that an nP has three terminal nodes: one for *n,* one for gender and an extra category, called *Declension Class*, corresponding to the main suffixes – Harris' word markers – which configure the edge of a Spanish noun. In Spanish there would be three main classes: Class 1: [o], Class 2: [a] and Class 3: [Ø/e] (see Roca 1989, Harris 1991, Oltra-Massuet 1999). Within this view, the declension class is a dissociated morpheme attached to *n* post-syntax. The result is a structure such as the following:

(10)

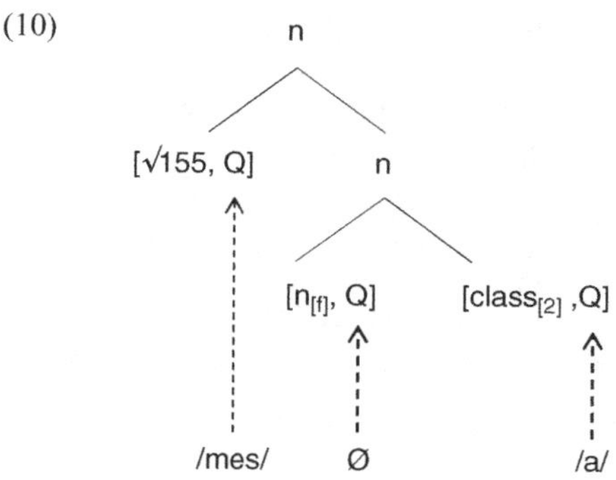

In this view, the Spanish word *mesa* 'table' is a feminine noun of class 2, *mano* 'hand' is a noun of feminine gender and class 1, while *llano* 'flat land' is of masculine gender and class 1. The rules of vocabulary insertion make sure that the right vowel matches the right declension class, rather than the right gender – gender itself never has an exponent. The probability that a member of class 1 is masculine is captured by means of general VI rules (see Kramer 2015, Oltra-Massuet and Arregi 2005).

In some analyses (see Oltra-Massuet 1999, Alexiadou and Müller 2008), the declension class is an inherent feature of the root and has to match the class of the dissociated morpheme – a problematic assumption in the context of a theory that adopts the hypothesis that roots have no grammatical properties. Kramer (2015) proposes an alternative that avoids assigning a root a class feature. Instead, the rules that insert the class features are contextually dependent. For instance, two separate rules introduce Class 1 in the structure: A very specific rule lists the roots that are selected by a $n_{[+f]}$ (√man-, √mot-, etc.) and a general rule introduces a Class 1 node in the context of $n_{[-f]}$. The same thing goes for Class 2 and Class 3.

It is hard to decide which analysis is best. Do we need class features? Kramer (2015: 237–238) argues that doing away with class features is an undesirable move because we end up with several rules of vocabulary insertion that result in the spell-out of [o], [a] and [e] (see 7), whereas in the system represented in (10) the three desinences are always the spell out of the same three declension classes. This consideration is convincing to the extent that the assumption of declensional classes in Spanish gives us empirical mileage – but in fact, it does not, since there are no actual declensions in Spanish nouns as are found in languages such as Latin. In Latin, the class of a noun decides its inflection for number and case. But in Spanish there is no case inflection and the plural morpheme [s] is independent of the desinence that precedes it. Thus, the construct of declension class for Spanish nouns provides no insight. I would argue that the system in (7) allows us to simplify the analysis in two ways: (i) we can dispense with the notion of declension class; and (ii) we don't need to sprout a dissociated morpheme in the post-syntactic component, in full-throated violation of the inclusiveness condition.

Gender in Spanish is expressed on determiners, quantifiers, and adjectives via concord with the noun. Example (11) shows the definite and indefinite determiners in Spanish:

(11) el : [def, –f]
la : [def, +f]
un : [indef, –f]
una : [indef, +f]
los : [def, –f, pl]
las : [def, +f, pl]
unos : [indef, –f, pl]
unas : [indef, –f, pl]

For all those nouns that do not follow the more general rules R7 and R8, the gender of a noun is only visible in concord with the determiners (as well as adjectives, if there are any):

(12) a. el puente
DEF.M bridge(m)
b. la fuente
DEF.F spring(f)

Following Carstens (2000), I take it that concord is a dependency that can be expressed using the Agree (probe, goal) presented in Section 3.1. The question of the probe for concord is complex. Recall that I argued in Section 3.1 that concord originates in K, which is therefore a repository of the unvalued gender and number features that trigger probing. The empirical argument that I presented in Section 3.1 (and in much deeper detail in López 2019) emerges from the fact that concord is possible if the right type of K head is present in the structure. I reproduce example (19) from Chapter 3 here as example (13) for the reader's convenience:

(13) Russian/*Kazakh*
Vyssh-*ij* shkol-*dï* *bıtır-d* *osïnda.*
high-M.SG.NOM/ACC school-ACC finish-3.PAST here
'He finished high school here.'

Auer and Muhamedova 2005: 43

In example (13), the Russian NP *vysshij shkoldî'* lacks gender concord, which would always be obligatory in a normal Russian DP. The reason for this lack of concord is that this DP is the complement of a Kazakh K and Kazakh is a language that has no form of concord. We also showed data in Turkish/German and Basque/Spanish code-switching that points in the same direction: if K is from a language that has no concord, concord within the DP disappears.

In Section 3.1 I argued that this empirical data should lead us to the conclusion that K is present in (at least some) languages that do not express it explicitly. Consider the following: if a Spanish DP appears as the complement of a Basque K, number concord within the DP disappears. If we take concord to originate in K, this empirical datum gets an easy account: the Spanish K has been replaced by the Basque K, with the result that concord within the DP is limited to what the Basque K allows. I take it then that gender and number concord in Spanish originates in K. However, as we know, the gender and number features show up on the D. I propose that K and D share these features – maybe through *feature inheritance*. The mechanism of inheritance makes a copy of the entire K bundle and merges it as a sub-label of D.

(14)

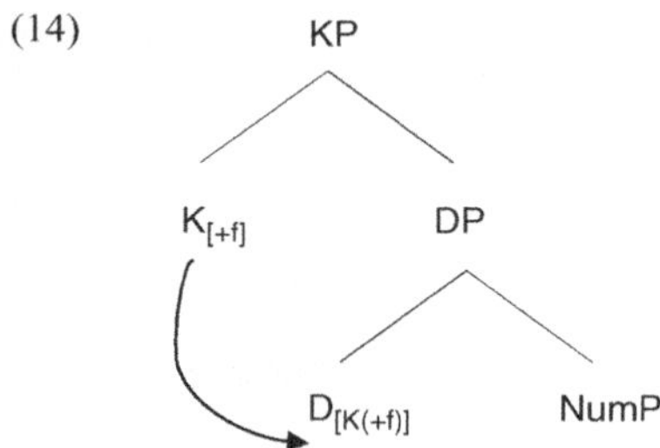

Spanish determiners consist of two or three terminals: One terminal for the (in) definiteness morpheme (which will spell out as */un/* for indefinite and */l/* for definite), one terminal for gender (*a* for feminine and *Ø* for masculine singular or *o* for masculine plural) and a terminal for plural, which spells out as *s*. The structure of a Spanish determiner is as follows:

(15)

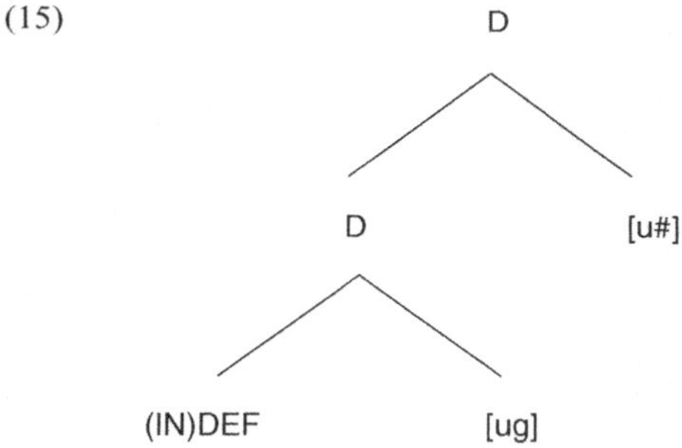

The unvalued gender and number features constitute independent probes and are valued using the familiar mechanism of Agree in the c-command domain of D. In the following examples, I arbitrarily choose the values plural and feminine:

(16)

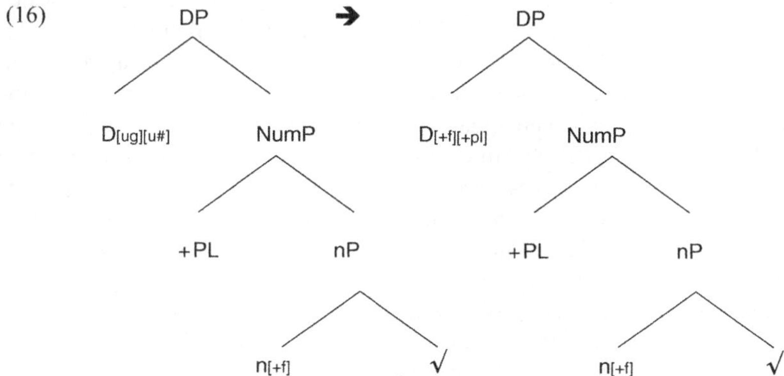

Since the features of D are now valued, D is ready for vocabulary insertion. These rules may take a shape like the following:

(17) VIRs for Spanish determiners (first pass)

1. DEF ←→ /l/
2. INDEF ←→ /un/
3. +f ←→ /a/
4. −f ←→ /o/ || _____ [pl]
5. −f ←→ Ø

The resulting structure after all features are valued and VIRs have been applied is in (18):

(18)

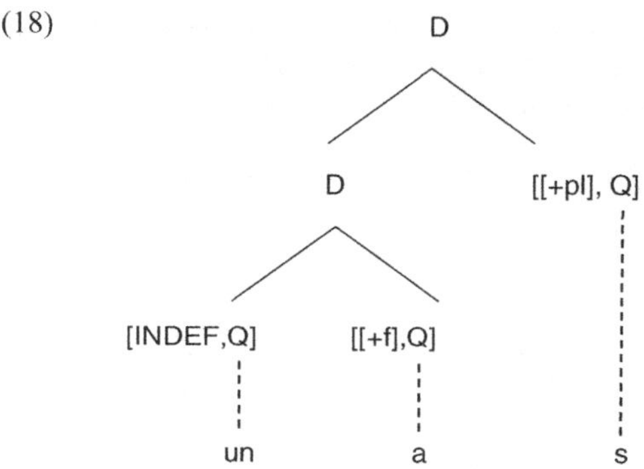

5.2 Gender in Basque/Spanish Code-Switching

In this section, I present some Basque/Spanish data that provides empirical evidence that the List 2 of a bilingual is one integrated system.

As Badiola and Sande (2018) show, the inhabitants of Gernika, in the Basque Country, are deep bilinguals who use Basque and Spanish regularly and code-switch between them. Their code-switching reveals an interesting feature of their linguistic competence. Basque is a language that does not express gender on the nouns (with only a few exceptional borrowings from Romance; see Hualde and Ortiz de Urbina 2003: 137, and my brief discussion to follow) and nouns can end in any consonant or vowel without any grammatical consequences. Spanish, however, is a language with masculine and feminine genders, which are associated with a variety of environments. The question that arises is: what happens when a Basque noun is merged as a complement of a Spanish in a code-switched discourse? What kind of concord will it trigger on the determiner?

Badiola and Sande (2018) presented a survey to bilingual speakers that included an acceptability judgment task and a forced choice task. Their research question was: what Spanish determiner would their subjects choose for a Basque noun? The result is that generally they chose the masculine gender, which confirms Roca's (1989) and Harris' (1991) analyses in which masculine is viewed as default (but see Parafita et al. 2015, for a different result with a different community of Basque speakers). The glaring exception is that if the word ended in [a] they consistently preferred the feminine determiner:

(19) *Spanish*/Basque
a. *la* makila (Spanish: el bastón)
DEF.F walking-stick
b. *la* gona (Spanish: la falda)
DEF.F skirt

The preference for feminine is cued exclusively to the word ending. Notice in particular that analogical gender plays no role: although the Spanish word *bastón* is masculine, the Basque equivalent *makila* collocates with the feminine determiner.[1]

The data uncovered by Badiola and Sande can be accounted for easily within a 1Lex theory. The VIR that links feminine with [a] is a VIR that is part and parcel of the linguistic competence of these speakers, not a rule of the *Spanish* of these speakers. In other words, there are no two separate sets of VIRs, but just one, which will operate whenever the environment is right, regardless of "language." I submit the data in (19) as empirical evidence in favor of the 1Lex theory and against the 2Lex theory. If indeed the bilingual speaker had two lexicons, or even two separate List 2, these data could not be accounted for: how could a Spanish rule affect a subset of the Basque lexicon?

Let me develop this in more detail. As mentioned, Spanish nouns ending in /a/ are in fact complex words, made up of a root and a little *n* with a [+f] feature. The desinence /a/ is the spell out of $n_{[+f]}$:

(20) falda $[[\sqrt{123}]+ n_{[+f]}] \rightarrow$ fald + a
SKIRT

Evidence that /a/ is not part of the root comes from derivational morphology. When a derivational suffix is added, it is added on the root √fald: *faldita* (small skirt), *faldón* (shirttail).

The Basque /a/ in words like *makila* and *gona* is also a separable constituent of the word. This can be seen in the following examples drawn from Hualde and Ortiz de Urbina (2003: 173), where the reader can find the entire paradigm (thanks to Karlos Arregi for a useful discussion):

(21) *hondartza* : 'beach'
*hondartz**ok***: beach.ABS.DEF.PL.PROX
*hondartz**etan***: beach.LOC.DEF

Interestingly, other vowels do not drop when adding suffixes. The noun *etxe* 'house' is inflected as *etxeok* not as **etxok*.

Thus, I believe it makes sense to propose that Basque /a/ is actually a desinence, the spell-out of *n* when *n* attaches to a particular set of roots, as shown in (22a). With this setup, it is very easy to see how *makila* and *gona* might trigger feminine concord on the Spanish determiner. It is only a question of letting the roots √makil, √hondartz, and √gon be inserted in an additional morphosyntactic frame, as shown in (22b):

(22) a. makila : $[[\sqrt{133}]+ n]$ ➔ makil + a
b. makila : $[[\sqrt{133}]+ n_{[+f]}]$ ➔ makil + a

This development causes no strain on the system and allows Basque nouns that end in /a/ to be assimilated into the VIR R7 (in (7)).

Some borrowings from Romance suggest that this analysis is on the right track. Hualde and Ortiz de Urbina 2003: 137) document that there is a small number of Spanish borrowings that appear in masculine and feminine form in some dialects. The short list includes the adjectives *majo/maja* (nice), *tonto/tonta* (silly), *katoliko/katolika* (Catholic). Within my terms, this means that these Basque adjectives are inserted in "Spanish" morphosyntactic frames a [±f]. Again, this is only possible if the two lexicons are integrated in the mind of a Basque/Spanish bilingual.

5.3 Gender in English/Spanish Code-Switching

We are now discussing examples in which a Spanish determiner is followed by an English noun (the *carro*) and vice-versa (*el* car). As is often the case in the field of code-switching, the literature does not fully agree on the description of the facts. Everyone agrees that Spanish D followed by English N is fine – so, (*el* car) is always fine.[2] The disagreement comes with English D and Spanish N – so, (the *carro*) is a source of controversy. Some of the literature argues that code-switching between an English D and a Spanish noun is less acceptable than the reverse (Belazi et al. 1994, Radford et al. 2007, Moro 2014) while others doubt that this is invariably the case (see Herring et al. 2010, which inspects corpus data). I conducted my own informal survey of three early and highly proficient Spanish/English bilinguals of the Chicago area with the goal of finding out if English D and Spanish N could indeed go together. I did indeed find an asymmetry, albeit one that is different from what has previously been described. The asymmetry that I found in acceptability judgments was confirmed via inspection of the Miami Corpus, gathered, transcribed, and made public by the Bangor Center for Bilingualism in Theory and Practice. The study of gender in English/Spanish code-switching provides additional evidence for the integrated approach because, as I shall show, the 2Lex assumption makes the incorrect prediction that some impossible outcomes should be acceptable.

5.3.1 The Data

The consultants were asked to read sentences like the ones in (23) and evaluate whether they found them acceptable or not. As they evaluated the sentences, I asked them to read the code-switched examples with two alternative pronunciations. The framing device that surrounded the code-switched DP was in English:

(23)
Juan forgot to bring us the *pez*. (pez=fish)
Before going to bed, María turned off the *luz*. (light)
To get to the dentist, you need to cross the *puente*. (bridge)
You can get some fresh water from the *fuente* (spring)
You got a stomach ache because you ate all the *queso*. (cheese)
You shouldn't drive the *carro*. (car)
When you open an account at the bank, they give you the *libreta*. (notebook)
Do me a favor, get me the *mesa*. (table)
This church is ugly, I didn't like the *restauración*. (restoration)
Sander thought he would bring us the *revolución*. (revolution)
The *resentimiento* prevented him from loving his brother. (resentment)
She didn't forgive him, despite the *arrepentimiento* that he showed. (regret)

The results are summarized in (24) with one randomly chosen example. What I found is that code-switching between 'the' and a Spanish noun worked alright, with only one restriction regarding the pronunciation of the DP, which is exemplified in the contrast between (24d) and (24e). (24d) shows that *the mesa* pronounced with English phonetics, is not acceptable to my consultants while (24e) shows that the same DP is acceptable if the entire DP is pronounced as if it were Spanish:

(24) Spanish/*English*
a. *Get me* la mesa.
the table
b. *Get me the table.*
c. √/? *Get me* la *table.*
d. */?? *Get me the mesa.* [ðə meɪsə]
e. *Get me the* mesa [da mesa]
f. */?? *Get me* el *mesa.* [el meɪsə]

Let's consider the sentences in (24) in turn. The judgments in (24a–b) fall in line with what previous researchers have found. With respect to (24c), my consultants express a preference to have *table* pronounced with English phonetics, but this preference seems not to be strong enough to regard the structure as unacceptable. With some hesitation, I regard (24c) as uniformly grammatical.

The contrast in (24d) and (24e), as far as I know, has not been discussed in earlier work. As shown in the transcriptions that accompany the examples, it is acceptable to have an English determiner followed by a Spanish noun provided that the whole DP receives a Spanish phonetics. The judgments in (24d) and (24e) were corroborated via a corpus investigation in Delgado (2019). Delgado inspected the Bangor Miami Corpus generously made public by the CBTP, University of Bangor, and found fourteen instances of 'the + Spanish NP':

(25)
The *boca* Herring8
'the mouth'
The *manguera* Herring9
'the hose'
The *costos* Maria27
'the expenses'
The *gringo* Sastre10
'the gringo'
The *capitana* Sastre10
'the captain (female)'
The *muebles* Sastre11
'the furniture'
The *harina* Zeledon6
'the flour'
The *maizena* Zeledon6
'the corn starch'
The *mosquitero* Zeledon6
'the mosquito net'
The *sala* Zeledon13
'the living room'
The *malicia* Zeledon13
'the malice'
The *espiritu santo* Herring17
'the holy spirit'
The real *espiritismo* Herring17
'the real spiritism'

He then trained an undergraduate research assistant to analyze the F1 and F2 formants of the vowel in the determiner and found that the vowel in 'the +Spanish NP' is indeed similar to the same speaker's /a/ in the Spanish determiner *la* and dissimilar to 'the' when it is followed by an English NP (the consonant /d/ could not be analyzed due to the fuzziness of the data). Pending a deeper investigation, it seems that the contrast between (24d) and (24e) is real and in need of explanation.

It is worth pointing out that corpora studies reveal that while the Spanish determiner + English noun combination is very common, the reverse is less frequent (see Liceras et al. 2016: 118 for a summary of the results). This would follow if it is indeed the case that the English determiner + Spanish noun combination happens to be more restricted than the Spanish determiner + English noun combination.

The data in (24d–e) are challenging for a 2Lex approach. Within a 2Lex theory that incorporates a distinction between code-switching and borrowing (see Section 4.4), (24d) should be grammatical under the following scenario. Consider the diagram in (26) and take Lex1 to be the "Spanish" lexicon and Lex2 to be the "English" lexicon. The word *mesa* /mesa/, a member of Lex1, may be borrowed into the Lex2 of the bilingual: it becomes the English word 'mesa', pronounced (/meɪsə/).

(26)

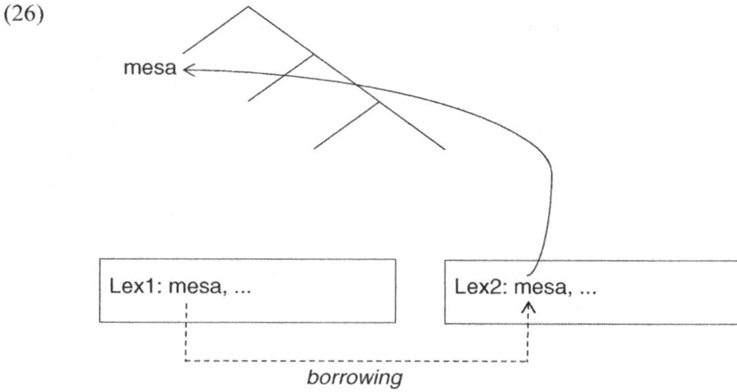

Once 'mesa' has become an English word, it should accept the determiner *the*, pronounced [ðə] – and this is how we incorrectly allow the unacceptable (24d). Unless we build up a constraint on borrowing from one lexicon to the other, in a 2Lex theory there is no restriction that would yield the unacceptability of (24d).

Let me now add another turn of the screw. DPs that look superficially like (24d) are indeed acceptable by bilingual speakers. As far as I can tell, they always involve Spanish-origin words that have become common currency in American English:

(27) a. John ate all the *tamales* yesterday. [ðə təmæləz]
b. I'm not drinking the *tequila* today. [ðə təkilə]

Thus, we need a formal theory that prevents (24d) in the general case while simultaneously allowing for the occasional development of what is exemplified in (27). Current theories seem to me to be too strict or too loose.

Moro (2014) (see also MacSwan 2005) is an example of an overly strict theory. In her approach, the entire feature structure of a functional category must be checked. She argues that examples like 'the mesa' are ungrammatical because the gender feature of the noun must be checked against the gender feature of the determiner: the unchecked gender features on the determiner in mixings such as 'la table' creates no such problem, following a particular theory of feature (sub)sets. Leaving aside that Spanish nouns can appear in monolingual speech without a determiner that could check their gender features (as in *Luis Enrique está buscando electricista* 'Luis Enrique is looking for (an) electrician'), Moro's theory does not capture the distinction between (24d) and (24e). In contrast, Liceras et al. (2008) can be presented as a theory that is too loose, since all possible D+N combinations are grammatical in their account, incorrectly allowing (24d) in the general case.

Finally, let me discuss (24f). The data in (24f) presents another interesting puzzle for the 2Lex theory. The inclusion of (24f) in this list might be surprising because, as far as I know, it has never been discussed. But the assumption of two lexicons with the added option of borrowing items from one lexicon to the other predicts that (24f) should be possible. (24f) represents the following scenario: the word *mesa* in Lex1 is imported into the Lex2 and therefore is selected by English *n*; thus *mesa* in Lex2 is a genderless noun because it is a noun of the English lexicon. If *mesa* can be turned into an English word, then it can be code-switched with a *Spanish* determiner. Which Spanish determiner? In Spanish, the default gender is masculine (and that's how we get *el building*, *el survey*, *el city hall*, etc., see Delgado 2018 and references therein). In such a scenario, the Spanish determiner could be *el*, which is the default choice when there is no agreement:

(28)

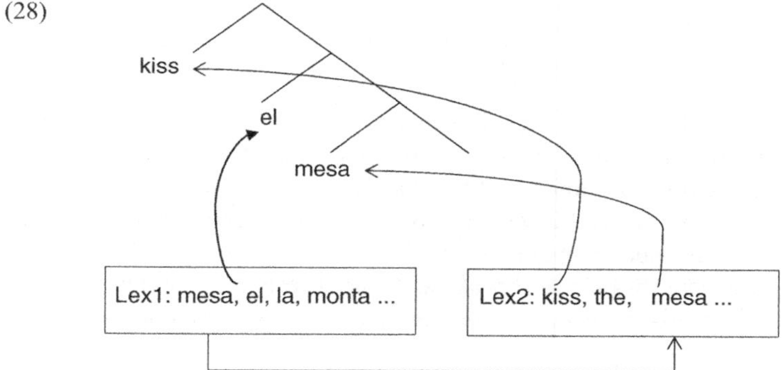

Thus, (24f) should be as grammatical as 'el building'. In fact, we should expect that Spanish feminine nouns should generally appear with a feminine determiner and with a masculine determiner – but this is not the case: with rare exceptions, gender assignment is fixed, among bilingual speakers as much as among monolinguals. This problem is inherent to any approach that assumes two separate lexicons and the possibility of borrowing from one to the other.

5.3.2 Analysis: Preliminaries

Let's start with the analysis. Building on the assumptions developed in Chapter 4, I take 'table' and *mes-* to be alternative spell outs of one root in List 1, here randomly assigned the index 145:

(29) List 1: √145
List 2: √145 ⟷ {table, mes-}

The root can then become the complement of a little *n*. As discussed in Section 3.2 as well as in Section 5.1, I take gender to be a feature of *n*. Let's posit three types or flavors of little *n*. The basic one is the "English" one, which has no extra properties. Spanish has two flavors of *n*, corresponding to the two genders:

(30) Little *n* in English: n
Little *n* in Spanish: $n_{[+f]}$
$n_{[-f]}$

As argued in Section 5.1, the connection between the gender feature and the noun desinence in Spanish is not trivial, involving a number of different rules. The summary I presented (see Section 5.1) stated that (i) the general rule is that /a/ spells out feminine and /o/ masculine, (ii) a number of more specific VIRs associate either gender to any vowel ending, and (iii) gender can also have a zero realization when the noun ends in a consonant.

For the time being, consider the following two structures. The first one shows the syntactic structure and spell out of the Spanish noun *mesa* and the second one shows the English noun 'table'. Thus, we have two VIRs:

(31)

(32)

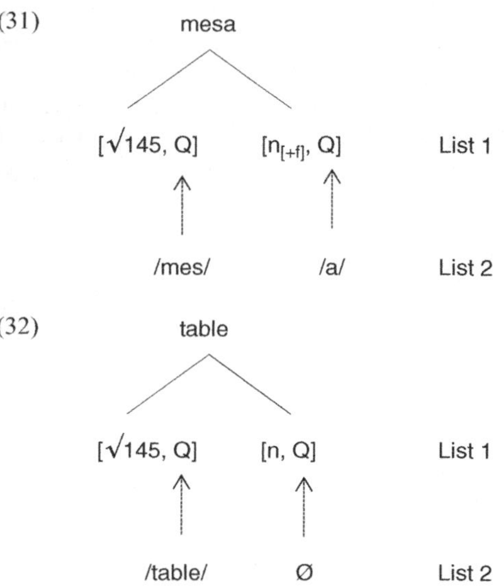

Obviously, these two VIRs are available to the bilingual speaker. But the data in (24) suggests that the bilingual speaker has additional options: /table/ can be selected by $n_{[+f]}$ as a possible spell out for √145 (yielding *la table*). The acceptability of *the mesa* suggests that a $n_{[+f]}$ can be selected by a featureless English determiner.

The morphology of determiners in English and Spanish is quite distinct. I take it that English 'the' is the spell out of the DEF feature while 'a' spells out INDEF. In Spanish, the DEF/INDEF features inflect for gender and number, as shown in (11). As described in Section 5.1, I take it that the features DEF/INDEF may carry an unvalued gender feature that gets to be valued as [±f] as a result of concord with $n_{[\pm f]}$. This DEF/INDEF with valued gender must spell out as *el/la* or *un/una*. But if DEF/INDEF[uGender] probes and only finds an *n* without a gender feature (an English *n*), the [uGender] of DEF/INDEF remains unvalued. Unvalued features do not lead to a crashed derivation but rather trigger default options (see Section 3.2, as well as López 2007 and Preminger 2014). Thus, when the VIRs kick in, it turns out that the subset principle decides that only 'the' can pair up with a DEF that has an unvalued feature: 'the' is a featureless determiner and the Spanish el/la have an additional gender feature that makes them too rich. This is how we get *the mesa*, where *mesa* maintains its Spanish structure with the noun desinence, as I shall detail. Likewise, only 'a' can spell out an INDEF feature with an unvalued gender feature.

After feature valuation, both the DEF/INDEF feature and the gender feature are independent terminals. /l/ spells out DEF, /un/ spells out INDEF, Ø spells out masculine and /a/ feminine (see 17). Thus, the syntax of determiners in English and Spanish is as follows (for the example I use only the DEF feature). English 'the' can be the spell out of a definite head with no gender features or with an unvalued gender feature. A determiner with feminine or masculine gender spells out as /l/ (in the following I omit the feature Q to unclutter the representations):

(33) a.

b.

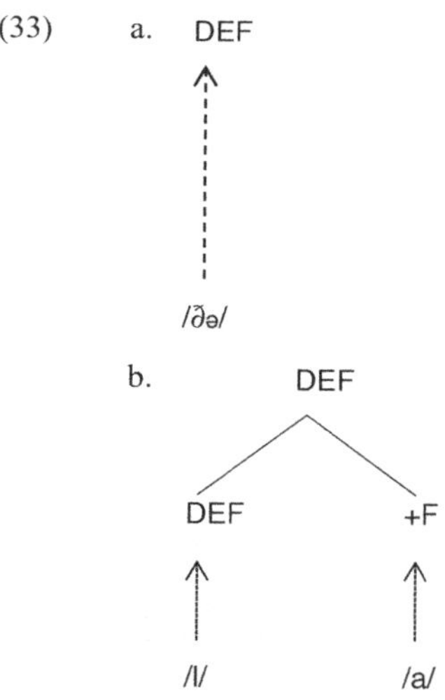

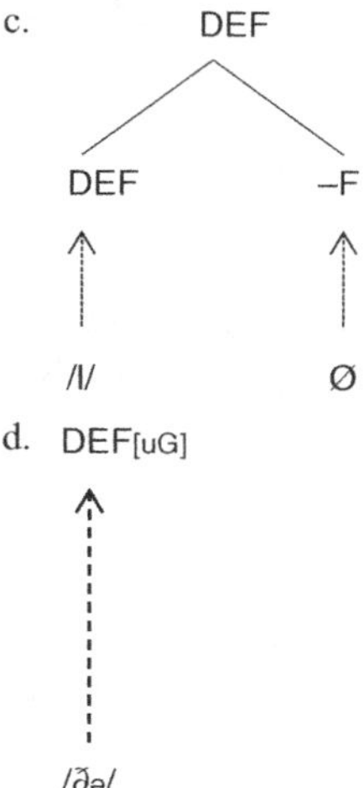

In subsequent trees, I generally simplify (33b) as $\text{DEF}_{[+f]}$ and (33c) as $\text{DEF}_{[-f]}$ if nothing in the analysis hinges on it. The corresponding spell-out rules for English and Spanish definite determiners for a bilingual speaker are as follows:

(34)
DEF ←→ /l/ || ___[gender]
DEF ←→ ðə
+F ←→ /a/
−F ←→ Ø
INDEF ←→ /a/
INDEF ←→ /un/ || ___ [gender]
−F ←→ /o/ || _____ [pl]

The Spanish exponents /l/ and /un/ can be inserted in a context in which they are adjacent to a valued gender terminal, otherwise the exponents /ðə/ and /a/ are inserted. The feature [−f] has no exponent (yielding *un* and *el*) unless it is adjacent to the plural node, in which case it is spelled out as /o/ (yielding *unos* and *los*). The feature [+f] is uniformly spelled out as /a/. The *e* in *el* is, I assume, a later readjustment rule.

Notice that imposing a condition on insertion of /l/ and /un/ is necessary to ensure that the desinence only affixes to /l/, not to /ðə/, and to /un/, not to /a/. Notice also that the grammar of a monolingual Spanish speaker does not require this contextual restriction. When constructing the VIRs of a monolingual who only has one exponent for definiteness, it is unnecessary to describe its context of appearance. Thus, the integrated assumption leads us to the conclusion that the grammar of a bilingual is indeed subtly different from that of a monolingual – reminding us of Grosjean's old dictum: "a bilingual is not two monolinguals rolled into one." This is a conclusion derived from the integrated assumption that may have far-reaching consequences, which I hope to explore in future work.

5.3.3 *Analysis:* la *table*

We are now in a position to begin the discussion of the puzzling code-switching data in (24c–f). Recall that we take the word 'table' and the root *'mes-* to be alternative spell-outs of the same root, which we will arbitrarily assign the index 145:

(35) List 2: √145 <--> {mes-, table}

Let's start with (24c), *la table*. The syntactic structure is represented in (36). In (36), the root merges with a $n_{[+f]}$ and the latter then merges with a D that has an unvalued gender feature. As a result of concord, the determiner values its gender feature as [+f]. The only vocabulary item available is */l-/*:

(36)

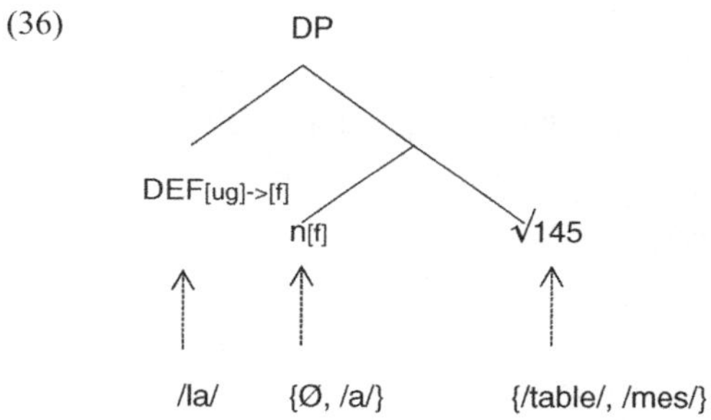

Recall my discussion in Section 4.2.1 about how the Germanic word *bior* (beer), which was neuter in the original and ended up becoming feminine in Italian and French. I propose that a similar process of analogical gender is available here: 'table' becomes the complement of a $n_{[+f]}$ in analogy with the other exponent, *mesa*.

As the reader may have noticed, there are several possible combinations of D, *n* and root. D could have an unvalued gender or no gender feature at all. *n* could have a valued gender feature or none at all. And there are two possible vocabulary items for the root. Some of these options are shown in (37). In (37), I consider only the spell out of the root as 'table'. As an instance of valued gender I arbitrarily choose feminine.

Let's start with (37i). (37i) is a regular English DP: the root that spells out as 'table' is selected by English *n*, and the latter is selected by the English determiner, without unvalued gender, and spells out as 'the'.

(37ii) recapitulates the analysis of (24c), *la table*. D has unvalued gender and *n* is feminine. Example (24c) is possible because 'table' is an available spell out for root √145 when it is selected by Spanish $n_{[+f]}$. As an option, $n_{[+f]}$ has no exponent.

Consider now (37iii). If the English *n* is selected by a determiner with gender features, the gender features remain unvalued. Since the Spanish vocabulary items *el* and *la* both have a gender feature, only the English *the* can be inserted, and this results in (37iii), for all purposes undistinguishable from (37i).

Finally, we consider (37iv): the Spanish n[+f] is selected by English DEF, without an unvalued gender feature, and then we have 'the table' again:

(37) Possible outcomes with spell out 'table':

i	DEF + n + [√145, /table/]	: the table
ii	$\text{DEF}_{[\text{uGender}]}$ + $n_{[+f]}$ + [√145, /table/]	: la table
iii	$\text{DEF}_{[\text{uGender}]}$ + n + [√145, /table/]	: the table
iv	DEF + n[+f] + [√145, /table/]	: the table

In parenthesis, allow me to point out that analogical gender is not obligatory in these configurations. In fact, bilinguals prefer the determiner *el* for words like 'survey' even though the Spanish equivalent, *encuesta* is feminine. For these speakers $n_{[+f]}$ cannot select the corresponding root, the root can only be selected by regular *n* or by $n_{[-f]}$. As Delgado (2018) argues, this is an accidental fact, the outcome of a particular sociolinguistic situation. As suggested, 'table' gets its feminine gender the same way that *birra* did, by analogic replacement, which in my terms involves adding an additional spell out option to the morphosyntactic frame. As Delgado shows, this happens with items of the familial environment. However, when bilinguals learn words outside the familial environment, such as 'survey', they learn them only as instances of the English morphosyntactic frame. If there is code-switching, and a Spanish $\text{DEF}_{[\text{uGender}]}$ is selected, the bilingual speaker has to choose the proper morphosyntactic frame and there is no Spanish analogue to guide her. More often than not, she chooses the default gender, [−f]. The determiner copies this value and it is spelled out as Ø, as shown in (34). (Relatedly, see Liceras et al.'s (2016) survey article.)

5.3.4 Analysis: the *mesa*

Consider now the more difficult examples of (24d) and (24e). Recall that (24d) ([ðə meɪsə]) is judged unacceptable while (24e) ([da mesa]) is acceptable. For the speakers who give these judgments, the word 'mesa' is necessarily a complex word, made up of the root √mes- and the word marker /a/. As pointed out above, the word marker is the spell out of $n_{[+f]}$. Therefore, the nP is necessarily feminine. In the following example, the determiner is "English style" without any gender features.

(38)

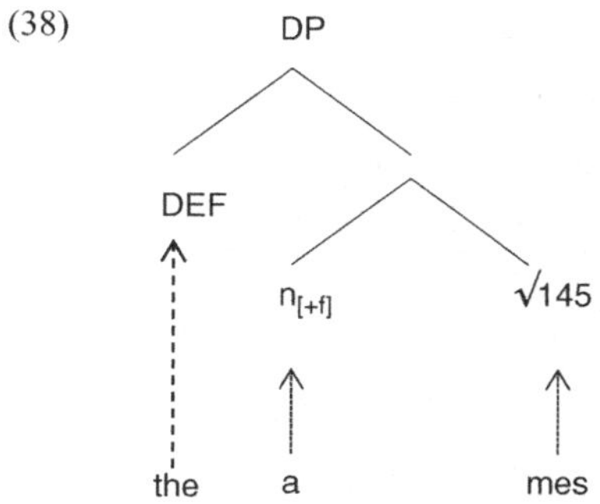

A determiner with no gender features can select for this $n_{[+f]}$, and it will spell out as 'the'. The interesting question now is why the entire DP must be pronounced in the Spanish way and not the English way. This is the more puzzling in contrast with 'la table', which does not seem to have the mirror requirement (or at least not to the same extent). My intuition is that the difference between *mesa* and 'table' lies in the complex structure of the former, which necessarily includes a particular type of *n*, namely, $n_{[+f]}$. I take the categorizing morpheme $n_{[+f]}$ to be the head of the word and therefore to decide which externalization system will be chosen. Recall that I have argued that since the root is devoid of any grammatical properties, including a label, it is also not able to project onto a higher category. It follows that the categorizer has to be the head of the word. This headedness can be expressed in Embick's (2010) model, according to which the categorizing head is the head of a phase (even if the transfer takes place at a later phase, as Embick argues). The pronunciation of 'the' as [da] comes about because the determiner and the categorizing head are units of the same phonological word and a phonological word must be sent to the externalization systems in one fell swoop (MacSwan 2000, MacSwan and Colina 2014). 'table', on the other hand can appear in any morphosyntactic environment – either *n* or n[+f] – and I believe this flexibility is the reason why it has the freedom to take on an English or a Spanish phonetics. For more on this issue, see Section 6.5.)

Example (39) considers the possible outcomes for the root *mes-* in combination with an *n* with a gender value and an *n* without it, as well as a determiner with or without unvalued gender. Since *mes-* requires a word marker, *n* must have a specification for gender. This disqualifies (37i) and (37iii). (37ii) is a regular Spanish DP. (37iv) is the interesting case: the *n* has a gender value while the determiner has no gender. Nothing makes this phrase impossible:

(39) Possible outcomes with spell out *mesa*:

i DEF + n + [√145, /mes/] : *the mesa

ii $\text{DEF}_{[uGender]}$ + $n_{[+f]}$ + [√145, /mes/] : la mesa

iii DEF[uGender] + n + [√145, /mes/] : *the mesa
iv DEF + $n_{[+f]}$ + [√145, /mes/] : the mesa

Let's now return to the following examples:

(40) a. John ate all the *tamales* yesterday. (cf. 27)
b. I'm not drinking the *tequila* today.

The examples in (40) contrast with (24d–e). There are no pronunciation restrictions on the determiner or the nouns in these examples. Descriptively speaking, the situation is as follows: bilinguals have created two morphosyntactic frames for these roots, a Spanish one with a gendered *n* and an English one without it. In effect, the words *tamal* and *tequila* have acquired full morphosyntactic flexibility. This is all the difference between the acceptable ðə təmæləz and the unacceptable *ðə meɪsə. Could *ðə meɪsə become acceptable in the model of ðə təmæləz? Certainly: a vocabulary item *mesa* could be created and inserted as the complement of English *n*; notice that this new creation does not have a word marker or any form of nominal desinence, the root would be √mesa, not √mes-. This is formally possible but somewhat unlikely. Why do *the tamales* and *the tacos* exist? We note one discriminating factor: *mesa* has an alternative "English" spell-out in the form of *table* while *tamal* does not. This makes the development of an English style morphosyntactic frame for *mesa* unlikely and one for *tamal* almost obligatory. I believe this is the factor that leads to two morphosyntactic frames for *tamal* while only one for *mesa*. (Having said this, the word 'mesa' does exist in the Southwest of the USA, as a word meaning 'plateau'.)

Finally, let's return to (24f), **el mesa*. Recall that I presented this example as an empirical challenge to the 2Lex model, which should allow the word *mesa* to be borrowed into the English lexicon and then become integrated in a Spanish phrase as a code-switched English noun. Within my assumptions, the reason why this phrase is rejected by my consultants is a failure of gender assignment, which is the same reason why monolingual speakers do not accept it either. Technically, we just need to posit that the root √mes- is selected by $n_{[+f]}$. Since √mes- is selected by $n_{[+f]}$, the determiner values its own UGENDER as feminine, and this spells out as *la*. Could there be a process of language change so that √mes- could end up being selected by $n_{[-f]}$? Formally, nothing prevents it, and this is the way it should be. Let's consider the possibilities of having the structure [$n_{[-f]}$ √mes-]. This structure could be fed into the most general spell out rule, which would yield *meso*. Alternatively, we could add the spell-out *mesa* to the list of exceptional spell outs for $n_{[-f]}$ (like other masculine nouns that end in /a/, such as *drama*, see (7)). Both options are formally possible, and I assume they may happen if the need arises. But generally, once words are fit into a morphosyntactic framework, this tends to remain stable. Historically, one can detect a few changes of this kind, but not many (in Spanish we see hesitation between a few words *el/la calor* 'the heat' *el/la mar* 'the sea', *el/la sartén* 'the frying pan').

To conclude Section 5.3.1–4: In these sections, I have developed an analysis of gender assignment and gender concord in Spanish/English code-switching within the 1Lex MDM framework. In particular, I have shown that the 2Lex system overgenerates unacceptable structures (see the examples in 24) while the 1Lex system avoids these pitfalls without any additional assumptions.

5.3.5 Earlier Approaches

As mentioned, there are many approaches to concord in English/Spanish bilingualism and I am not able to discuss them all here. But I would like to mention those whose theoretical assumptions are closest to my own framework: the one developed by Juana Muñoz Liceras and her colleagues (Liceras et al. 2008, 2016, Liceras 2016), as well as Pierantozzi (2012).

Liceras and her colleagues used as subjects of their experiments Spanish-dominant bilinguals who may have quite a different profile from my own heritage subjects – consequently, their results and mine may not be comparable. Be that as it may, allow me to say a few words about their work. Their starting point is a contrast between (41a) and (41b) and they claim that both are possible but (41a) is substantially more common:

(41) a. *la* house
b. the *casa*

Recall that my claim is somewhat different: (41b) is acceptable if the pronunciation is fully adapted to Spanish. Liceras and colleagues suggest that a notion of *Internal Dominance* accounts for the pattern in (41). Since both forms are attested, they argue that a grammatical analysis should be abandoned and a processing analysis adopted instead. The internally dominant language is the language that contributes the most grammaticized features to the structure. Thus, the Spanish determiner wins over the English determiner because it has gender. This predicts that 'la house' is more common than 'the casa', although the latter is not impossible. The ultimate reason behind this is the *Grammatical Features Spell-out Hypothesis*: a processing condition that says that you want to spell out functional categories that are more visible because they express more grammatical features.

Notice that once we take phonology into consideration, we are led to assume that the difference between (41a) and (41b) is indeed a grammatical one, but the grammatical conditions are of a different nature: the acceptability or not of code-switches relies on the types of morphosyntactic frames in which roots can be merged and the subsequent pronunciation that the morphosyntactic frames give rise to.

A discussion of Pierantozzi (2012) will provide additional insight into the assumptions and analyses adopted here. Pierantozzi (2012) assumes a DM framework similar to mine, with the important difference that, for her, gender is an inherent feature of the noun. This assumption is crucial because it makes it impossible to adopt an integrated system. Let's see why.

In Pierantozzi's (2012) framework, in a language that has gender, a noun is a syntactic terminal with the feature specification N[g] as evidenced by concord on the determiner, adjective, etc. In the linguistic system of a bilingual – say, a English/Spanish bilingual – two vocabulary items could be inserted in this terminal: for instance, /house/ or /casa/. The Spanish vocabulary item /casa/ has a gender feature that matches the one in N[g] but /house/ does not. Both *la casa* and *la house* are acceptable to bilingual consultants, despite the fact that /casa/ is a better match for N[g] than /house/ is. It follows that /casa/ and /house/ are not in competition. And this entails that /casa/ and /house/ must be lodged in distinct independent List 2. In contrast, my analysis does not require that the bilingual speaker have separate lists of exponents for each of their languages – the only crucial assumption that allows *la house* is the notion that gender is not inherent to a root but rather it emerges from the morphosyntactic structure. Crucially, neither the roots nor the exponents have any gender features: these are housed in the functional categorizer *n*. The vocabulary items /house/ and /cas/ can spell out the same root R, and R is in a morphosyntactic environment that includes $n_{[+f]}$. *La house* is possible to the extent that the vocabulary item /house/ can be selected by $n_{[+f]}$, just as any other form of gender assignment.

5.4 Gender in Nahuatl/Spanish Code-Switching

The analysis of noun class in English/Swahili code-switching, as well as the analysis of gender in Basque/Spanish and English/Spanish code-switching, is based on the overarching assumption that nouns can fit more than one morphosyntactic frame. This is certainly a feature of "monolingual" grammars: Swahili roots can show up in more than one noun class (recall: *mtoto* 'child', *kitoto* 'small child', *matoto* 'big child'), some nouns in Spanish can be both masculine or feminine (*estudiante* 'student'), some nouns in Romanian have different gender in the singular and the plural. Thus, it is not surprising that the same phenomenon happens in "bilingual" grammar. This is the reason why we find that, for example, the Basque noun *makila* may be selected by a $n_{[+f]}$ as well as the regular Basque little *n*. It is not surprising but, then again, it is not obligatory either. Issues of what is usually referred to "gender assignment" – in our terms, selection of a root by a particular flavor of *n* – are somewhat arbitrary and once choices are made, they tend to be rigid. It should be interesting to see what predictions we would make for a language that did not allow for gender assignment flexibility.

Let's assume code-switching between Lx, a language with gender, and Ly, a language that has no gender and no assignment flexibility. In this language, Dy + NPx would work along the lines of *the casa*. However, Dx + NPy would never work. The NPy would never have a gender feature and therefore Dx would end up without valuing its gender feature. If the gender feature is not valued, an exponent with a valued gender feature would be too specified and would not fit. The only possible spell out for an unvalued gender feature would be a genderless exponent of Ly.

This abstract scenario is instantiated in Nahuatl/Spanish code-switching, as discussed in MacSwan's study of D+NP combinations in this language pair (MacSwan (1999: 244–250). As we know, determiners in Spanish inflect for gender and number; the interesting part is that determiners in Nahuatl do not. According to MacSwan, the D+NP code-switching combination is acceptable if the determiner is Nahuatl and the noun is Spanish, but not the other way around.

(42) Nahuatl/*Spanish*

a. neka *hombre*
'This man'

b. * *este* tlakatl
'This man'

c. se *hombre*
'a man'

d. * *aquel* tlakatl
'that man'

MacSwan 1999: 244–245

The contrast between (42a) and (42b), as well as the acceptability of (42c) and the unacceptability of (42d) can be accounted for in the sort of analysis that I presented in the previous sections with the added assumption that Nahuatl roots do not accept being selected by a Spanish *n*. Let's see how.

(43) Nahuatl/*Spanish*

a. neka/se *hombre*
D + $n_{[-f]}$ + [√23, hombre]

b. * *este/aquel* tlakatl
D[ug] + n + [√23, tlakatl]

(42a) and (42c) can be accounted for along the lines set up in previous sections. The little *n* has the gender feature [−f] and the (IN)DEF feature is brought in without unvalued gender features. The spell out for this (IN)DEF is the Nahuatl determiner, as shown in (43a).

As for (42b) and (42d), the unacceptability arises when an (IN)DEF with an unvalued gender feature selects for a Nahuatl *n* without a gender feature. The gender feature of (IN)DEF reaches the VIRs with the gender feature unvalued. At that point, it can only be spelled out by the Nahuatl determiner because Spanish determiners, which do bear a [+f] or [−f] feature, are too specified. This is shown in (43b).

(42b) and (42d) would only be possible if the Nahuatl noun could be inserted in a Spanish frame with a $n_{[\pm f]}$, in the model of *la house*. Apparently, this possibility has not developed in the I-language of Nahuatl/Spanish bilinguals. Ultimately, the reason why (42b,d) are ungrammatical is a simple issue of gender assignment.

MacSwan's account of the Nahuatl/Spanish situation is (roughly) based on the notion that the ϕ–features of D need to be checked while those in N do not. Following MacSwan's reasoning, a Spanish D will require a Spanish N and a Nahuatl N would be unacceptable because it would not have the requisite valued features. But a Nahuatl D does not require a Nahuatl N because the Nahuatl D has no features to check. This analysis is based on the notion that unvalued features lead to unacceptability, which, as discussed in Section 3.2, is probably a mistaken assumption. Moreover, it leaves many of the examples discussed above without an account: for instance, why should *la house* be possible?

5.5 Gender in Spanish/German Code-Switching

Gender in the Spanish/German variety called *Esplugisch* is discussed in detail in González-Vilbazo (2005). These data came out of González-Vilbazo's field work at the German School of Barcelona over a period of several weeks, where he gathered data informally, recorded some dialogs and presented consultants with acceptability judgment tasks. He also confirmed these judgments with other Spanish/German bilinguals. The data presented in this thesis will help bolster my argument that an integrated view of bilingual grammar is preferable to the 2Lex worldview that remains dominant.

The data presents a high degree of intricacy. For instance, it is generally possible to have a German noun with a Spanish determiner:

(44) *Spanish*/German
El brötchen
DEF.M bread(n)

In the opposite direction, it is possible with some combinations but not others. For instance, code-switching is possible in (45a), with a dative determiner, but not in (45b), with a nominative one (see also Sections 5.2, 5.3):

(45) German/*Spanish*
a. Dem *cuaderno*
DEF.M/N.DAT notebook(m)
b. * Der *cuaderno*
DEF.M.NOM notebook(m)

The purpose of this section is to account for the restrictions on German/Spanish code-switching within the DP. The solution relies crucially on the MDM model presented in these pages and provides a proof of concept that it can handle complex data sets. I start presenting a short tutorial on German gender in Section 5.5.1 and I present González-Vilbazo's findings in Section 5.5.2. I then develop an analysis in Section 5.5.3.

5.5.1 Spanish and German Gender

As was described in Section 5.1, Spanish nouns are divided into two genders, traditionally referred to as masculine and feminine and which I refer to as [+feminine] and [–feminine].

(46) el : [def, –f] (see Section 5.1, ex (11))
la : [def, +f]
un : [indef, –f]
una : [indef, +f]
los : [def, −f, pl]
las : [def, +f, pl]
unos : [indef, −f, pl]
unas: : [indef, −f, pl]

The German system is a three-gendered system: feminine, masculine, and neuter. Following González-Vilbazo, I take the German system to form a feature hierarchy with three possible values. The feminine gender has the feature [+f], masculine is [−f, +m] and neuter is [−f,−m] (see also Section 4.3):[3]

(47)

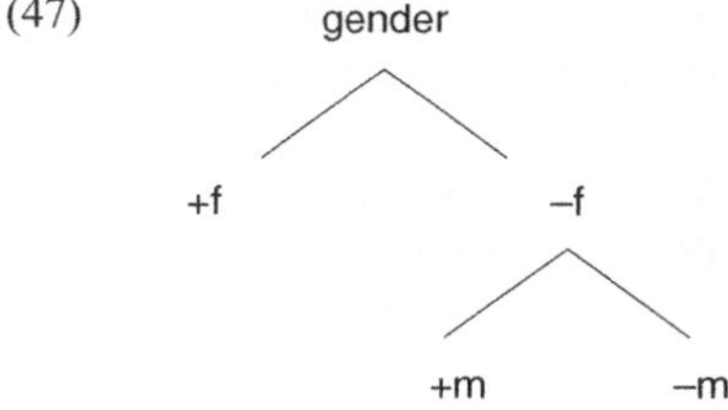

This yields three possible morphosyntactic frames for German nouns:

(48) a. $n_{[+f]}$ √ {frau (woman), stadt (city), gabel (fork) . . .}
b. $n[_{-f,\ +m}]$ √ {löffel (spoon), stuhl (chair), mann (man) . . .}
c. $n[_{-f,\ -m}]$ √ {messer (knife), hemd (shirt), kind (child) . . .}

The German D copies the gender and number features of *n*. It also inflects for morphological case, which distinguishes nominative, accusative, dative, and genitive. Gender, number, and case are all expressed in the determiner, albeit with numerous syncretisms. The following is a table of nominative, accusative, and dative singular masculine, feminine, and neuter German determiners:

(49) Some singular determiners in German

	DEF			INDEF		
	M	N	F	M	N	F
NOM	der	das	die	ein	ein	eine
ACC	den	das	die	einen	ein	eine
DAT	dem	dem	der	einem	einem	einer

The plural determiners only inflect for case. There is no gender morphology associated with the plural determiners in German.

(50) Some plural determiners in German

	M	N	F
NOM	die	die	die
ACC	die	die	die
DAT	den	den	den

Notice that there are several places where the exponents for the [−f] determiners are the same. Let's classify nominative and accusative together as [+structural] and dative as [–structural] (while keeping genitive out for the time being). With this information, we can analyze the feature structure of each determiner as in (51). I present the feature structures in a semi-formal way, mixing privative and binary features; in a more formal presentation, nominative should be [+structural, –accusative] and accusative should be [+structural, +accusative]. Additionally, I have not tried to account for all the apparent syncretisms, thus allowing the phonological strings /der/, /die/, and /den/ to expone two distinct morpheme bundles; finally, I use orthographic rather than IPA representations to facilitate the discussion (as I do in other sections of this monograph):

(51)
1 /der/ : [nom, def, −f, +m] [nominative=+structural-accusative]
2 /das/ : [+structural, def, −f, −m]
3 /die/ : [+structural, def, +f]
4 /den/ : [acc, def, −f, +m] [accusative=+structural+accusative]
5 /dem/ : [–structural, def, −f]
6 /der/ : [–structural, def, +f] [–structural=dative]
7 /ein/ : [+structural, indef, –f]
8 /eine/ : [+structural, indef, +f]
9 /einen/ : [acc, −f, +m]
10 /einem/ : [−structural, −f]
11 /einer/ : [−structural, +f]
12 /die/ : [+structural, def, pl]
13 /den/ : [−structural, def, pl]

Let's focus on the gender feature. Some of the determiners in (51) are [+f] (3, 6, 8, 11). Plural determiners have no gender feature: /die/ works for all nominative and accusative nouns and /den/ for all dative nouns. Notice also that there are some determiners with the feature structure [−f, +m] or [−f, −m], while others seem to be only [−f]. The determiner in (51.1) (/der/) only works with masculine nouns and the one in (51.2) (/das/) only works with neutral nouns. It makes sense therefore to assign to them the features [+m] and [−m] respectively. On the other hand, the dative determiners in (51.5) (/dem/) and (51.10) (/einem/) are used with masculine and neuter nouns. Thus, I assume that (51.5) and (51.10) only have the gender feature [−f], with no specification for [±m].

The indefinite determiners (51.7–11) demand a little more attention. Notice that /ein/ can be used for nominative masculine and neuter and for accusative neuter. For accusative neuter, we have a specified determiner, /einen/. Thus, I have taken the latter to have the feature [+m] while I take /ein/ to be [+structural] (therefore able to fit in nominative and accusative terminals) and [−f], without specification for [±m]. This feature structure allows it to fit into syntactic terminals with the feature structures [nominative, ±m] as well as [accusative, −m].

German determiners include two terminals. There is a terminal for the (in) definiteness feature (*d* for definite, *ein* for indefinite) and another terminal that has either a plural value or a gender value (I abstract away from case at this point). I take it that the German D has a terminal with an unvalued ϕ-feature, which is not specified for type:

(52)

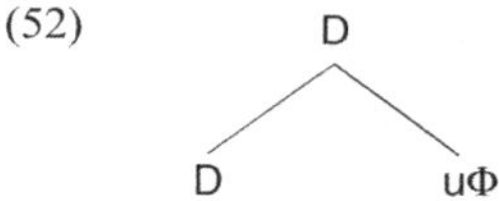

The structure of the German D contrasts with the Spanish D, repeated here for the reader's convenience, as the latter has separate terminals for gender and number:

(53)

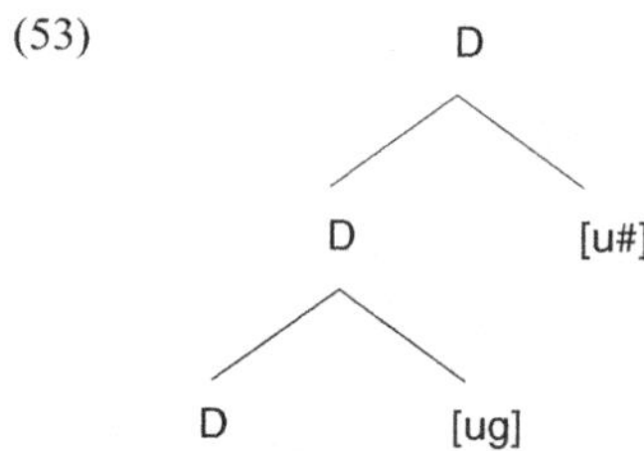

Consequently, the German D has a unique probe, which consists of an unvalued ϕ-feature, which will seek any valued ϕ-features it can find in its c-command domain. Let's see how it works. Assume that a singular noun phrase is a noun phrase without a Number head (i.e., singular is the absence of number). In this circumstance, the probe [uΦ] finds the gender features in *n* and copies them. Assume now that the noun phrase is plural (i.e., there is a plural feature projecting a Number Phrase between D and *n*). The probe in the German D finds this plural feature and copies it. This ends the probing: the probe has its ϕ-feature valued and there are no additional probes in D. This is how the German D never exhibits any gender features in the plural.

Finally, we are now in a position to formulate the rules of vocabulary insertion that characterize the I-language of the Esplugisch speaker. At this point it is important to note, as is often done, that a bilingual is not two monolinguals rolled into one. If a speaker has a linguistic system, call it La, with only one exponent for definiteness, the rule of exponence will be maximally simple. A "multilingual" individual may have several exponents for definiteness whose context of appearance may be complex. For instance, a Spanish/German bilingual has two exponents of definiteness, */l-/* and */d-/*. Morphologically, they are clearly distinct: The former is associated with additional terminals for gender and number while the latter is associated with only one terminal for all its ϕ-features. Thus, the VIRs for *l* and *d* that I propose exploit this fact.[4] For the time being, let's focus on the Esplugisch speaker.

(54)					
	1.	def	←→	/l/	‖ [D ______ T1 T2]
	2.	def	←→	/d/	
	3.	indef	←→	/un/	‖ [D ______ T1 T2]
	4.	indef	←→	/ein/	
	5.	+f	←→	/a/	‖ ______ [#]
	6.	–f	←→	/o/	‖ ______ [pl]
	7.	–f	←→	Ø	‖ ______ [#]
	8.	pl	←→	/s/	‖ ______ [g]
	9.	+f	←→	/ie/	‖ [+structural] def ______
	10.	+f	←→	/e/	‖ [+structural] indef ______
	11.	+f	←→	/er/	
	12.	–f,+m	←→	/er/	‖ [+structural] ______
	13	–f,+m	←→	/en/	‖ [+accusative] ______
	14.	–f,–m	←→	/as/	‖ [+structural] ______
	15.	–f	←→	/em/	‖ [–structural] ______
	16.	–f	←→	Ø	‖ [+structural] indef ______
	17.	pl	←→	/ie/	‖ [+structural] ______
	18.	pl	←→	/en/	

(54.1) and (54.3) say that */l/* and */un/* insert in nodes that have the feature definite or indefinite, respectively, and that are found within a Dmax that includes two other terminals. The two-terminals requirement is simply the environment that distinguishes the German and the Spanish determiner. The German /*d*/ and /*ein*/ are inserted elsewhere, as shown in (54.2) and (54.4).

The batch of rules in (54.5) to (54.8) define the "Spanish" spell out for gender and number on the determiner: (54.5) says that a feminine terminal spells out as /a/ if it is sitting next to a number feature (either a number feature valued as plural or an unvalued number feature.) This correctly defines the environment that spells out /a/ as feminine because none of the "German" gender exponents is adjacent to a number feature. (54.6) defines the spell out of masculine as /*o*/ if the determiner is plural, yielding *los* and (54.7) tells us that masculine has no exponent in the singular, and so we have *el* (I assume that the *e* is epenthetic).

The rules (54.9) to (54.11) define the contexts of the "German" [+f] terminals, yielding *die*, *eine*, and *der* respectively. (54.12) and (54.13) define the contexts of the masculine determiners *der*, *den*, and *einen*, while (54.14) defines the neuter determiner *das*. (54.15) and (54.16) define the determiners that have the feature [−f]: the dative determiners *dem* and *einem* as well as the nominative indefinite *ein* and accusative indefinite neuter *ein*. Finally, (54.17) and (54.18) define the plural determiners *die* and *den*.

5.5.2 *Esplugish Data*

Let me now present the Esplugish data, as originally brought to the attention of code-switching researchers by González-Vilbazo (2005: 158–167).

Esplugish speakers do not seem to resort to analogical gender. Thus, the determiner concords with the noun that spells out, not the equivalent in the other language.

When the determiner is Spanish, code-switching is always possible. German feminine nouns take the feminine Spanish determiner while masculine and neuter nouns take the non-feminine determiner (recall the discussion of clitic left dislocation in Section 4.3):

(55) *l-a* hose
DEF−F pant(f)

(56) *el* gürtel
DEF.−F belt(m)

(57) *el* brötchen
DEF.−F bun(n)

(58) *un-a* hose
INDEF−F pant(f)

(59) *un* gürtel
INDEF.−F belt(m)

(60) *un* brötchen
INDEF.–F bun(n)

When the determiner is German, we need to pay attention to case morphology as well as to definiteness. We start with definite determiners. If they are in nominative or accusative case, the feminine determiner can collocate with a feminine Spanish noun. But if the Spanish noun is masculine, it cannot collocate with any nominative or accusative German determiner:

(61) d-ie *torre*
DEF–F.NOM/ACC tower(f)

(62) ?? d-er *tenedor*
DEF–M.NOM fork(–f)

(63) ?? d-as *tenedor*
DEF–N.NOM/ACC fork(–f)

(64) ?? d-en *tenedor*
DEF–M.ACC fork(–f)

However, if the determiner is in dative case, it is grammatical in all genders:

(65) d-em *interruptor*
DEF–M/N.DAT switch(–f)

(66) d-er *torre*
DEF–F.DAT tower(f)

With indefinite determiners, we find the following situation: Code-switching is always possible in the nominative case.

(67) ein *interruptor*
INDEF.M/N.NOM switch(–f)

In the accusative case, it remains possible as long as we use the neuter determiner, not the accusative one:

(68) ein *interruptor*
INDEF.N.ACC switch(–f)

(69) ?? ein-en *interruptor*
INDEF–M.ACC switch(–f)

Code-switching is always possible with an indefinite feminine determiner (González-Vilbazo provides no examples but it follows from the discussion).

Finally, code-switching is always possible between a plural determiner and a noun:

(70) a. d-ie *tenedores*
DEF–PL forks(–f)

b. l-a-s frauen
DEF–F–PL women

As we can see, there are some surprisingly unacceptable forms (examples (62), (63), (64), (69)) but some of the acceptable forms are surprising too, within a 1Lex framework.

Here is the gist of the analysis that I develop in Section 5.4.3. Consider the list of rules in (51). By looking at this list, we can see that there are some German determiners that have the same gender structure as some Spanish ones. *Dem*, *ein*, *einem* all have only the feature [−f], just like Spanish *el*. *Die(3)*, *der (6)*, *eine*, and *einer* just have the feature [+f]. We can predict that the German [−f] and [+f] determiners should all be interchangeable with the corresponding Spanish determiners. On the other hand, some German determiners have a more complex gender structure than Spanish determiners: *der(1)*, *das*, *den (4)*, *einen* are all [−f, ±m]. This feature composition is too rich to fit a syntactic terminal that has only a [±f] feature. Thus, we can predict that these German determiners cannot take a Spanish n as a complement.

5.5.3 *Analysis*

Now we have all the ingredients to study the code-switching data presented in González-Vilbazo (2005). Recall that we have two different structures for determiners, one with terminals for gender and number and another one with just one terminal for phi features. We also have the VIRs listed in (54). The goal is to exclude code-switching between a Spanish singular masculine noun and a German nominative or accusative definite determiner or a masculine accusative indefinite determiner, while allowing all the other combinations.

All the feminine nouns, in either direction, are always grammatical in code-switching. This is the structure of a feminine DP:

(71)

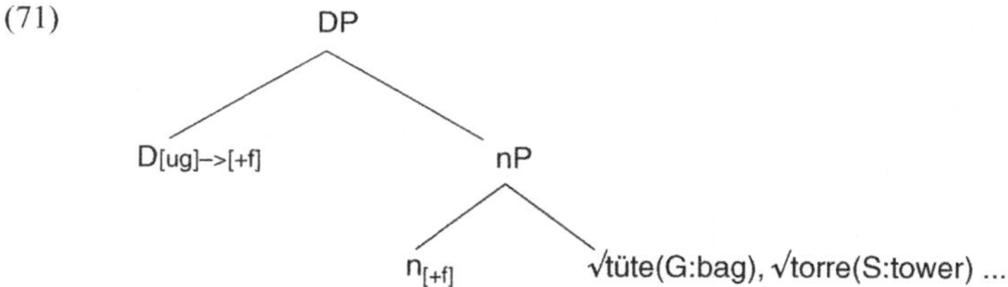

The example in (71) shows the morphosyntactic structure of a German noun like *tute* 'bag' or a Spanish noun like *torre* 'tower'. The *n* has a [+f] feature, which values the unvalued gender of D after Agree. Let's assume we have merged a "Spanish" D with two terminals [D D, [ug], [u#]]. As a result of probing, we have a structure as follows: [D D, [+f], [u#]]. This is the environment in which we can insert *la* or *una*, following VIR (54.5). Let's assume that we have merged a "German" D with only one terminal in (71), [D D, [uΦ]]. Then we have [D D, [+f]]. (54.5) cannot apply in the absence of a number terminal, and so one of the other rules to spell out [+f] must apply (54.9, 10, 11). The result is that code-switching between D and nP is always fine if the noun is feminine.

The case of German masculine and neuter definite determiners with a Spanish noun presents an interesting example of how the MDM in a 1Lex assumption works. Recall that a German definite nominative or accusative determiner does not collocate with a Spanish noun while a German dative determiner or a German indefinite determiner does. This is the relevant structure:

(72)

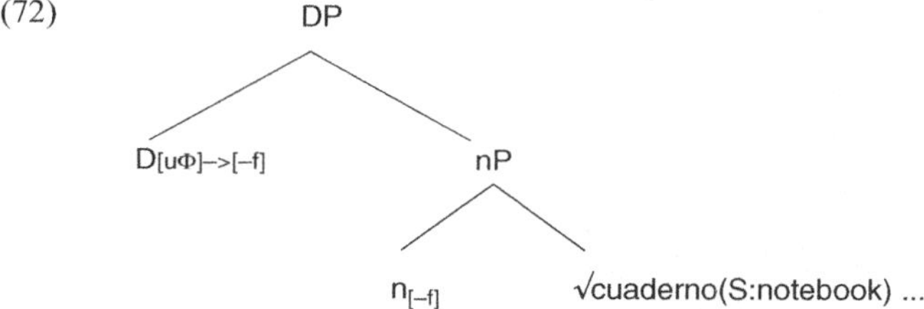

Let's assume we have merged a "German" determiner with only one terminal for ϕ-features, as shown in (72). The Spanish *n* in this structure only has a [−f] feature, which gets copied onto the determiner. In this structure, vocabulary items that have a [−f] feature can be inserted: German *dem* and *ein* (as well as the Spanish determiners), which are only [−f] (see 51). Crucially, the determiners *der*, *das*, *den*, and *einen*, which have the more complex structure [−f, +m] or [−f, −m], are too specified. This accounts for the grammaticality of (65), (67), (68) and the unacceptability of (62), (63), (64), (69).

Let's now consider the case of the Spanish determiner with the German masculine or neutral noun. The syntactic structure of these examples is the following:

(73)

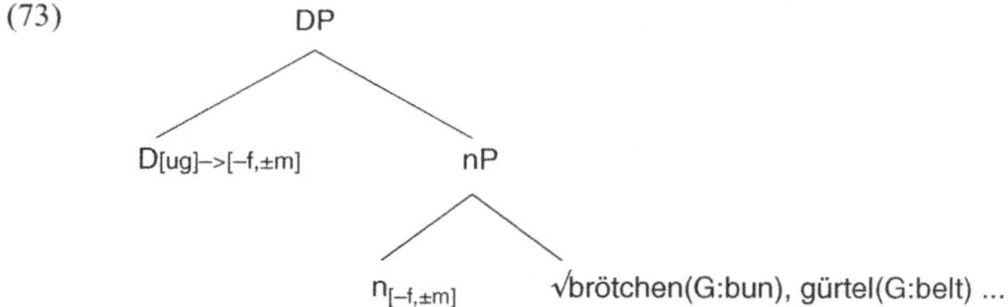

The *n* in this structure has the feature composition [−f, +m] or [−f, −m]. This feature structure is copied onto D after Agree. Assume that a "Spanish D" has been merged, that is, a D with two terminals [D D, [ug], [u#]]. In this configuration, the subset principle ensures that the Spanish exponent *el* can be inserted because *el* is only [−f]. The exponent /*l*/ is not in competition with the German /*d*/ given the specificity of the environment with two terminals which ensures that /*l*/ always beats /*d*/. The German vocabulary items *der*, *das*, *den*, etc. can show up if we merge a "German" D with one terminal.

The same strategy can be applied to the plural forms in (70). Recall that code-switching between determiner and noun is always possible in the plural. The following is a possible structure, with a "Spanish" D with two terminals and a German noun:

(74)

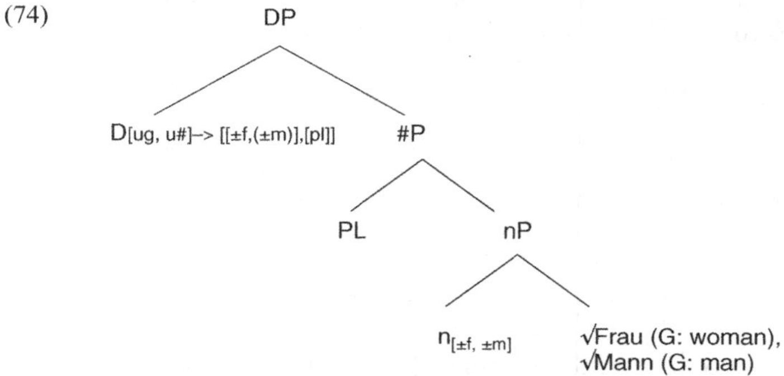

The two terminals can probe separately and agree with Number and with *n*. The Spanish exponents *las* and *los* fit right in. *los*, whose gender feature is only [−f], can be inserted thanks to the subset principle once again. Thus, we have the acceptable *las frauen* and *los männer.* Consider now the option of a "German" D, with only one terminal and a Spanish noun:

(75)

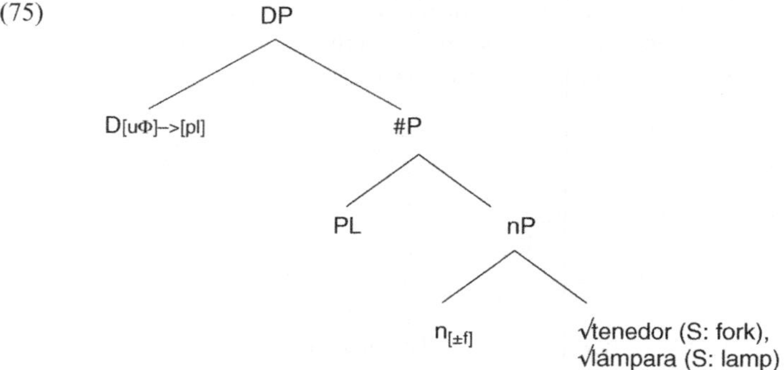

The unique ϕ-probe of D finds Number and copies its plural feature, without probing any further. The result is the acceptable *die tenedores* 'the forks' or *die lámparas*.

The only data presented by González-Vilbazo that I have not yet discussed involves genitive case. In German, determiners can inflect for genitive case. When that happens, code-switching with a Spanish noun is not possible:

(76) * ein-es tenedor
INDEF-GEN fork

It is not immediately obvious why this is the case (and González-Vilbazo provides no analysis either). One possible approach is the following. Genitive case in German triggers concord on the noun (which does not continually spell out):

(77) ein-es Mannes
INDEF-GEN man.GEN

This genitive morpheme on the noun should probably be regarded as a dissociated morpheme sprouted and cliticized after syntax. Quite possibly, the unacceptability of (76) comes about because Spanish nominal exponents do not accept such a dissociated morpheme.[5]

5.5.4 Discussion and Precedents

The analysis of the Esplugisch data shows how we can construct an integrated system within a MDM framework and design it in such a way that even very intricate restrictions can be accounted for without appealing to separate lists. Of some interest is the fact that determiner exponents with poor feature structure can be inserted in a syntactic terminal with a richer feature structure (subset principle) while exponents with a rich structure cannot be inserted in terminals with a poor structure. That is, we have *el brötchen* 'the bun', where the Spanish determiner with only a [−f] feature can be inserted in a terminal with features [−f, ±m] while we also have that a determiner with a [−f, ±m] feature composition cannot be inserted in a terminal that only has the [−f] feature, as in *der interruptor* 'the switch'. This is an insight that is elegantly derived from the MDM principles and the 1Lex hypothesis; as far as I can tell, it would not be easily accommodated in a lexicalist framework, particularly one that takes a 2Lex hypothesis as a starting point.

Before I close this section, I need to refer to two previous analyses that have approached this same data.

González-Vilbazo (2005) introduced these data to the community as well as a wealth of data and analyses of Esplugisch. The analysis he developed is similar to mine in that it uses feature structures to account for the compatibility of determiners and nouns in the two languages. His model is lexicalist: instead of using DM, he proposes an algorithm to introduce determiners and spell them out, with results very similar to a DM approach. However, he does not assume

1Lex; rather, Spanish and German determiners are defined as such in the lexicon and the DP is therefore defined as a German or Spanish DP.

DenDikken (2011) also briefly approaches the Esplugisch data, within a DM framework that is very similar to mine. However, his choice of feature structures for the German articles lead him to wrong results. First, he is interested in capturing the fact that *die* appears both as singular feminine and as plural for all genders (see the tables in (49) and (50)). He claims that this is a phenomenon of syncretism and the German article *die* has no plural or gender feature. This may work well to describe the grammar of a German monolingual, but it does not do so well for a bilingual German/Spanish speaker because the Spanish article *la*, specified with gender, would always beat the German *die*. In order to circumvent this problem, he proposes that the structure of the Spanish DP includes an extra functional category Gender and therefore *die* and *la* are never in competition (although, as far as I can tell, this structural difference is not fully justified). Second, he defines *das* as simply [−f], which makes it equivalent to *el*. However, this would predict that **das cuaderno* should be grammatical, which is not (as he himself acknowledges). Although entirely in the right track in the general approach, DenDikken's approach is inadequate in the details of the analysis.

5.6 Conclusions

This section on gender has provided additional arguments to discard a 2Lex approach to code-switching and embrace the integrated MDM system instead.

With regard to the Basque data, a separationist approach to bilingual grammar cannot account for the fact that Basque words that end in /a/ can be merged with Spanish feminine determiners. This can only be approached within a system in which there is a unique set of List 2 rules and not two separate ones. Likewise, the Spanish/English code-switching is also incompatible with a 2Lex theory. A 2Lex theory incorporating borrowing as separate from code-switching such as that in MacSwan (1999, 2000 i.m.a.) cannot account for the impossibility of *[ðə meɪsə] or *el mesa. The Nahuatl/Spanish data discussed in MacSwan (1999) receives a natural analysis within 1Lex assumptions, while the analysis proposed by MacSwan within a 2Lex framework conflicts with what we know of other code-switching data. Finally, the apparently intractable Esplugisch data has turned out to be quite amenable to the framework presented here.

The analysis of earlier analyses gave us additional context. In particular, the contrast between the current framework and Pierantozzi (2012) showed us that the 1Lex approach is tied to the independently supported hypothesis that gender arises in a syntactic structure and is not an inherent feature of a noun.

This chapter is aimed at showing that the 1Lex MDM framework is capable of accounting for code-switching data emerging from different language pairs. This is a novel feature, since all previous work had concentrated on one language pair and had designed analyses tailored to this language pair without making sure that the analyses presented were consistent with other known databases.

Having said this, gender assignment and gender concord remain active fields of research in code-switching and will remain so for the foreseeable future because all work to date – including this chapter – has only scratched at the surface. For instance, Cocchi and Pierantozzi (2017) investigate gender concord outside the noun phrase with relative pronouns or participles, obtaining intriguing results, such as the one exemplified in (78):

(78) German/ *Italian*
Das Haus *è stat-a dipint-a.*
The(n) house(n) is been–F painted–F
(In Italian: *casa*(f))
'The house has been painted.'

At least some of their consultants, accepted sentences in which the German DP would trigger normal gender concord within the DP but then would trigger agreement on the participle following the analogical gender strategy. Food for thought.

6 1PF in MDM

6.1 The Layers of PF

The separationist framework takes it for granted that a bilingual person should have two PFs. Let's call this the 2PF assumption. This assumption is argued for explicitly in MacSwan (1999, 2000). The following diagram summarizes MacSwan's proposals (from example (2) in Chapter 2):

(1)

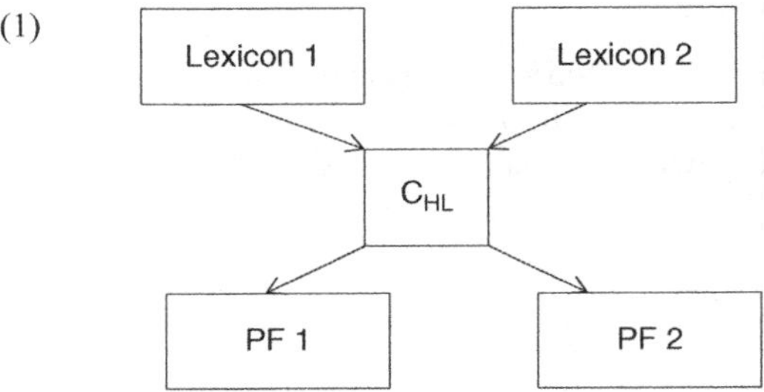

The purpose of this chapter is to present empirical evidence that the PF of a bilingual forms an integrated system, thus rounding up my argument that a bilingual person possesses a single, integrated, linguistic competence.

Crucial to the argument is the assumption that PF consists of a derivational sequence of operations, as in Embick and Noyer (2001, 2007), from the moment of transfer – when the structure detaches itself from the Lexicon-LF computation – to the point when it is ready to access the articulatory-perceptual mechanisms. First, there are syntactic operations of displacement that affect particular types of morphemes and alter their ordering even within a word. A classic example is the lowering of T to v in English. Some of these syntactic operations might take place after VIRs have applied.

Second, there are operations that alter the feature composition of terminals. The most important for us is impoverishment, which I exemplified with clitic clusters in Chapter 3. Clitic cluster simplification is going to play a stellar role in this section.

After all operations on terminals have taken place, the next derivational step involves VIRs replacing the Q features on terminals, as shown in detail in

Section 3.2. After vocabulary insertion, there are three more processes that need to happen. A linguistic structure needs to be assigned nuclear stress as well as prosodic structures. According to an influential tradition, there are three levels of prosodic structure that we can label phonological word, prosodic phrase, and intonation phrase (Selkirk 1995). Nuclear stress is sensitive to word and phrasal structure. Likewise, prosodic phrasing is built on syntactic boundaries – even though the output is quite different from phrase structure. Additionally, the syntactic structure needs to be linearized to accommodate the demands of the S-M interface. Finally, some morphophonological rules may apply to the vocabulary items, including readjustment and assimilation. Here is a diagram from Section 3.2, repeated here for the reader's convenience:

(2) *Distributed Morphology framework* (see Chapter 3, ex 35)

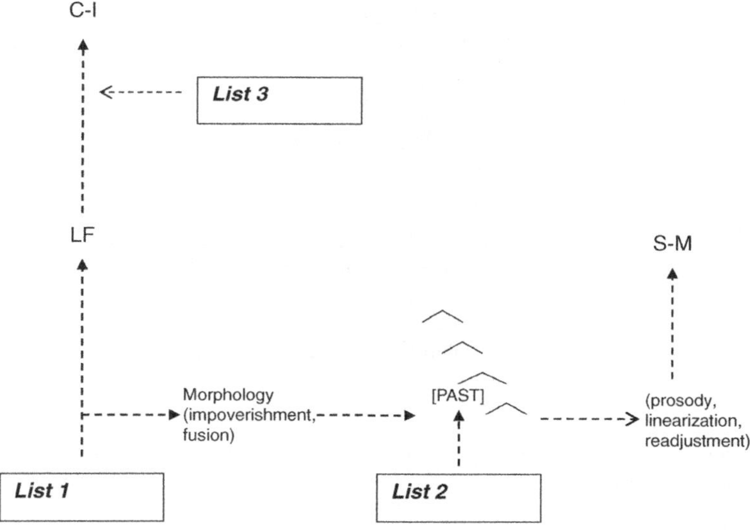

The question now is: which steps of this derivational PF should be regarded as integrated and which should be separated? I have already argued that List 2 is integrated – recall, in particular, the discussion revolving around gender and code-switching presented in Chapter 5. Thus, arguing for an integrated PF means, at this point, arguing that the grammatical rules that apply before and after vocabulary insertion are also integrated.

This is in fact what I do in Sections 6.2 and 6.3. The argument revolves around rules that apply or are active in the "wrong language." Take languages Lx and Ly. Let's assume that the (monolingual) grammar of Lx includes a post-syntactic rule Rx. If the grammatical system of a bilingual is really integrated, we should expect Rx to apply in a Ly structure, if the environmental conditions are right. Another plausible expectation is that Rx would be active even when Ly is being processed. Both expectations are fulfilled. This would be totally mysterious if the two grammatical systems were separate. Additionally, in Section 6.4, I present an Occam's razor type of argument that even linearization and prosody construction are integrated. With this architecture in place, in Section 6.5 I shed new light on a well-known phenomenon in code-switching research: Poplack's (1981) ban on word-internal switches.

6.2 Clitic Combinations among Catalan/Spanish Bilinguals

Let me now present some evidence that the impoverishment rules are not separated in two sets. The argument that I present here revolves around pronominal clitic combinations among Catalan/Spanish bilinguals.

The clitic combination [3rd.dat] + [3rd.acc] is subject to rules of impoverishment in both Spanish and Catalan. As shown in the work of Bonet (1995) and Halle and Marantz (1994), among others, the rules are somewhat different in each language. I already mentioned in Section 3.2 the Spanish one. Pronominal clitics in Spanish have the feature structure summarized in (3) (the complete list of Spanish clitics is in Section 3.25):

(3) le : third person singular dative (see Section 3.25)
la : third person singular accusative feminine
lo : third person singular accusative masculine
les : third person plural dative
las : third person plural accusative feminine
los : third person plural accusative masculine
se : third person

When two third person clitics are together, the dative one becomes *se*, as shown in (4).

(4) Spanish
Pedro [**le** **lo**] dijo ➔ Pedro **se lo** dijo.
Pedro 3.DAT 3.ACC said
'Pedro said it to him.'

As Halle and Marantz (1994) explain, *se* is the least marked clitic pronoun in Spanish, being deprived of person or case features. The rule that yields *se* for *le* can be represented as (5):

(5) CL[dative] ➔ CL || ____ [accusative] (cf Section 3.2, (33))

That is, the feature [dative] is erased from the syntactic terminal when it is adjacent to an accusative third person clitic. The syntactic terminal ends up with no features and only /se/ can spell out such a terminal.

In colloquial Catalan the output of impoverishment is somewhat different. As can be seen in (6), the combination of the dative clitic *li* and the accusative clitic *ho* yields a form spelled out as *l'hi* that sounds exactly like a dative clitic in isolation:

(6) Catalan

El Pere [**li**	**ho**]	va	dir	
the Pere 3.DAT	3.NEUT.ACC	PAST	say	
→ el Pere **l'hi** va dir.				l'hi : /li/

'Pere said it to him.'

Despite the opaque spelling, it seems that the simplest way to account for this impoverishment rule is that the accusative clitic is subject to a version of radical impoverishment, what Arregi and Nevins (2012) call *obliteration*, an operation that simply erases the syntactic terminal. The example in (6) involves a neuter clitic. In (7) I write examples with feminine and masculine clitics:

(7) Catalan

Li	la	va	donar →	l'hi (/li/) va donar
3.DAT	3.F.ACC	PAST	give.INF	
Li	lo	va	donar →	l'hi (/li/) va donar
3.DAT	3.M.ACC	PAST	give.INF	

'(s)he gave it to her/him.'

The following formulates the Morphology rule:

(8) CL[accusative] → ø || [dative] ____

Interestingly, the environmental conditions for the Catalan and Spanish rules of impoverishment are identical: a third person dative clitic and a third person accusative clitic in the same clitic cluster. Thus, under the assumption that PF is integrated in the bilingual I-language, we should not be surprised to find impoverishment rules applied to the wrong items. In fact, the following is heard often in colloquial Catalan (these examples were found in the Internet):

(9) a.

El Pere [**s'**	**ho**]	va	dir
the Pere SE	3.NEUT.ACC	PAST	say.INF

'Pere said it to him/her.'

b.

Se'l	vaig	enviar	juntament amb les fotografies.
SE 3.M.ACC	PAST.1	send.INF	together with the photographs

'I sent it to him/her together with the photographs.'

c.

Se la	vaig	donar	fa	tres o quatre dies.
SE 3.F.ACC	PAST.1	give.INF	do.3	three or four days

'I gave it to her/him three or four days ago.'

It is easy to see that the forms shown in (9) result from applying the "Spanish" impoverishment rule that delinks the dative feature and spelling out the resulting terminals with Catalan exponents (yielding results that Catalan teachers find deplorable, as revealed by a google search). This is only possible if the rules of impoverishment are not split in two PFs in the minds of Catalan bilinguals but are part of one single morphology.

Bilingual Spanish/Catalan speakers may also say (10):

(10) Pedro le dijo.
Peter CL.DAT said
'Peter said it to him.'

This suggests an application of the "Catalan" impoverishment rule to the "Spanish" clitic combination with the result that the accusative clitic is obliterated. A factor that confounds this analysis is that the structure shown in (10) is very common throughout the Spanish-speaking world (although not in the dialects geographically close to Catalonia). Consequently, I cannot conclude with certainty that (10) is the output of applying the "Catalan" clitic simplification rule although it is certainly consistent with this analysis.

To conclude: clitic cluster simplification among bilingual Spanish/Catalan bilinguals suggests that morphological operations that take place in the "inner PF" before spell-out are integrated in the I-language of the bilingual.

6.3 Welsh Mutations in English

Consonant mutation in Welsh is a phonetic change in the shape of a consonant that takes place in specific syntactic environments. Since the rule necessarily applies after Vocabulary Insertion, it belongs in the "outer" PF area. A recent article by Vaughan-Evans, Kuipers, Thierry, and Jones (2014) has shown that Welsh-English bilinguals activate the mutation rule even when they are processing English. They argue that this is evidence that "abstract syntactic rules transfer anomalously from one language to the other, even when such rules exist only in one language" (Vaughan-Evans et al. 2014: 8333). Rather, I take it as evidence that the outer PF is also fully integrated in the bilingual competence system.

Let's see what consonant mutation is. It is a phonetic process that affects the initial consonant of a word in some specific syntactic environments, particularly in the boundary of a maximal syntactic category (see Hannahs 2013 for an overview of consonant mutation in Welsh). The result of the process is that a consonant becomes "softer": the voiceless stop becomes voiced and the voiced stop becomes fricative (there are in fact three types of mutations but for our purposes this is all we need). The following is an example in which a voiced consonant becomes fricative:

(11) Lladd-odd y brenin ddraig. [draig] ➔ [ðraig]
Kill-PAST the king dragon
'The king killed the dragon.'

Hannahs 2013: 127

The following two examples are relevant to understand Vaughan-Evans et al.'s experiment. The possessor *ei* triggers mutation on [c] (/k/), yielding /g/, while the determiner *r* does not:

(12) a. ei gynnwys
its contents
b. r cynnwys
the contents

Vaughan-Evans et al. 2014: 8334

It is plausible to assume that consonant mutation is a process that takes place after vocabulary items have been inserted. If it applied earlier, there would be no consonants to mutate. Thus, it belongs in the "outer" PF area.

Bilingual Welsh/English speakers were given sentences in English to read that included normal English words (such as the word 'contents'); English words mutated as if they were Welsh – so "gontents" for 'contents' after a possessive pronoun; English words mutated in contexts in which Welsh would not allow for mutation – so "gontents" for 'contexts' after a definite determiner; and aberrant forms, such as "dontents" for 'contents'. It is important to note that the entire experiment was conducted in English and therefore it cannot be said that the subjects were in a "bilingual mode." While reading the crucial words the subjects' electrophysiological response was measured. Vaughan-Evans and colleagues found that those words that were "correctly" mutated were significantly easier to process than both words mutated in the wrong environment and aberrant words. That is, from the point of view of these speakers' processor, it did not matter if a word that was subject to mutation was "Welsh" or "English" or even whether the environment of mutation was "Welsh" or "English"; in particular, it didn't matter that the determiner or possessor was English. This datum suggests that the mutation rule is part of the linguistic system of these speakers – it is not a grammar rule of the "Welsh" of these speakers, just as the clitic simplification rule does not belong to one particular grammar. In normal speech, the mutation rule must be systematically inhibited when speaking in English. Vaughan-Evans et al., looking at these data from a separationist prism, suggest that the mutation rule must have been active even when English was being processed. From an integrationist perspective, I take it to be clear evidence that the outer PF area of the bilingual I-language is fully integrated.

6.4 Word Order and Prosody

Let's now turn to the most external part of PF: the derivational stages in which linear order and prosodic structure are defined. In order to approach this issue, allow me to reintroduce light verbs again:

(13) *Sranan*/Hindustani

a. *plafond* *boro* kare
ceiling bore.through do
'hit the ceiling'

Muysken 2000: 254

Spanish/*German*

b. Hizo *nähen* *das Hemd.*
do.PAST.3 sew.INF the shirt
'She/he sewed the shirt.'

González-Vilbazo and López 2012: 35

Recall what made these data so interesting to the theoretical linguist. The Sranan VP *plafond boro* in (12) exhibits OV order, although Sranan is a VO language. So, *plafond boro* is not a Sranan VP, even if the internal constituents sound Sranan. The reason why the VP has this apparently alien structure is the selecting light verb *kare*, drawn from Hindustani, which imposes the OV order on its complement. The German VP in (13) is VO although a German VP with an auxiliary or modal should be OV. The culprit is again the light verb that selects it – in this case, the Spanish *hacer*, which imposes a VO order on its complement.

Additionally, the prosody of the "German" VP is Spanish-like, not German-like (as argued in González-Vilbazo and López 2012). What does this mean? As Büring and Gutiérrez-Bravo (2001) point out, in some languages the verb and the object form a prosodic unit (an accentual phrase, a prosodic phrase, or a minor phrase) while some languages build two separate phrases each with their own nuclear stress. Büring and Gutiérrez-Bravo (2001) have argued that German belongs in the first category while Spanish exemplifies the second, as shown in (14):

(14)

```
(                    x      )I   (               x            )I
(x  )(      x  )(    x      )Φ   (x  )(          x            )Φ
JUAN ha venDIdo los LIbros        JUAN hat die BÜcher verkauft
Juan has sold      the books      Juan  has the books   sold
'Juan has sold the books'
```

Interestingly, in the light verb construction the verb and the object form separate prosodic units, even if both are spelled-out with German material (see the detailed discussion in González-Vilbazo and López 2012):

(15) *Spanish*/German
Juan ha hecho ($_{\Phi}$verKAUfen) ($_{\Phi}$die BÜcher).
Juan has done sell the books
'Juan has sold the books.'

In separationist models, such as MacSwan's, it is claimed that the Spanish constituents go to the Spanish PF and the German constituents go to the German PF. But word order and prosody in light verb constructions provides evidence that this is in fact not true. If we were to interpret (13) and (15) in terms of a separationist architecture, we would have to conclude that the German VP goes to the Spanish PF and the Sranan VP goes to the Hindustani PF. Only an integrated model can approach an understanding of these phenomena.

The underlying culprit of the peculiar properties of (13) is the light verb, an exponent of the functional head *Voice*, which is the head of the phase. Thus, following González-Vilbazo and López 2012, I argue that the head of the phase has two crucial properties (among others): The first is that it decides which direction the constituents within the phase will go regardless of the provenance of these constituents – in fact, since they all come from the same List 1 and List 2, the "language" of the constituents makes no difference. Second, the head of the phase also decides which prosodic properties its complement may have:

(16)

Since patterns of prosody and word order are dependent on properties of a functional head *we can posit a unique PF* also in the most external derivational stage. This unique PF can find an instruction in a "German" Voice according to which the word order of the vP should be OV and can also read an instruction in a "Spanish" Voice according to which the order should be VO. Positing a split PF is unnecessary.

I conclude then that the entire derivational process up to the sensorimotor interface is integrated as a single competence system. What happens from then on? Should we require separate externalization systems to account for the different phonetic properties of both languages? I don't really have an argument one way or another. I would only like to point out that there is no necessary link between an externalization system and a "language." Let me explain this point with an example (see Hoot and López 2012, for a first presentation of this idea). Take a Spanish/English bilingual. Normally, this speaker will use Spanish phonetics for Spanish utterances and English phonetics for English utterances. However, it is perfectly possible to mix them, and speak Spanish with an English "accent" and vice-versa – usually, for comic effect. Additionally, a reviewer for Cambridge University Press pointed out that Spanish heritage speakers in the USA use an English pronunciation for English-origin words that denote items related to education but adapt food words to Spanish phonetics, which highlights the independence of pronunciation and language. Thus, if there are indeed two externalization systems for the bilingual, they are not bound to an entity that we may call a "language" but are simply alternative paths that connect the competence system to the performance systems.

6.5 The PF-Interface Condition

Let's now explore one consequence of the derivational PF presented in these pages. PF plays an important role in one interesting issue in the code-switching literature: the (im)possibility of code-switching within the word. Poplack (1980) and MacSwan (1999), among others, argue that code-switching within the word is not possible. This is exemplified in the following example, probably the most oft quoted in the history of code-switching research. The English verb 'eat' is suffixed with the Spanish gerund morpheme:

(17) *English*/Spanish
* *Eat*iendo.
'eating.'

Poplack 1980: 586

MacSwan and Colina (2014: 191) propose that the reason why (17) is ungrammatical is the following:

(18) *PF-interface condition* (PFIC)
Avoid ranking paradoxes

(In fact, MacSwan and Colina's proposal is more elaborate, but (18) suffices for our purposes). They adopt a constraint-based phonological theory in which constraints are universal, but defeatable, and different languages rank constraints differently. MacSwan and Colina's idea is that the "word" (defined in a traditional lexicalist form) is the unit that is submitted for phonological parsing. Since the different morphemes of a word, coming from different "languages," have different constraint rankings, code-switching within the word would likely yield a paradox. The result is that code-switching within the word is prohibited.

However, there are counterexamples to the ban against code-switching within the word. Here are a few:

(19) Nahuatl/*Spanish*
Ne ni-k-*amar*-oa in Maria
I 1sg.3sg.love-vsf IN Maria
'I love Maria.'

MacSwan 1999: 276

(20) German/*Spanish*
Er war ganz schön *cabre*iert
he was completely pretty angered
'He was pissed off.'

González-Vilbazo 2005: 132

(21) English/*Telugu*
I *katt-inc-kon*-ified this house
build-do-self.
'I had this house built for myself.'

Bandi-Rao and Den Dikken 2014: 163

MacSwan (2000: 46–47) argues that apparent counterexamples do not exemplify code-switching but borrowing (although in MacSwan and Colina 2014 this deflection is not mentioned). Recall MacSwan's claim concerning the difference between code-switching and borrowing. In code-switching, W(a) is taken from Lex(a) and drawn into the computational system directly. In borrowing, W(a) is taken from Lex(a) and copied onto Lex(b). It is then drawn into the computational system as an item from Lex(b):

(22) Sample of a tree with borrowing. LIs from Lex1 are borrowed into Lex2

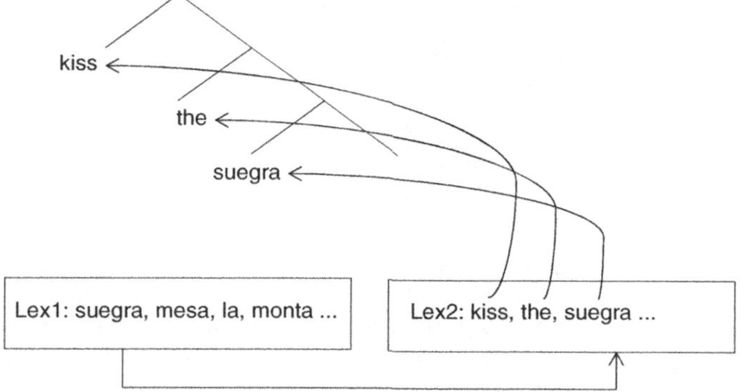

A consequence of this analysis is that in any of the examples (19) to (21), the word would have a homogeneous phonology because all the components of the word come from the same lexicon. Let's evaluate this proposal.

Notice that the PFIC hides an implicit assumption: the scope of the application of phonological rules/constraints is the word. But there are a number of phonological rules/constraints that go beyond the word and apply within the boundaries of phonological phrases/minor phrases. Well-known examples are Italian *radoppiamento sintattico* as well as Chichewa vowel lengthening. Consider now the following scenario. Lx has a high-ranked phonological constraint Cx, which applies outside word boundaries, say at the edges of phonological phrases. Ly does not have Cx (or, in a universalist approach to constraints, it is ranked very low). In this context, the PFIC would prevent code-switching that could involve Lx. However, this prediction is not fulfilled.

For instance: take Japanese/Brazilian Portuguese code-switching. Japanese builds prosodic boundaries on the left edge of syntactic phrases (Selkirk and Tateishi 1991) while Brazilian does it to the right (Sandalo and Truckenbrodt 2002). These opposite prosodic requirements should give rise to points of conflict in code-switching. Consider now the following example from Kato (2003), also Veenstra and López (2016: 326):

(23) Japanese/*Brazilian Portuguese*
Segunda-feira-ni *telegrama*-o *manda* shimashita.
monday-on telegram-ACC send do.PAST
'He/she sent the telegram on Monday.'

Since Brazilian Portuguese and Japanese have contradictory requirements on prosodic structure, (23) may be subject to two possible phrasings:

(24)

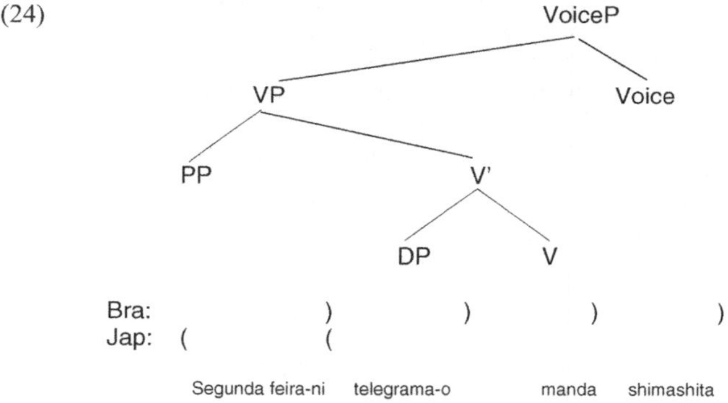

Brazilian prosodic structure requires a prosodic boundary between *telegrama-o* and *manda* and another one between *manda* and *shimashita* while Japanese prosodic structure would rule them out. MacSwan's PFIC should forbid this code-switching example because the requirements of the different languages involved are paradoxical. But the code-switch is just fine – and it is phrased as in Japanese, which is the language that provides the Voice head (Mary Kato p.c.).

Consider also the Esplugisch examples mentioned in Section 3.1, repeated here:

(25) Spanish/*German*
Hizo *nähen das Hemd.*
do.PAST.3 sew.INF the shirt
'She/he sewed the shirt.' (Cf. 1.4b)
González-Vilbazo and López 2012: 35

As discussed in González-Vilbazo and López (2012), German and Spanish have different prosodic structures, Spanish requiring a boundary between the direct object and the main verb. Again, this paradoxical requirement should lead to unacceptability, but this is not the case. These examples show that languages have tools to overcome the problem of conflicting phonologies. In the particular examples in (23) and (25), the Voice Phrase – exponed by the light verb – determines how the constituents of the VP are phrased. I suggest we pursue the idea that phasal heads fix the grammatical properties of their complements.

Let's now turn to (17) and the phenomena that the PFIC is supposed to account for. As far as I know, it seems to be a true generalization that words have a homogeneous phonology, as argued for by MacSwan (1999), González-Vilbazo (2005), Stefanich and Cabrelli (2018). For instance, in example (20) *cabreiert* is pronounced in the "German" way, with both /r/ pronounced as velar trills (González-Vilbazo, p.c.).[1] Example (26) formulates this puzzle:

(26) Puzzle 1: Within words, phonology is homogeneous.

This would seem to confirm the PFIC in this narrow domain. However, (26) gives rise to an additional question that the PFIC is not designed to account for: when code-switching takes place between a root and a derivational morpheme, the phonetics of the word is that of the derivational morpheme:

(27) Puzzle 2: a. The root takes the phonetics of the derivational affix.
b. The derivational affix does not take the phonetics of the root.

This was pointed out in González-Vilbazo (2005). Returning to example (20), the root √cabre- is Spanish, but it is pronounced as if it were German, including the very salient pronunciation of the vibrant consonant as velar rather than alveolar.

Stefanich and Cabrelli's (2018) experimental design is particularly apt to show the point. They use English nonce words such as *zarp* and they elicit from bilingual subjects the production of these words with a Spanish morphology, as in *zarpeando*. The point is how they pronounce the initial segment: as a voiced fricative (English phonology) or as a voiceless fricative (Spanish phonology). Their results show that bilinguals strongly prefer to pronounce *zarpeando* with a voiceless initial segment: the affix has influenced the pronunciation of the root.

Stefanich (2019) has expanded on Stefanich and Cabrelli (2018), testing the results with two additional segments and giving subjects a production and a judgment task. The segments tested were the front high lax [ɪ], which does not exist in Spanish (in this language there is no tense/lax opposition); the /z/ v. /s/ opposition; as well as English [θ], which also does not exist in the Spanish dialect that her subjects speak. In their judgment task, the subjects learned new English words such as *pif,* /pɪf/, thomp /θomp/ as well as 'zarp'. They were then asked to evaluate the hispanized version of them: *thompear, pifear*, etc. Their results show that when the "English" root of a nonce word includes a substitute (/s/ for /z/, /i/ for [ɪ] and /t/ or /s/ for [θ]), subjects rated the result better than the alternatives that included the English phonemes. In a production task, they always adapted the lax vowel and the voiced alveolar fricative. However, on occasion, some of the subjects used [θ] instead of adapting the consonant to Spanish as /s/ or /t/ – the reasons for this nonconsistent result are now being investigated. In any case, the overwhelming amount of data supports (24) and I continue to assume it in the following.

Other than the work just cited, there aren't many descriptions in the literature of how code-switched segments are pronounced and therefore not much evidence that Puzzle 2 is real. Fortunately, Akinremi (2016) is a very useful reference in this context. This article is a detailed study of how English verbal roots are integrated into Igbo morphosyntactic frames and the accommodations that need to occur for the integration to be successful. For instance, she shows how the English vowel /ɚ/, which does not exist in Igbo, is adapted as /ɔ:/:[2]

(28) Igbo/*English*
gà-à-*work* /wɔ:k/
FUT-epenthesis-work
'she/he will work.'

Akinremi 2016: 69

Akinremi's work suggests that Puzzle 2 is a general fact of intra-word code-switching.

Puzzle 2 falls out of the scope of the PFIC because the PFIC only requires the pronunciation to be homogeneous, it makes no prediction as to whether the root or the grammatical morpheme should win out. In particular, the borrowing concept does not require that the "borrowed" part of the mixed word be the root and not the derivational affix.

Let's see how the 1Lex framework approaches this problem. First, I would like to mention once again that in the 1Lex model just presented, no distinction between borrowing and code-switching can be formulated (see Section 4.4). If W(a) is pronounced as if it belongs in L(b), this cannot be accounted for by claiming that W(a) was borrowed into the lexicon of L(b). It should instead be accounted for under the assumption that it went through the L(b) externalization system. Conceptually, I take it that eliminating the distinction between code-switching and borrowing is desirable.

The solution to this puzzle can already be found by putting together our assumptions on word morphology in Section 3.2 as well as our analysis of the pronunciation of the code-switched form *the mesa* in Section 5.3. I argued that the categorial morpheme was the head of the word – in fact, our assumptions would make it impossible for a root to be the head since a root does not even have a label. The same reasoning applies here: the categorial morpheme is the head of the word and therefore supplies the phonology for the whole word. Embick (2010) argues that category morphemes are phase heads and we have already seen that phase heads play an important role in the PF side of the grammar: word order and prosody structure are dependent on the phase head, as we saw in Section 3.1.

With this much in mind, consider the derivation of a code-switching word like *cabreiert* (example (29)):

(29) $\sqrt{\text{cabre}}]\ \text{ier}\ _{v}]\ \text{t[3rdsg]}\ _{ptc}]$

Since the categorizer is German, it forces the root to adopt the "German" phonology. As for the inflectional affix, it follows suit due to the selectional requirements discussed in Section 4.2. This entails that the entire word must follow the German phonological patterns (see López et al. 2017 for a more complete account only partially compatible with the present framework).

To summarize this section: I have shown that the 1Lex theory can account for the same data that the PFIC is meant to account for without making any principled distinction between borrowing and code-switching. Additionally, the MDM model that I assume can account for the role that derivational morphology has in the phonology of the entire word.

6.6 Conclusions

In this chapter, I have presented empirical arguments that the PF of a bilingual is unified and not split in two modules, as argued by MacSwan (1999 et seq.). The PF model that is assumed is the DM-type of PF, consisting of a sequence of derivational operations that prepare a linguistic structure for the externalization mechanisms. Two pieces of empirical evidence presented here show that PF rules of "one language" can apply in a context that looks to be of the "other language": reduction of clitic combination among Catalan/Spanish bilinguals and the processing of mutated English consonants by Welsh bilinguals. Moreover, once we understand that constituent order and prosodic structure are features of a phase head, the need to have separate PFs disappears. MacSwan's PF-Interface Condition is discussed and I show that the integrated MDM model presented here can provide a satisfactory solution to the empirical observation.

7 Lexical Questions: What Do You Learn When You Learn a Word?

The theory presented here is a theory of linguistic competence – a theory of the formal properties of humans' I-languages. Psycholinguists are more concerned with processing, production, and acquisition than the underlying system. Although the goals of both leagues of scholars often do not intersect, there is some psycholinguistic work that seems to have some bearing on the ideas proposed in this monograph. The purpose of Chapters 7 and 8 is to explore this work and, hopefully, enlarge its scope as well as the possible audience for the ideas presented here.

I understand that, by entering a field that I am not a specialist in, I can fall into the trap of amateurism – and its concomitant professional ridicule. But it seems to me that the potential benefits of building the bridge between linguists and psycholinguists outweigh the disadvantages. I am willing to take a first step here, assuming that I probably misunderstand basic questions, hoping to initiate a dialogue rather than providing convincing solutions.

In Section 7.1, I present an overview of the MDM model with some extensions regarding the Encyclopedia, which was left undeveloped in previous chapters. With this development in place, I explore what happens when someone learns a word in Section 7.2 from the perspective of the MDM. In Section 7.3, I present a brief discussion of current psycholinguistic models of bilingual lexicons and argue that the MDM is a useful tool to approach some of the problems that those models try to account for. Section 7.4 switches gears and discusses lexical co-activation briefly. Finally, I present some conclusions. The result of this tentative exploration is that the 1Lex MDM model proposed in these pages will come out reinforced.

7.1 The MDM: The Role of the Encyclopedia

The model that I have been developing can be represented in compressed form in (1):

(1)

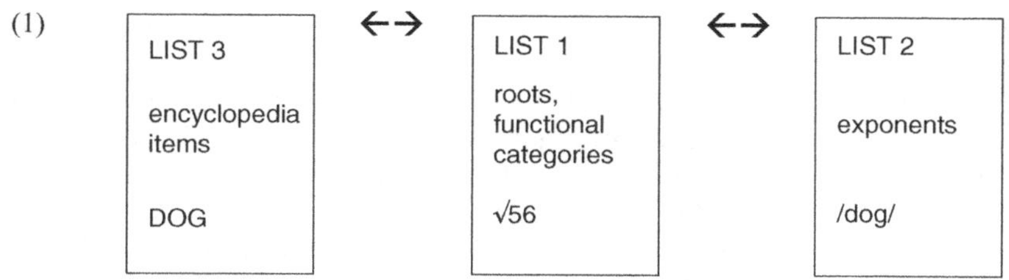

To summarize some of its outstanding features: There is no theoretical primitive corresponding to the Saussurian notion of word, a mapping of a *signifiant* with a *signifié*. Instead, we have three separate lists linked by the computational system of human language, C_{HL}. List 1 consists of a set of roots and functional categories. The roots in this system are nothing but formal indices that help us link the items in List 3 and in List 2. These indices are devoid of any grammatical information; since they do not have a label, they cannot project onto fully fledged phrases.

I also adopt the wide-spread assumption that functional categories are listed in List 1 (although, as far as I can tell, for my purposes they could also be listed as indices). Functional categories are drawn from a Universal Features Inventory (Embick 2015). The idea is that a subset of items from the UFI are activated in a particular I-language and consequently are able to select roots or other functional categories and have an exponent. List 2 consists of a list of rules of exponence – called VIRs in DM -, discussed in detail in Section 3.2.

The meanings of words are listed in List 3, what usually is referred to as the Encyclopedia. I take it that the Encyclopedia is the set of slices of the conceptual structure of the human mind that find an indexed structure in List 1. Recall that I argued that the items in List 3 map onto syntactic structures that minimally include a root (=an index) and a categorizing morpheme:

(2)

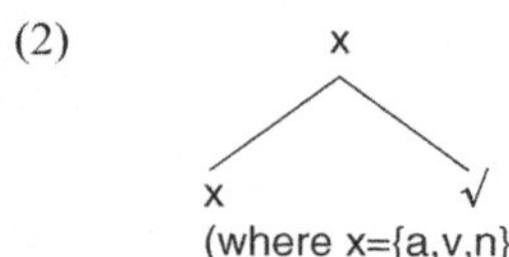

Other than this, I don't have much to say about the conceptual structure in this monograph but a few comments might be in order. First, I understand that a good chunk of conceptual structure is not indexed by a root – in other words, many concepts in a particular human's mind are not linguistic or at least not expressed in the grammar of his or her language. There is a pervasive idea that this affects abstract concepts but it seems to me that it affects even the most concrete and mundane ones. For instance, the concept "drinking receptacle with a handle" exists in the minds of everyone in the western world, but not every language may have a specific term for this concept: In Spanish we have the words *taza* and *jarra*, both of which designate drinking receptacles with a handle but a *jarra* is as wide at the top as at the bottom and can be full of beer or wine but not coffee while *taza* cannot be used to drink beer or wine and the bottom can be narrower than the top. There is no word in Spanish that denotes "drinking receptacle with a handle" *tout court*. The English word 'mug' denotes a receptacle with a handle but a 'cup' may also have a handle (but does not have to have a handle) and the small drinking receptacle that I use to drink my morning espresso has a handle but can never be called a 'mug', and so on (see Malt et al. 2015 for a summary discussion of cross-linguistic differences on how languages parse the conceptual structure).

Finally, I do not have much to say about the structure of what I call conceptual structure itself. There are some intriguing recent proposals, including the possibility that there are two levels of conceptual structure for analogic concepts and parametric concepts, as in Evans (2015). Fortunately, I don't need to go into this.

Under the assumption that the Universal Feature Inventory is a subset of conceptual structure, in this model, conceptual structure feeds List 1 and List 2. I am not sure if this is a bug or a feature of the system – in any case, functional categories could easily be reanalyzed as indices too.

The main conclusion of this chapter is that learning vocabulary in a second language is not qualitatively distinct from learning vocabulary in a first language – from the point of view of the competence system, learning new words involves the same sorts of adjustments to the linguistic system: learning new ways to structure a set of concepts into an encyclopedia item that maps onto an index and an exponent, finding new exponents for old encyclopedia items, restructuring some portion of the conceptual system, or adding grammatical information to old words. Before I start the discussion in Section 7.2, I would like to highlight that I am not attempting to account for the *process* of word learning, how the *gavagai* problem is resolved and so on. Rather, the discussion is focused on a much narrower question: what do you learn when you learn a word? That is, I am focusing on the impact that a new word has in the linguistic system.

7.2 Learning New Words

Let's say this writer, a mechanical ignoramus, is shown a strange object and told that it is a *carburetor*, a word he has never heard of. Neither had he ever seen the object before. Moreover, he is taught what the carburetor is for and – surprise! – he understands the explanation. He has acquired a new word, *carburetor*. What exactly has he acquired?

In the traditional, Saussurian view of word, a word consists of a *signifiant* and a *signifié*. Learning the new word consists of learning this new meaning/form mapping. In my terms, the process looks more complex: the learner has to acquire a new exponent in List 2 and an encyclopedia item in List 3, develop a new index in List 1 to link the two and set the morphosyntactic environment in which the index can be used. Is this complexity warranted? Obviously yes. For instance, consider that the Spanish equivalent of *carburetor* is masculine but neuter in German: this is a simple example that learning the new word involves more than the meaning/form mapping. This is captured in the MDM system quite nicely because the MDM system integrates the new information into the C_{HL} – learning a new word entails learning the index as well as the grammatical environment in which it may occur: a masculine *n* in Spanish, a neuter *n* in German.

Let's say the writer knew the word *carburetor* but all he knew is that it is a piece of an engine but had no idea what its shape is or what it is for. Let's now say that someone explains everything about carburetors to the writer and – surprise again! – he actually understands it. What has he learned? Before the patient mechanic's explanation, the writer already had an index – say, √99 – and a vocabulary item for 'carburetor', as well as some very fuzzy List 3 representation. After the explanation, two things have happened simultaneously: (i) the writer's Encyclopedia has been enriched with a new, more precise, representation and (ii) the indexed structure now links to the new richer representation in the conceptual set.

Finally, let's assume that this writer goes to the garage and overhears someone say, "the carb in this car is not mixing well." The writer has never heard the word *carb* but in this particular context, he realizes that 'carb' refers to the same thing as 'carburetor'. What has he learned? A new vocabulary item for an old List 1 and List 3 item:

(3) Before learning: CARBURETOR ⟷ √99 ⟷ /karburetor/
After learning: CARBURETOR ⟷ √99 ⟷ {/karburetor/,/karb/}

I assume my carburetor examples represent generally what is learnt when we learn vocabulary in a first language: a lot of it involves learning the whole word from scratch: new index, new morphosyntax, new encyclopedia item, new exponent. Sometimes, it is about tinkering with things that are already there in sketch: the learner expands and slices the conceptual structure, creates new vocabulary items, and fixes the indexed structure that connects them.

Let's see now what happens when you learn words in a second language. We are now supposing that the writer, a Spanish speaker, learns the English word *planet* as well as the Chinese word *xíng xing*. He realizes that they all refer to the same concept, which we may represent as PLANET. What has he learned? The extension of *planet, planeta*, and *xíng xing* is the same: whenever the proposition 'x is a planet' is true, the propositions 'x is a planeta' and 'x is a xíng xing' are also true. We can then take it that what this person has learned is new phonetic forms for an encyclopedia item (but see fn 3, chapter 4):

(4) Before learning: PLANET ⟷ √89 ⟷ /planeta/
After learning: PLANET ⟷ √89 ⟷ {/planeta/, /planet/, /xíng xing/}

Additionally, this person will also have to learn that *planet* and *xíng xing* are selected by a bare *n* in a language in which *n* bears no gender features. We can further assume that becoming more and more proficient in English and Chinese won't lead to changing this relation between the List 3 and the List 1 items. That is, there is no need to create a redundant meaning/form representation for each of 'planet' and *xíng xing*. Is this substantially different from the way we learn words in a first language? When we learn a first language, we typically learn a matching of index, encyclopedia item, and exponent, while in a second language, at least at the beginning, we seem to match old concepts to new exponents. But we do this when we learn our first language too, as shown with the 'carb' example.

Let's now assume that an English speaker learns the German word *gefallen*. It means exactly the same as English 'like', so that if it is true that 'y likes x' it is also true that 'x *gefällt* y' and vice-versa. Notice that the positioning of x and y has been changed, purposefully, between the English and German examples. This is because the German word requires that the person who likes appears as a complement in dative case while the thing liked appears as a subject in nominative case. According to fairly standard analyses, (see Arad 2003, among many others) this difference in the distribution of case and grammatical function is directed by the flavor of *v* that selects the root. Thus, in this example, learning a new word requires acquiring a new exponent and a new grammatical structure for the index. The Encyclopedia, on the other hand, does not need to change:

(5)	List 3	List 1	List 2
	LIKE	[√56] $v_{[ger]}$	/gəfalən/
		[√56] $v_{[eng]}$	/laɪk/

Is this something that we do only when we learn our L2? Again, I don't think so. The German child has to learn the verb *mögen* together with *gefallen* – both mean the same but they are inserted in different morpho-syntactic structures – *mögen* works like English 'like' with the liker in nominative case and the likee in accusative case. Thus, the German child learning *gefallen* is not in a different place than the English-speaking adult learning the same word.

One more mini-story. The writer, a Spanish speaker, learns the English word *jealousy*. Now, it so happens that the word *jealousy* denotes two very different emotions: it denotes what I feel when someone flirts with my spouse and it denotes what I feel when someone gets a promotion that I desired for myself. In Spanish, two different words are used for the two emotions: *celos* and *envidia* (the latter a cognate of the English word *envy*). The I-language of this Spanish speaker looks like (6a), with distinct roots and vocabulary items for the two List 3 items. As he begins to learn English, this Spanish speaker initially takes *jealousy* to mean the same thing as *celos*. His I-language now looks like (6b), with both /θelos/ and /dʒɛləsi/ as possible spell-outs for CELOS. Later he realizes the two words are not equivalent and /dʒɛləsi/ is also used with the meaning of ENVIDIA: he has learned how to use *jealousy* in the same contexts as an English speaker. What has he learned? The conceptual structure has not changed, the two emotions CELOS and ENVIDIA are List 3 items. But now there is a new phonetic form that can be applied to two old concepts. In our terms: the root √99 can spell out as /embidja/ or /dʒɛləsi/ and the root √98 can spell out as /θelos/ or /dʒɛləsi/:

(6) a. Before learning: CELOS ⟷ √98 ⟷ /θelos/
ENVIDIA ⟷ √99 ⟷ /embidja/
b. After learning (1): CELOS ⟷ √98 ⟷ {/θelos/, / dʒɛləsi/}
ENVIDIA ⟷ √99 ⟷ /embidja/
c. After learning (2): CELOS ⟷ √98 ⟷ {/θelos/, /dʒɛləsi/}
ENVIDIA ⟷ √99 ⟷ {/embidja/, /dʒɛləsi/}

Again, one could ask if this process is something that we do as we learn our first language. We certainly do. As we acquire our first language, we are constantly reshaping the connections between List 3 and List 2. A child learning English as a L1 might think that 'high school' and 'college' are synonymous words and only later realize that their conceptual scope is somewhat different – which involves a process strictly parallel to what we see in (6).

This is the last of the flash short stories. Let's say the writer, a Spanish speaker, learns the Quechua word *supay*. It is the name of a deity that does not exist in the Christian theology, which is the only one the writer is familiar with. Initially, he may try to assimilate it to a familiar concept, say the DEMON concept of Christian tradition. This is shown in (7a), where the word /supai/ is just another spell out for DEMON. Eventually, the writer may construct a new concept (possibly built out of previous conceptual primitives) in his Encyclopedia and link it to a new index and the new phonetic representation, as in (7b). In fact, the learning of what this word means will not be completed until the whole mythological structure – a new conceptual structure – has been put in place:

(7) a. Before learning: DEMON ⟷ √2 ⟷ {/demonio/, /supai/}
b. After learning: DEMON ⟷ √2 ⟷ /demonio/
SUPAI ⟷ √3 ⟷ /supai/

I think these examples suffice to make two points:

(i) the MDM model allows us to understand more clearly what is involved in learning a new word: sometimes what appears superficially to be "learning a new word in the L2" is just learning a new exponent; sometimes the learning does embrace a new concept; sometimes it entails only a new morphosyntactic structure for old concepts; sometimes it involves expanding the range of grammatical environments in which an index can be merged. Of all these processes, adding new exponents seems to be the easiest one, since it requires no alteration of grammar or conceptual structure. This expectation is confirmed by anecdotal evidence – Spaniards who colonized Peru initially identified *supay* with the Christian devil and seemed unable to create a new conceptual structure for the new exponent. It is also confirmed by experimental evidence, as I explain in a minute.

(ii) The acquisition of an L2 vocabulary is not fundamentally different from learning the L1 vocabulary: there will be processes like the ones I just described of creating or altering exponents, conceptual structures, and grammatical frameworks. It follows that one should create a single model to represent our lexical knowledge and learning, in particular, we should avoid positing dedicated models to represent our L2 knowledge or our L2 learning of new words. This conclusion follows directly from the integrationist framework that I propose in this monograph.

7.3 Psycholinguistic Models of the Bilingual Lexicon

Psycholinguistic research has uncovered a number of properties of bilingual lexicons, which have led to proposing a series of models that seek to capture them. In particular, the models of the bilingual lexicon that I have consulted are mostly concerned with understanding the sort of errors that L2 learners make (see in particular the informative overviews in Pavlenko 2009, Williams 2015). There seem to be two distinct approaches to the problem, the terms of the debate neatly summarized in Brysbaert and Duyk (2010) and Kroll, van Hell, Tokowicz, and Green (2010). The first one proposes that the L1 and the L2 lexicons are stored separately, they are asymmetrically connected and they are, likewise, asymmetrically bound to the conceptual structure (see Kroll and Stewart 1994 for the classic proposal). On the other side, connectionist models propose that bilingual speakers have only one lexicon. It would seem that the latter approach is more germane to my own proposals; however, the theoretical assumptions are so different that it looks as if we have reached conclusions that only look similar at the most superficial level. In essence, as a linguist, I am interested in the lexicon as a component of the I-language of a speaker and I try to figure out how it interacts with the computational system and the interface systems: The word "lexicon" means things like transitivity, events, noun classifications, and so on. The co-activation work inspired by connectionism seems to be mostly interested in how words are stored in our long-term memory. If an English word that begins with the syllable 'can' as in 'candle' activates a Spanish word that begins with the same syllable, this tells us something about how information is stored but not something about how our linguistic competence – the connections between our List 1, List 2, and List 3 – works.

A good model of the bilingual lexicon should be able to account for properties of the bilingual lexicons that have been uncovered in recent years, in particular, that bilingualism affects the organization of the L1 lexicon. In the terms of my framework we could summarize it as follows: let's assume that a monolingual person of Language x has a List 1 root *r* that maps onto an item *i* of List 3. For this individual, continuous contact with Language y will affect this relationship so that *r* will map onto an item *i'*, which covers a slightly different area of the Encyclopedia from *i*. Here are some examples: Athanasopoulos (2009) shows that the semantic space for blue color in Greek, which is divided into different roots (*ble* and *ghalazio*), is *shifted*, maintaining a proportional distance, among those who have lived extensively in an English-speaking country. There is also *reverse transfer*: as documented in Pavlenko and Malt (2011), bilingual L1 Russian/ L2 English speakers tend to classify containers ('cup', 'glass', etc.) in their L1 more like English speakers than like monolingual Russian speakers (this effect was more noticeable among early bilinguals). Finally, there is also *attrition*, when a conceptual distinction in your native language disappears in an intense contact situation (Athanasopoulos et al. 2010). It seems that these findings are fully consistent with the MDM 1Lex framework; they are in fact built into this grammar organization: if the new vocabulary has to negotiate the real estate with the old, it is to be expected that there will be readjustments in both directions. On the other hand, a theory that assumes that a bilingual has two compartmentalized lexicons does not predict shifting, reverse transfer, or attrition.

Some research on priming points to the conclusion that the lexicons of bilinguals are set in a *compound* organization: the words in each language are connected to a common conceptual structure. For instance, it can be shown that an Italian-English bilingual will recognize the Italian word *sedia* faster if it has been primed by the English 'chair' (Basnight-Brown and Altarribia 2007, Williams 2015). If we look at this result from the MDM perspective, it is consistent with the assumption that both *sedia* and 'chair' are exponents of the same List 3 and List 1 items.

Some other research points to a *subordinate* organization: the words in the L2 seem to take a detour through the L1 before reaching the conceptual structure, at least among low proficient learners. In the present context, let me introduce the most cited model of bilingual lexicons: The Revised Hierarchical Model (RHM; Kroll and Steward 1994). The proponents of this model want to capture the

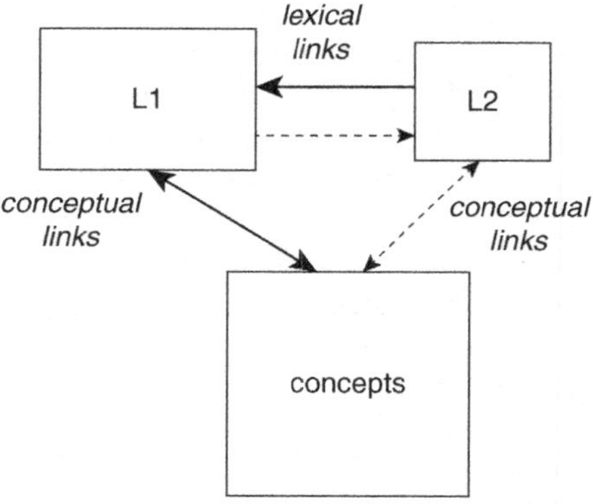

Figure 7.1 The Revised Hierarchical Model
Kroll and Stewart 1994

insight that in the early stages of L2 acquisition "L2 words are more strongly connected to their L1 translation equivalents than to concepts … as L2 proficiency increases, the links between L2 words and concepts become stronger" (Pavlenko 2009: 143; see Kroll and Stewart 1994, Kroll and Tokowicz 2005, and Kroll et al. 2010, among many others.) The RHM, represented in Figure 7.1, captures this idea. As you can see in Figure 7.1, the words in L2 pass through the L1 before reaching the conceptual structure. The connections between L2 and conceptual structure do exist but are weaker, as shown by the thinner line. Once the L2 learner becomes more proficient, more direct connections between L2 and conceptual structure are possible.

The intuition underlying the RHM is captured nicely in the MDM, as shown in the 'planet' example (see (4)). As experienced by language learners the world over and witnessed by generations of language teachers, the initial learning of L2 "words" is really the addition of new exponents/vocabulary items to the List 2, while the rest is left unchanged. The English speaker who learns Spanish learns that *perro* means 'dog', *pájaro* means 'bird' and so on. Notice that this strategy does not have to be discarded, as many words in different languages do denote the same thing (planet, dog, cat, mouse, horse, tree …), as previously argued. For many other new words this equivalence breaks down: *celos* is not the same as 'jealousy'. When the non-equivalence is detected, a new mapping of items in List 3 and in List 1 must be developed: in this particular context, 'jealousy' may be a possible spell out for two distinct List 3 and List 1 items (see (6)). The original RHM claims that the figure in (8) only reflects the beginning of learning a second language and it is later abandoned. But Thierry and Wu (2007) show that even among advanced learners there is evidence that the strategy is used to some extent while other works show that even at the beginning level, access to conceptual access is possible (see Brysbaert and Duyk 2010).

There is more to the RHM than the initial intuition. The main empirical motivation for the RHM is the experimental finding that translation from the L2 to the L1 is significantly faster than translation from the L1 to the L2. The RHM accounts for this by assuming that L2 words are directly connected to L1 words whereas the latter can only reach the L2 words through conceptual structure.

However, Athanasopoulos (2015) shows that the RHM cannot account for conceptual shift or reverse transfer because of its compartmentalized structure. Additionally, as Brysbaert and Duyk (2010: 365) point out, the RHM would lead to expect a high priming effect of L2 to L1 and a much weaker priming effect in the opposite direction, a hypothesis that has been tested using masked priming paradigm (Schoonbaert et al. 2009). In fact, priming effects from L2 to L1 seem to be very hard to find. Proponents of the RHM can counterargue that theirs is a model of language production, not language processing. One could wonder if there is a model that can account for both.

Schoonbaert et al. (2009) propose an account of their priming results within a connectionist framework. The starting point is that the L1 word has a richer semantic representation than the equivalent L2 word which, in their model, is shown by the activation of more nodes in the semantic level. This is shown in Figure 7.2.

The L1 word activates a higher percentage of semantic features than the L2 word: in this model, semantic features are represented as nodes in the semantics level. An L1 prime activates a high percentage of nodes connected to an L2 target but an L2 prime only activates a smaller percentage of nodes connected to the L1 target. This results in stronger priming of L2 by L1 and very little priming of L1 by L2.

Unfortunately, Schoonbaert et al. (2009) do not explain what they mean by "semantic features" and they do not provide an example. They obviously do not mean semantic features in the sense in which linguists use the term (see my discussion of furniture and drinking receptacles in Chapter 4). As far as I can tell, both 'taste' and *smaak* should evoke the same semantic features in an English/Dutch bilingual. Figure 7.2 seems to suggest that *smaak* has some semantic features in the minds of Dutch L1 bilinguals that 'taste' does not have, but the authors of the model don't tell us what these features are. Thus, it seems to me that semantic features is the wrong way of looking at it. I would argue that the priming effects that Schoonbaert et al. (2019) discuss are not a consequence of weaker L2 semantics: it is the L2 exponent – the vocabulary item in the List 2 – that is weaker due to less usage, fewer contexts, etc.

Additionally, it is not clear to me that this model has anything to say of the translation experiments that are the focus of Kroll and Stewart (1994). Recall that Kroll and Stewart found that it takes longer to translate from L1 to L2. It seems to

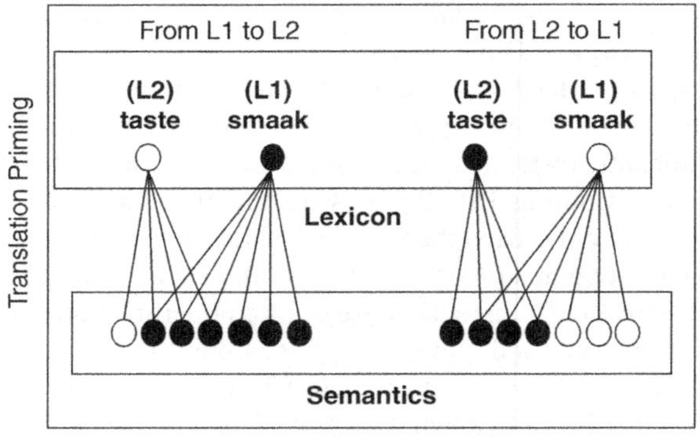

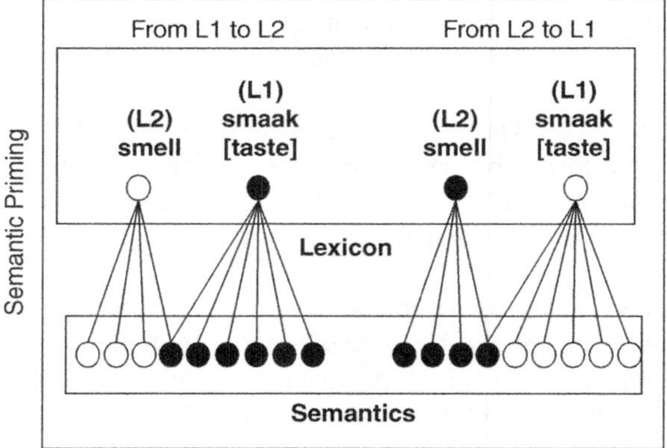

Figure 7.2 A connectionist model of the bilingual lexicon (Schoonbaert et al. 2009:581)

me that the Schoonbaert et al.'s (2009) model predicts that translation from L1 to L2 should be faster than vice-versa, precisely because the overlap in semantic features should favor it. So, it seems that the translation and priming experiments yield results that appear paradoxical at first sight. It looks like a good area where we can check the usefulness of the MDM.[1]

The starting point of my proposal is that the translation and masked priming experiments elicit alternative exponents to the same List 1 and List 3 element. Further, let me suggest that the L1 exponents are more strongly activated than the L2 exponents. This can in fact be incorporated into the MDM by adding probabilistic weights to the different exponents (see Adger and Smith 2010 for an analysis of dialectal variation based on probabilistic weights). These probabilistic weights are certainly necessary independently. Consider our favorite example, how *birra* displaced *cervesia*. In order for this displacement to take place, there has to be an increasing probability among speakers to choose the new exponent over the old until the point that the old exponent's probability is 0. So, let's assume that the Dutch person who has English as L2 has both 'taste' and *smaak* as vocabulary items but the former has lower probability. I represent probability with a shadow representation:

(8) List 3 ←→ List 1 ←→ List 2
TASTE √566 {**smaak**, taste}

As mentioned, Kroll and Stewart (1994) found that translation from the L2 to the L1 was faster than the opposite direction. Translation from L2 to L1 is faster because the subjects were given the weaker exponent as input and had to return the stronger one. The stronger and more likely exponent is easier to find in long-term memory than the weaker one and therefore it is easier to access in a translation task. Translation from L1 to L2 is slower because the subjects were given the stronger exponent as input and were asked to retrieve the weaker one. Consider now the masked priming experiments, which yielded a stronger priming effect going from L1 to L2. I surmise this is also because the L1 representation is stronger and therefore it has a stronger evocative power.

A question raised by the RHM is the following. In the model in Figure 7.1, both the L1 and the L2 are linked to a module called concepts. I am not certain that I know what these concepts are: are they the meanings of words or are they part of a language of mind? Other questions that can be raised by this: Are those concepts "there" beforehand? Is learning a new language just finding new links to these concepts? What happens when the new language distributes the conceptual space differently (i.e., seats, drinking receptacles)? These issues are discussed at length in Pavlenko (2009), as well as Jarvis and Pavlenko (2008).

Consider Pavlenko's Modified Hierarchical Model (MHM), shown in Figure 7.3. It retains the triangular shape of the RHM but adds complexity in the conceptual space, with a box for L1 concepts, another one for L2 concepts, and an overlapping area.

Notice some characteristics of this model. First, the concept box is divided in three sub-categories: L1-specific categories, L2-specific categories, and shared categories. As a consequence, the arrows linking one box to another have also become more complex. We have the lexical link from L2 to L1 that we saw in the Kroll and Stewart (1994) model. Quite naturally, we have conceptual links between L1 words and L1 categories as well as L2 words and L2 categories. But we also see that there are instances of transfer: L2 transfer (using L1 words for L2 categories) and L1 transfer (using L2 words for L1 categories). On the downside, as Athanasopoulos (2015) points out, the MHM does not quite address the empirical problem of reverse transfer.

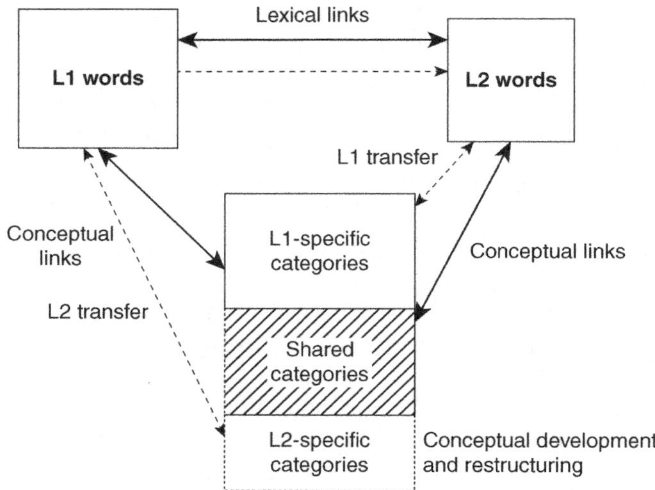

Figure 7.3 The Modified Hierarchical Model
Pavlenko 2009: 147

What does the MHM do for us? Pavlenko (2009) offers a couple of examples and a distinction between *semantic transfer* and *conceptual transfer*. Let's say a Finnish speaker says *he bit himself in the language*, where *language* is pronounced instead of *tongue*. In Finnish, the word *kieli* has the same semantic scope as *tongue*, referring to the body part and to *langue*. According to Pavlenko, this error is an example of *semantic transfer*, which occurs at the point when a word is mapped onto a concept. But it seems to me that the error does not involve the conceptual structure itself because Finnish and English have the same (or similar) categories.

An example of an error in *conceptual structure* is the usage of an English speaker who uses the Russian word *chashka* ('cup') to refer to a paper cup, which in Russian is denoted with a different word. Pavlenko describes this error as a mistake in understanding the conceptual range of *chashka*. This would be an example of *conceptual transfer*.

The sort of model that MDM exemplifies is perfectly suited to handle Pavlenko's examples, although the solution provides quite a different insight. Consider the Finnish example first. Recall that, as reported, the Finnish speaker says 'language' when he means 'tongue'. According to Pavlenko, this is a problem of semantic transfer, the word 'language' has mapped to the wrong meaning. Within MDM, this is conceptualized as follows: The "error" would come about as the assignation of the wrong exponent to a particular index and encyclopedia item:

(9)

	List 3 ←→	List 1 ←→	List 2
Before learning	TONGUE	√44	{/kieli/, /læŋgʊɪdʒ/}
	LANGUE	√45	{/kieli/, / læŋgʊɪdʒ/}
After learning:	TONGUE	√44	{/kieli/, /tʌŋ/}
	LANGUE	√45	{/kieli/, /læŋgʊɪdʒ/}

For this speaker, the root √44, which maps onto an item in the Encyclopedia that could be defined as "TONGUE "or "MUSCLE IN THE MOUTH" has the exponents {/kieli/, /language/}. The root √45, which maps onto a List 3 item that we may call LANGUE, has exactly the same exponents. After learning the actual usage of the English words, the Finnish speaker has 'tongue' as the exponent of √44 and 'language' as the exponent of √45. Learning to use 'tongue' for 'language' with the meaning of TONGUE simply entails a change in the VIRs – and therefore it is not in fact a semantic error.

As for the English person learning Russian, the error is of the same type as the initial misunderstanding of *supay* (see example (7)): approaching the learning of words in a second language as learning new vocabulary items for old concepts. Eventually, learning the correct semantic range of the word *chashka* involves an alteration in the Encyclopedia: the learner will eventually have to figure out that *chashka* does not link with the old concept CUP (with exponent /kʌp/), but will have to develop a new concept, call it CUP2, with the extension of Russian *chashka*, as well as a new index:

(10)

	List 3 ←→	List 1 ←→	List 2
Before learning	CUP	√57	{/kʌp /, /tʃaʃka/}
After learning:	CUP	√57	{/kʌp/}
	CUP2	√58	{/tʃaʃka/}

With this I finish my discussion of the models of bilingual lexicons. I am fully aware that I have barely scratched the surface of the problem. However, I hope to have shown that the MDM 1Lex framework can provide excellent tools for analysis. I also hope to have aroused the curiosity of scholars with expertise in this field.

One more note before I move on. As mentioned, the RHM is explicitly designed as a production model (particularly emphasized by Kroll and Tokowicz 2005) – in other words, it is a model of L2 speakers' performance (although Williams 2015 classifies it as a comprehension model). This raises another issue. The RHM leads to the conclusion that if an English speaker learning Spanish uses the word *celos* where he should use *envidia,* this is a performance error. I think this is misguided: this usage reflects an aspect of this person's knowledge of their L2 (i.e., the meaning that *celos* and *envidia* have in their mental lexicon). Generally, systematic errors reveal something about the competence system while occasional, sporadic errors are due to performance. In particular, the assumption that the L2 words are equivalent to L1 words is a fairly systematic strategy in learning an L2 vocabulary, a fact that is not captured in a model that seeks to be a performance model. On the other hand, the MDM is a competence model: it seeks to understand how our knowledge of language is structured. Systematic errors must be caused by properties of the competence system. The inappropriate usage of the English word 'jealousy' by a Spanish speaker reflects something about the organization of the lexicon of that person, as shown previously.

7.4 Co-activation

There is now a wealth of studies on lexical *co-activation*, embracing almost every aspect of the phenomenon (see Williams 2015 for a useful overview). For instance, take the following experiment (Nas 1983, cited in Dijkstra 2005). Nas asked Dutch-English bilinguals to decide if words from a list were English words or not. Some of the non-English words sounded like Dutch words, others did not. The ones that sounded Dutch were rejected more slowly, suggesting that the Dutch vocabulary is also active for subjects who are accomplishing a task dealing with the English lexicon. Assuming that a bilingual has two "languages," lexical co-activation studies argue that bilinguals do not entirely shut off the lexicon of one language when using the other – rather, it seems clear that both lexicons are fully awake when a speaker processes or produces one of them. This has been shown with many different methods and tasks (see Kroll et al. 2015, Dijkstra 2005).

There is, of course, an alternative interpretation of these results. One could simply assume, as I do in these pages, that the effect of a person having "two languages" is an illusion since all normal humans are in possession of a unified linguistic competence. A direct consequence is that there is no such thing as "co-activation" because there are no separate lexicons in the bilingual's mind. Kroll et al. (2015: 377) seem to approximate this idea when they reach the conclusion that "all the languages that are known and used become part of the same language system" (although I would question the idea that *lexical* co-activation data can provide generalizations concerning the whole linguistic system.) This is also, of course, the conclusion reached by all the scholars who approach the lexicon from a connectionist perspective.

A lot of the research on co-activation involves orthography, partial phonological identity, and a number of other notions. For instance, using the English word 'steak' activates the Dutch word *sterk* 'strong' (see the overview in Dijkstra 2005). This suggests that co-activation is involved with every feature of how words are stored in long-term memory, including connections among these lexical items that do not normally enter the linguist's assumptions concerning the structure of the speaker's I-language. As I said at the introduction, when linguists thinks of the "lexicon" of a language, they normally think of the meaning of words, the phonological exponent, their morphosyntactic environment. This entails that the issue of lexical co-activation goes way beyond the sort of phenomena that linguists try to describe – including the MDM argued for in these pages. There is, it seems to me, some room for collaboration for scholars from different perspectives.

7.5 Conclusions

Let me now summarize what we have learned in this chapter. I have elaborated on the List 3 side of the grammar in Section 7.1 in preparation for a discussion on word learning in Section 7.2. The conclusion that I reached at the end of Section 7.2 is that the outcome of first and second language vocabulary acquisition in an individual's I-language are not that different because vocabulary acquisition always involves the same outcomes: creation of new List 1 items and/or new morphosyntactic frameworks for them, creation of new List 2 items, and shaping and reshaping List 3 items.

In Section 7.3, I discussed some psycholinguistic approaches to second language vocabulary acquisition. All of these models take for granted that acquiring vocabulary in a second language is fundamentally different from acquisition of the first and, as a consequence, acquisition of bilingual vocabulary requires models specifically designed for it distinct from models of monolingual vocabulary. I have shown that the integrated MDM model can provide insight into the research questions that occupy psycholinguistics scholars and suggested that the distinct-models approach is not necessary. Finally, in Section 7.4, I have very briefly discussed the by-now-abundant literature on co-activation and claimed that it largely confirms the 1Lex hypothesis.

8 Psycho-Syntactic Questions: Acquisition, Priming and Co-activation, and a Note on Processing Cost

Chapter 8 continues with my engagement with the psycholinguistic literature in light of the MDM model presented previously. Before I start the discussion, some *caveat lector* is in order. To start with, both linguists and psychologists would agree that the connection between linguistic theories and psycholinguistic models is not a trivial matter. Part of the problem is that we do not seem to share an understanding of what the design of language is. In the discussion that follows, we will see that what I call 'syntax' and what the psycholinguistics literature calls 'syntax' are often quite different things. In the psycholinguistics literature on co-activation and priming, word order is central to syntax and sometimes it seems that syntax is only about order; whereas in my view, shared by many linguists, order is resolved at the interface with the S-M, and pragmatics, as well as prosody, play as important a role in order as syntax. Grammatical constructions are analytical primitives for the authors I will discuss, whereas many linguists would join me in claiming that they are epiphenomena. Finally, psycholinguists in this tradition do not mention aspects of syntax that many linguists do find central: dependencies, scope, selection, functional categories, and so on. I am not going to try and bridge the issue, which is way beyond my strength – more modestly, I simply zero in on what seems to be relevant for my purposes.

In Section 8.1, I discuss bilingual acquisition and the Separate Development Hypothesis (SDH). Many scholars working on bilingual acquisition argue that it involves the development of two separate linguistic systems. The basic argument is based on *functional separation*, the fact that (at least some) bilinguals can speak in one or the other language without mixing them up. This seems to contradict my proposal that bilinguals' linguistic system is fully integrated (as well as the psycholinguistic literature on co-activation and priming). I discuss the arguments that have been presented for the SDH and show that the facts that they point out are amenable to the integrated system that I defend in these pages.

In Section 8.2, I discuss some work on syntactic co-activation and priming that seems to support or at least be compatible with my proposals, although with some reinterpretation of their results. Finally, in Section 8.3, I present a brief discussion on whether code-switching entails a processing cost and to what extent this cost impinges on my integrated proposal.

8.1 Bilingual Acquisition and the Separate Development Hypothesis

The proposal sketched in these pages runs counter to the mainstream opinion among linguists and psycholinguists that investigate bilingual language acquisition. In this field, the dominant opinion is the so-called *Separate Development Hypothesis* (SDH), briefly discussed in Chapters 1 and 2. According to the SDH, bilinguals have two fully separate grammatical "systems" in their head (interestingly, this approach collides with the work of other psycholinguists who study priming, as described in Section 8.2). The SDH is, in effect, a variant of the separationist assumption that I have argued against throughout. In this section, I argue that the evidence presented to support the SDH, based on functional separation, does not really support a split linguistic competence; in fact, it can be reanalyzed along the lines developed in this monograph.

The SDH has two versions, a strong one and a weak one. According to the weak one, influence is possible from one grammar to the other, albeit only at the interfaces (Hulk and Müller 2000). According to the strong one, there is no influence. Here I focus on the strong version, which is the one that appears to most directly contradict my proposals. For this discussion, I focus on De Houwer (2005), which presents a convenient summary of the main arguments.

De Houwer (2005) presents two formulations of the SDH, one that I find unimpeachable, and another one that I disagree with. They can be summarized with these quotes:

(1) The morphosyntactic development of the one language does not have any fundamental effect on the morphosyntactic development of the other.
De Houwer 2005: 33 (from De Houwer 1990: 63)

(2) In acquiring two languages from birth, children are undergoing a sort of "double" acquisition process in which two morphosyntactic systems are acquired as fundamentally separate and closed systems.
De Houwer 2005: 43

De Houwer herself seems to think that (1) and (2) are truth-conditionally identical, since both are used as alternative definitions of the SDH. But their import is actually quite different.

I understand the statement presented in (1) as meaning that a bilingual child learning English and Dutch acquires English and Dutch, not a debased version of either language – the word 'fundamental' is crucial here. This person, as a bilingual child or adult, will be in full possession of the expressive resources of both languages. This seems right, provided that the societal conditions allow for the flourishing of both languages.

The hypothesis presented in (2) is the one of concern and the one that I would like to question: is it true that bilinguals have two separate systems (instead of a unique competence as just argued)? Let's consider what empirical evidence has been used to support SDH. The empirical argumentation in favor of SDH has the following general structure: in order to accomplish function F (question, assertion, negation, etc.), L1 uses structure S1 while L2 uses S2. Once we control for other factors, we find that bilingual children and adults use S1 when using L1 and they do not use S1 in L2 or vice versa. Thus, L1 and L2 are separated. Let's call this the Structure/Language Pairing argument (SLP).

The SLP should not be confused with the *Functional Separation* hypothesis (FSH), according to which bilingual children must have two languages in their head because children who are raised in the *one parent – one language* paradigm know when to use each of their languages. Versions of this argument have been presented in various forms many times over the years. One classic reference is Genesee, Nicoladis, and Paradis (1995), where it is argued that even bilingual children at the one-word stage know when and with whom to use words of one language or the other. I discuss the FSH later in this section, now I focus on the SLP.

As an example, consider yes/no questions in English vs Dutch. As De Houwer explains, yes/no questions in English require do-insertion if there is no auxiliary in the clause, as shown in (3a). Instead, in Dutch we have subject/verb inversion, as shown in (3b):

(3) a. Do you want some tea?
b. Wil je thee?
Want you tea

Now, if bilingual English/Dutch children were not subject to separation, one should be able to expect seeing do-support in Dutch yes/no questions and lexical verb movement in English. This does not happen, which according to De Houwer leads to the conclusion that the grammatical systems of English and Dutch are separate in the child's mind. The empirical fact is real and therefore a purported argument for an integrated system needs to address it.

One question we could ask is, is it always the case that the two languages of the bilingual remain as impermeable as De Houwer argues? Some literature on acquisition and an abundant literature on contact and historical linguistics disagree.

Some studies on bilingual children show that the two systems cannot be impermeable, since there is clear influence of one on the other. For instance, Yip and Mathews (2000) show that a bilingual Cantonese/English child uses prenominal relative clauses in English, which can only be due to influence from Cantonese. But this phenomenon (as well as others) seems to disappear after a few years if the two languages develop normally. This had led to the claim that children start out with one "fused" grammatical system that eventually splits into two (see Köppe 1996 for a critical evaluation of this proposal).

Students of historical and contact linguistics often discuss how particularly dense contact situations do indeed yield influence from one grammar to the other, sometimes driving language change (see Aikhenvald 2006 and references therein). Consider the following example from Sánchez (2003):

(4) Lamas Quechua
Abrasaykan achkitanta.
He.is.hugging his dog

The word order in most varieties of Quechua is SOV. However, in Lamas Quechua, the objects can appear in post-verbal position, as in this example. This is attributed to influence from Spanish, which is an SOV language. Sánchez also discusses the disappearance of case markers and the development of indefinite articles as consequences of the contact situation (for more on Spanish/Quechua contact linguistics, see Muysken 2012, Muntendam 2013). Quechua also influences the Spanish of these bilingual speakers. But the assumption that the two grammatical systems grow in the minds of speakers as separate systems is incompatible with the fact that bilinguals show clear signs of interference and convergence.

Meisel (2011) confronts the apparent contradiction that bilingual children are able to acquire two languages without a glitch with the diachronic evidence that linguistic contact leads to language change. His hypothesis is that language change may take place when children acquire a second language at a relatively young age and presents a plausibility argument that certain grammatical features (e.g., gender) are hard to acquire even by very young children. The assumption that gender is acquired late does not seem to hold, as shown in Radford et al. (2007), where an overview is presented. Of course, even if it were true that gender is late to be acquired, there is no evidence that this is actually what triggers linguistic change.

In light of this discussion, consider now the following datum.

(5) US Spanish
Una caja conteniendo zapatos
'A box containing shoes'

The noun phrase in (5) is acceptable to every Spanish speaker that I have been able to consult with and who has grown bilingual in the USA. Although this datum has not been obtained by means of a controlled experiment, I take it as a real fact of US Spanish – and easily available for inspection for anyone with access to speakers of US Spanish. But this sentence is not acceptable to Spanish speakers who are not bilingual in English. It looks like (5) is the result of English influence and has found its way to the adult grammar. The Spanish suffix /ndo/ is a gerund, and can be used as a verbal or clausal adjunct but, for speakers of Spanish outside the USA, it cannot be used as a noun modifier. English /ing/ is used for many other functions, including both as a verbal and nominal adjunct. What seems to be the case in (5) is that the Spanish /ndo/ has expanded its usage so it can be used as a nominal adjunct, almost certainly as a calque of /ing/. Thus, the two grammatical systems must be porous enough to allow for this sort of expansion. Incidentally, notice that we can hardly call this phenomenon an instance of attrition or incomplete acquisition (see Montrul 2004 on incomplete acquisition): these speakers also allow nominal modifiers with relative clauses, just like speakers of non-USA Spanish. It looks more like the opposite of attrition, call it expansion, since they have an additional ingredient in their grammars.

The data in (4) and (5) contradict other claims found in the literature. Hulk and Müller (2000) and Meisel (2012), among others, claim that apparent instances of influence of one grammar over the other do not affect the bilinguals' internalized grammars but rather, this influence is only something that occurs at the point when this knowledge is activated. I do not think this line of thinking can apply to (4) and (5), where we can see a real change in the speakers' linguistic competence. Likewise, Hulk and Müller (2000) suggest that influence of one grammar over the other takes place at the interfaces – but, again the data shown in (4) and (5) can hardly be described as interface phenomenon.

Moreover, in previous chapters of this monograph we have already seen some empirical data that should be interpreted as counter-evidence against (2). For instance, consider the clitic simplification data discussed in Section 6.2. As I showed at that point, bilingual Spanish/Catalan speakers may simplify a Catalan clitic combination following the Spanish rather than the Catalan rule. This should not be possible if the two languages were indeed watertight.

Code-switching, in particular, should be regarded as an area of difficulty for the SDH. If the two grammatical systems are separate and closed, we get into the same series of empirical problems that MacSwan's approach to code-switching presents, including, for example, the problems of mixed selection and noun class assignment (see Sections 2.2 and 4.1). The other code-switching data I have discussed in this monograph, in particular the rich array of data that emerged from code-switching between D and NP in Chapter 5, likewise constitute direct counterevidence to the SDH. At this point, it is interesting to see how De Houwer (2005) dismisses the code-switching evidence:

(6) Children's mixed multiword utterances consisted mainly of free morpheme insertions of the guest languages into the host language. These free morpheme insertions were most often nouns.

De Houwer 2005:43

Her point seems to be that children's "mixed-utterances" consist of nouns of one language inserted into a sentence constructed in the other language. Thus, she views code-switching in terms of lexical items inserted into an alien discourse, a view of code-switching that I criticized in the Introduction. In particular, she does not acknowledge the possibility that code-switching may involve the integration of grammatical resources. However, Cantone (2007) presents abundant evidence that children's code-switching is not fundamentally different from adults' and that this code-switching involves integration of linguistic resources. Consider the following example:

(7) Italian/*German*

Mama io	voglio	la	*überraschung.*
mama I	want	the.F	surprise(f)

'Mom, I want the surprise.'

Cantone 2007: 175

This sentence was produced by a child who was three and half years old at the time. Notice that the Italian article that precedes the German noun exhibits feminine morphology because the German word is feminine. Thus, we see that in children's code-switching, as in adult code-switching, the constituents that form part of the structure establish dependencies with one another, in contradiction with the insertionist view of children's code-switching.

As I have concluded previously, I believe that only one competence system grows out of humans' language faculty. The empirical evidence seems to support this hypothesis and provides numerous challenges to the SDH. It seems to me that the SDH is born out of a consideration of bilingualism in particular European environments. The environmental conditions, in particular the exposure to the sort of schooling that places emphasis on metalinguistic awareness and prescriptive rules, may conspire to ensure that the resulting production skills of the bilingual do indeed resemble the output of two watertight grammatical systems. When such an influence from the schooling system is weak or absent, we notice contact phenomena like what we saw among Quechua/Spanish in Perú and

English/Spanish bilinguals in the USA. That is, the facts the De Houwer and others noticed do not reveal anything about bilingual acquisition or bilingual linguistic competence, all they reveal is the output of a particular educational system.

A second reason why the SDH has been assumed for so long might be educational. Unenlightened teachers and some monolingual parents worry that exposing a child to two languages from birth might cause confusion. Thus, the SDH may be used to assuage those fears with scientific authority. But we have plenty of living and breathing evidence that within appropriate societal and educational conditions a bilingual child will become a bilingual adult with full skills in both languages. Consequently, we do not need the SDH to make the case for child bilingualism, particularly since we know that its empirical foundation is wobbly.

In the following, I use the 1Lex MDM model to account for the apparent separateness of the Dutch/English bilingual and disassemble the SLP argument. That is, I will present a capsule analysis that shows how an integrated competence system may live in one mind while providing the necessary tools so that, for example, a bilingual English/Dutch speaker will not use *do*-support when speaking Dutch. I also write a few lines showing how the linguistic expansion of the Spanish/English bilingual that we have seen and exemplified in (5) could take place.

Let's see how (3) can be accounted for in the model of grammatical competence developed in this book. Here I present a very skeletal example: I won't try to present an analysis of all the instances of do-support or the regular declarative sentences in which there is T-lowering. The idea is simply to present the outlines of how the system works.

The paradigms for the present tense for the Dutch verb *willen* and the English verb 'want' are as follows:

(8)

	willen			*want*		
	Root	T	ϕ	Root	T	ϕ
1	wil	Ø	Ø	want	Ø	Ø
2	wil	Ø	t	want	Ø	Ø
3	wil	Ø	Ø	want	Ø	s
Pl	wil	Ø	en	want	Ø	Ø

In earlier chapters I discussed the role that morphosyntactic frames play in understanding code-switching data, in particular gender and noun class. For instance, when discussing the phenomenon of English nouns that are inserted in Swahili sentences, I proposed that English nouns may appear in two morphosyntactic frames. Here we have the opposite situation: the Dutch verbs appear only in Dutch frames, the English only in English frames. Let's posit then that Dutch/English bilinguals have two instances of *v*:

(9) *Dutch/English* bilingual

List 1: T
v1
v2

The grammars of these bilinguals are set up in such a way that all and only pairs of a root and a "Dutch" vocabulary item can be found in the v_1 frame, while pairs of a root and an "English" vocabulary item can only be complements of v_2.

(10) √199 can have two spell-outs: {want, wil-}

√199 ←→ /wil/ || ___ v_1
√199 ←→ /want/ || ___ v_2

What is the difference between v_1 and v_2? It is generally assumed that the grammatical difference reflected in (3) relies on a particular property of T, which has the ability to attract v in Dutch but not in English (see Zwart 2011, among many others). Both languages have T-to-C in interrogative sentences but only Dutch drags v+√ along with T because only Dutch has v+√ as a constituent of T. In English, T-to-C does not drag a lexical root and hence *do* is inserted at PF as a support of the T morpheme if no auxiliary or modal is available.

(11) Dutch: C [T [v]] v-to-T→
C [[T+v] [t_v]] T-to-C→
[C+[T+v]] [t_T [t_v]]

English C [T [v]]
[C+T] [t_T [v]] T-to-C→
[C+ *do*] [t_T [v]] *do*-insertion

Let's take it that v_2 and T have no special properties. v_1, on the other hand, we define as having the special property that defines Dutch sentences (i.e., being attractable by a higher head). This set up ensures that Dutch verbs raise to T while English verbs do not. Instead, English grammar allows for lowering of T-to-v, which can be taken to be a default lowering mechanism that takes place as a last resort in PF if v-to-T is not possible in syntax and T is an affix (see Embick and Noyer 2001). The result of T-to-v is a node dominated by *v* while v-to-T is a node dominated by T. In our specific example, the root √199 that is governed by v_1 and spells out as /wil/ finds itself within the complex word T while the root √199 that is governed by v_2 and spells out as /want/ does not.

As a consequence, a Dutch bilingual person may have two possible syntactic representations for T. T may be isolated (English type, as in 12a) or it may have an incorporated v_1+√ (Dutch type, as in 12b). Now there might be one of the following syntactic terminals, T or T[v_1]:

(12)

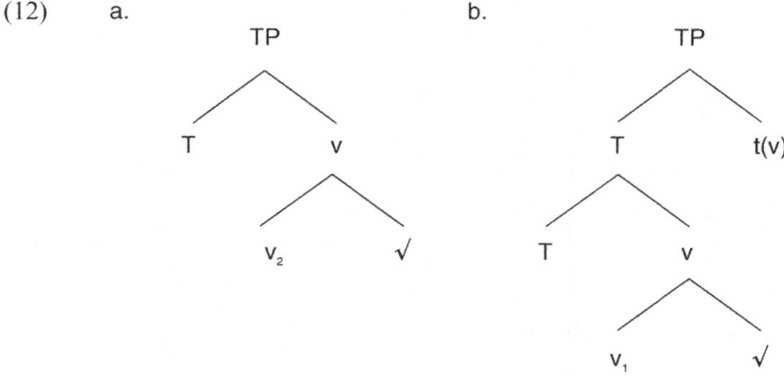

At this point, the interrogative complementizer attracts T, yielding two possible structures: either C[T] or C[T[v_1]]. This is what is fed to the VIRs.

The VIRs have the following tasks: (i) affix /t/ to the Dutch verbs in second person singular; (ii) affix /en/ to the plural Dutch verbs; (iii) spell out the English T in C as [do/ and (iv) attach /s/ to the English verb in third person. In List 2 are the four relevant VIRs:

(13) *Dutch/English bilingual*

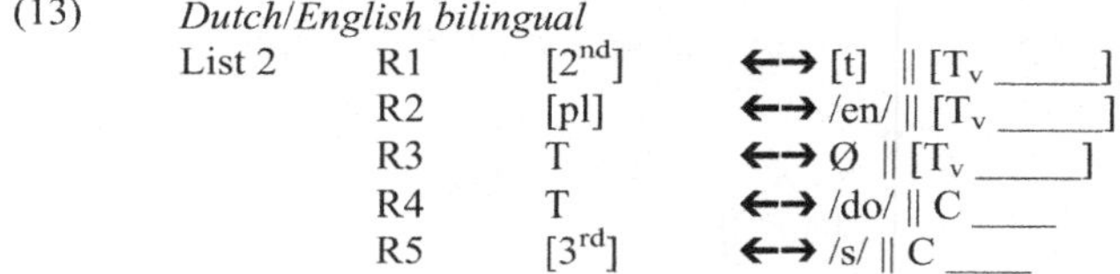

List 2	R1	[2nd]	←→ [t] ‖ [T_v ____]
	R2	[pl]	←→ /en/ ‖ [T_v ____]
	R3	T	←→ Ø ‖ [T_v ____]
	R4	T	←→ /do/ ‖ C ____
	R5	[3rd]	←→ /s/ ‖ C ____

R1 says that the Dutch suffix /t/ spells out a second person terminal when T dominates v. The structure in which R1 applies is the following:

(14)

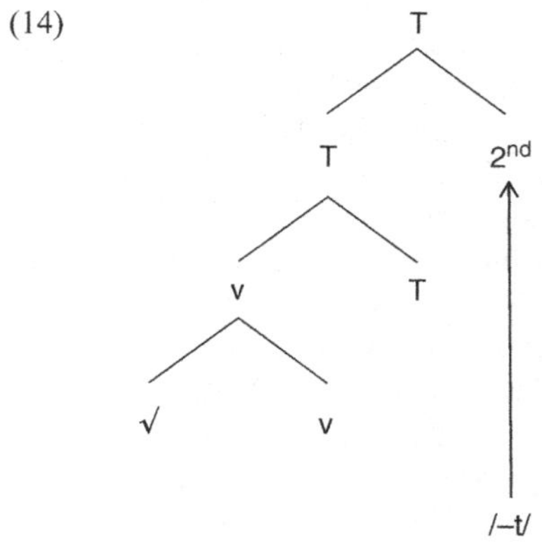

In (14), the root has incorporated into *v* and the latter has incorporated into T. Notice that the rule does not specify that *v* is v_l because v_1 is the only type of *v* that raises to T and therefore this specification is not necessary in the spell-out rule. R2 does the same thing with the plural suffix /en/. Otherwise, R3 says that T has zero spell out if it dominates v. Notice that none of R1–R3 affect "English" structures because they are defined to apply only when a *v* is in a complex word dominated by T. Consequently, R4 and R5 can only apply to "English" structures. R4 spells out T as /do/ when it is dominated by C. Finally, R5 inserts /s/ in a third person singular 'do'.

An interesting result of this analysis is that although the output of the bilingual is undistinguishable from that of a monolingual, the competence system is somewhat different: A monolingual Dutch person will not need a contextual rule like R1 but just a general rule to insert verbs. We already found this situation when discussing Esplugisch in Section 5.5. I present (13) as a hypothesis of how one single system of linguistic competence can handle the data presented in (3) without the need to posit two encapsulated systems.

It is again important to highlight that having a set of rules like (13) is not something peculiar about bilinguals. Roeper (1999 et seq.) argues that everyone has multiple grammars in their head: what he calls *universal bilingualism* (see Section 2.4). For example, English is a fairly rigid SV order – even when an object is topicalized the resulting order is OSV. However, with a small set of quotation verbs it is possible to produce OVS:

(15) "Nothing" said the UN ambassador.

Roeper (1999) takes examples such as (15) to claim that monolingual English speakers are bilingual, to the extent that they have a systematic class of exceptions to the SV rule.

The analysis that I can propose for this kind of sentence is very parallel to (15). There is a "Dutch" *v* in the I-language of monolingual English speakers that can be attracted by T, but only a few roots can be selected by attractable *v*. The example of quotation verbs confirms that it is not necessary to posit separate linguistic systems to account for De Houwer's observation: apparently contradictory rules can co-exist in one linguistic system without comingling in production.

Let's now turn to (5). The question now is how our system handles what is usually referred to as "linguistic influence." Recall that a strict version of SDH cannot handle it because it posits that the two grammatical systems are fully independent, which prevents any influence of one on the other. However, the 1Lex approach proposed here can easily handle (5). Let's assume that in English there is a morpheme, call it [adn] for adjunct nominal. This morpheme takes a vP as a complement and projects an adjunct phrase (adnP). This adnP can function as a noun phrase modifier:

(16) A box $[_{adnP}$ [adn] $[_{vP}$ contain shoes]]

The morpheme [adn] spells out as /ɪŋ/. In our model, this means that there is a VIR in List 2 such as the following:

(17) List 2:
[adn] ←→ /ɪŋ/

Monolingual Spanish speakers do not have [adn]. However, bilingual Spanish/English speakers have it. The phenomenon that we see in (5) suggests that these speakers have two rules to spell out [adn]:

(18) List 2 (bilingual Spanish/English)
[adn] ←→ {/ɪŋ/, /ndo/}

Thus, (5) can be accounted for simply by adding one additional VI rule to the repertoire of Spanish/English bilinguals.

Finally, let's consider some broad consequences of adopting the SDH. Consider a bilingual child whose two languages are typologically similar in some respects (as is always the case, probably), say, a Spanish-French bilingual. These two languages look very different in the surface but both are SVO, both have adjectives generally following nouns, both have object clitic pronouns, both have dislocations doubled by a clitic, both use the auxiliary *have* to form compound forms of a verb (although the meaning is somewhat different, as well as the list of verbs that are selected by this particular auxiliary), both use forms of *be* to construct passives, etc. Are bilingual speakers going to have two duplicate SVO rules? Generally speaking, are they going to have two encapsulated systems with a considerable amount of grammatical rules in common? This is what the SDH would lead us to expect. And what about the Creole continua? As far as I can tell, none of these questions can be answered within the SDH. I suggest that the SDH be abandoned.

Now we can return to the FSH. Recall that the FSH states that children have two separate systems because they know in which circumstances and with which interlocutors they can use one language or the other. Once we understand how a system like the one sketched in (11) to (13) allows us to maintain a unified system without "mixing," we can see that the environmental awareness of the bilingual speaker does not entail separate competence systems. Instead, I suggest that we understand functional separation as a phenomenon linked to our performance systems – the fact that our performance systems are capable of surprising feats of inhibitory control and thus allow us to activate certain aspects of our competence while inhibiting others.

8.2 Co-activation and Priming

Research on syntactic co-activation and priming is relevant for our purposes because it seems to point in the same direction as this monograph.

Let's start with some recent work on syntactic co-activation: Both Hatzidaki, Branigan and Pickering (2010), which has turned out to be a seminal work in this area, and Sadounaki and Thierry (2014), a very different experiment with regard to methodology and linguistic variables investigated, converge with the 1Lex model that I argue for in these pages.

Hatzidaki et al. (2010) test the possibility that syntactic features of L1 may be present when trying to produce a constituent in the L2 in situations of code-switching. Consider the following example:

(19) *Greek*/English
Τα λεφτα is/are useful.
The money

The noun *λεφτα* 'money' is plural in Greek. You would expect it to trigger plural agreement on the English verb. In a production task experiment, Hatzidaki et al. (2010) found that bilingual Greek/English subjects occasionally gave incongruent answers, which the authors account for under the assumption that the syntactic features of the English noun are activated when producing a Greek noun phrase.[1] Purmohammad (2015) reaches a parallel conclusion with a very similar experiment involving the position of adjectives and nouns in Persian/English code-switching.

Notice that Hatzidaki et al.'s (2010) results are almost expected under the view of bilingual grammar developed in these pages. We could posit that these subjects have a root √899, which means 'money' and has two possible spell-outs, depending on the properties of the *n* that selects it. In production, it is not surprising that the VIRs get mixed up:

(20) LIST 1 √899 'money'
LIST 2 √899 ←→ /money/ || ____ $n_{[-pl]}$
√899 ←→ /λεφτα/ || ____ $n_{[+pl]}$

Sanoudaki and Thierry (2014) report on an experiment that, they claim, provides evidence that bilinguals have both grammatical systems co-activated when processing monolingual data (see also the replication in Luque, Mizyed, and Morgan-Short 2018). I propose to reinterpret their results in the terms laid out in this monograph and present it as evidence that syntax is processed independently of the phonology associated with syntactic terminals. Given the difficulty of defining the term "grammatical system" coherently, my interpretation of their results is advantageous. One good thing: there is no doubt that the participants in the experiment are deep bilinguals as described here.

Sanoudaki and Thierry's experiment involves an inspection of event related potentials (ERP) of English/Welsh bilinguals as well as English monolinguals at the time of processing phrases that are grammatical in Welsh but not in English. In particular, they looked at the relative order of adjective and noun in both languages. In English, adjectives normally come before the noun they modify (red book, not *book red), while in Welsh they are always postnominal. In an acceptability judgment task, the Welsh bilingual subjects rated English noun phrases like monolingual English speakers, that is, they accurately rated 'red book' as grammatical and '*book red' as ungrammatical.

In the ERP study, the variable they looked at is the N2 component, which is a marker of response inhibition that shows up across types of tasks, linguistic or non-linguistic (e.g., N2 can show up in a task consisting of counting vertical lines in a landscape in which there are horizontal and vertical lines). In order to create the conditions for N2 to be expressed, they designed an experiment with instructions in the go/no-go format: if you see an X with these characteristics, do Y. Otherwise, do nothing.

The subjects saw an object in a computer screen: it could be, for example, a red book, a blue book, a red car, or a blue car. Then the subjects saw a sentence such as *the red book was on the left*. The instruction was that if they saw that something red was on the left (or wherever the sentence said), they had to press a YES button but if they saw it on the right they had to press a NO button. Likewise, if they had seen a book on the left side of the screen, they had to press YES, if they saw it on the right they had to press NO. If no book or no red object was seen, subjects were asked to not respond. Notice that subjects could respond after seeing the adjective if there was a match. If the adjective did not match the picture, subjects had to wait to hear the noun to see if it matched. The inhibition necessary to avoid responding triggers a significant N2 amplitude.

The crucial twist that Sanoudaki and Thierry (2014) added to the experiment was the following: sometimes subjects were exposed to sentences in which the order of noun and adjective was reversed: *the book red was on the* left. What happens under this condition? What happens when subjects are exposed to the sentence *the book red was on the left* after seeing a red car in the screen?

It turned out that for English monolinguals, inhibiting a response (a NO response in this case) after hearing 'book' was difficult because *book* closes the noun phrase. This difficulty was reflected in a N2 curve that was of similar size whether the noun matched the picture or not. Welsh bilinguals would be more open to inhibit the response because they are used to the N+A order in their native language and therefore a noun does not necessarily close a noun phrase. Consequently, for bilingual speakers the N2 curve was bigger for nouns that mismatched the picture than for nouns that matched the picture.

Sadounaki and Thierry's explanation is based on the traditional notion of co-activation. They claim that when the bilingual speakers process an English sentence, the Welsh grammatical system is co-activated. But the assumption of separate grammatical systems does not take us very far, as I have argued.

My explanation is, I believe, simpler. Recall that one of the basic tenets of this monograph is that bilinguals host one grammatical competence and this grammatical competence engages syntactic structures whose terminals are populated by abstract features. The smaller N2 curve suggests that Welsh speakers have equal facility processing a N+A or an A+N structure, because their syntactic system allows for both. The fact that the syntactic terminals carry English exponents does not particularly affect the processing of the syntactic structure, which is apparently blind to the phonetic content of the exponents. Syntactic processing therefore can take place over disembodied grammatical structures – it is only in PF that linearization takes place.

Let's now move on to syntactic priming. Syntactic priming refers to the following effect: hearing a certain syntactic structure primes the usage of the same structure in a later sentence. In a typical experiment, subjects hear and repeat a sentence and then are asked to describe a picture. It is generally found that when describing the picture, subjects will use a structure that parallels the one they just heard. The working assumption is that if processing one stimulus affects the processing of another stimulus the two stimuli must share some aspect of their representation. (See Pickering and Ferreira 2008 and Branigan and Pickering forthcoming for overviews on syntactic priming.) For our purposes, we are interested in bilingual priming: when perception of a structure S1 in L1 primes the usage of a structure S2 in L2 such that S1 and S2 are regarded as equivalent.

Investigations on bilingual syntactic priming support or are consistent with the integrated proposal presented in these pages (see also Serratrice 2016). The structure of the argument is as follows. We can see that exposure of a bilingual subject to a sentence in one language *primes* the production of a sentence with the same structure in the other language. For instance, a Spanish/English bilingual who has been exposed to a passive sentence in Spanish is more likely to produce a passive sentence in English in a picture-naming task (Hartsuiker, Branigan, Pickering 2004). Therefore, they conclude, some aspect of the representation – lexical or syntactic – is shared between the two languages. We can take the priming data to the next step and claim that there is in fact one computational system that creates syntactic representations. Moreover, once again we find that syntactic processing takes place detached from the vocabulary items found in the terminals, consistent with the MDM.

Hartsuiker et al. (2004) present an explicit model of bilingual language production that, they claim, can account for bilingual syntactic priming as well as code-switching. It is represented in Figure 8.1. As can be seen in the diagram, their starting point is a connectionist model of the lexicon, which they

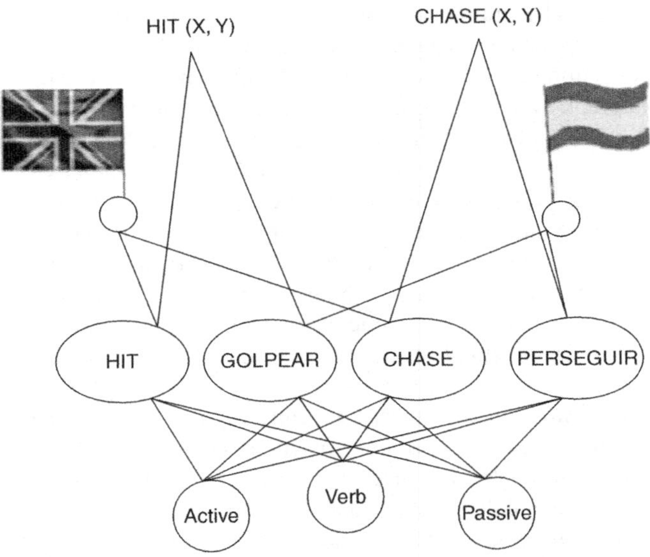

Figure 8.1 A connectionist model of syntactic priming
Hartsuiker et al. 2004: 413

call a *lemma* stratum. This lemma stratum includes nodes that represent lexical items (what we would call roots). In Figure 8.1, we are peering into the mind of an English-Spanish bilingual. She has a vocabulary that includes chase, *perseguir*, hit, *golpear*. They are all related to just two pre-linguistic concepts, the CHASE concept and the HIT concept. Lemmas are tagged for language. Those that are shared are tagged for both languages (Pickering and Branigan 1998). Lemma nodes are also linked to category nodes (such as 'verb', 'noun', etc.) as well as *combinatorial nodes* that encode information about syntactic constructions, such as 'active' or 'passive'. Thus, if the lemma *chase* and the passive node are selected, the result is a passive sentence. The system presented in Figure 8.1 is integrated: we have English and Spanish words connected to the same category nodes and combinatorial nodes. Because the syntactic nodes are integrated, we understand how syntactic priming happens (as well as code-switching: the latter is simply a question of which lexical items get to be connected to the construction nodes.)

As you can see, Hartsuiker et al. (2004), (as well as Pickering and Ferreira 2008 and other examples of the syntactic priming literature I have consulted) claim that speakers contain a repository of representations for syntactic constructions in the same manner that they hold a lexicon of lexical items. Consistent with the MDM, I do not assume that there is a long-term repository of syntactic constructions in the lexicon (or the lemma stratum) of native speakers. In fact, I don't think that the assumption of a layer of combinatorial nodes is necessary to account for priming. Let me show why. The priming literature shows – in particular, the bilingual priming literature – that a conversation exchange must contain some linguistic information in short-term memory: an abstract representation of the event being mentioned, the participants of the event and the grammatical relations held by the participants. That is, the interlocutors remember a sentence both as a specific proposition (the bullet hit the bottle) but also as an abstract representation (x did y to z) with variables for the participants as well as the grammatical relations sustained between them so that the abstract structure can be recycled in subsequent discourse with new variables replacing the old ones. I suggest this information could be formalized in the form of a discourse representation structure (see Kamp and Reyle 1993 for a textbook introduction to discourse representation structures).

That is, a speaker who has just heard 'the bottle was hit by a bullet' will have a discourse representation with the following information:

(21) The bottle was hit by a bullet.

1. ∃e Agent(x,e) & Patient (y,e) & PAST(e)
2. e=hit
3. x=bullet
4. y=bottle
5. [$_{TP}$ y T [$_{vP}$ e t(y)] by x]

The discourse structure of both interlocutors will have the following information: there was a transitive event (21.1) which is a hitting event (21.2) such that the agent of the hitting x is a referent that I identify as a bullet (21.3) and the patient y is a bottle (21.4). Additionally, the interlocutors carry in their mind the structure in (21.5), in which y is the subject and x is the object of the preposition 'by'.

Since the passive structure has been stored in the discourse, it is accessible when the following piece of discourse is parsed. In particular, it is crucial that the passive structure be represented in discourse with variables for the participants of the event so that it can be retrieved onto the next discourse representation with new values for the variables: this is what we call priming. And this is the reason why bilingual syntactic priming provides evidence for the integrated system and the MDM model. First, priming requires that syntactic terminals be stored in discourse stripped of their phonological and even semantic content, as predicted in MDM (see Serratrice 2016 for remarks along these lines). Second, if something like (21.5) is accessible by the following discourse in any of the languages of the bilingual, there is a good chance that (21.5) does not have any marks that identify it as belonging to one language or the other – and this supports the integrated hypothesis.[2]

To conclude, the research in bilingual syntactic priming is consistent with the integrated approach advocated in these pages. It is also consistent with a more complicated theory in which some portions of the syntactic knowledge of a bilingual are shared while others are not. But this complication seems unnecessary.[3]

8.3 On the Cost of Code-Switching

One of the richest research agendas in bilingualism research explores the possibility that switching involves a processing cost (see Van Hell, Licofsky, and Ting 2015 for a useful review of the literature on the topic). This research would seem to impinge on my own proposals: if code-switching involves using resources freely within an integrated system, should a conclusion that code-switching is costly constitute empirical counterevidence? The answer is, not necessarily: it depends on whether the additional cost is caused by initiating or by terminating code-switching.

Most of the research on switching costs consists of experimental settings in which subjects are asked to respond to a word that shows up in a screen in complete isolation – not a design that involves the processing of a word in a discourse and therefore not a research that taps the I-language of a native speaker. That is the case with many of the experiments reported in Van Hell et al. 2015, which seem to be about retrieving information from long-term memory and not about finding properties of the structure of the linguistic system. From that point of view, this class of experiments seems to have little bearing on my research questions.

Having said this, there are a number of experiments that do place code-switching in a sentence and measure eye movements, speed of processing, or electrophysiological patterns. These experiments also find that there is a cost in code-switching: slower reading, slower eye-movement, ample N400 curve. There are, however, two caveats to these experiments. The first caveat involves the participants. It seems to me that, generally speaking, the participants were not deep bilinguals and only sometimes could they be regarded as highly proficient in both languages. As mentioned in the Introduction, intra-sentential code-switching is predominantly a phenomenon of the I-language of deep bilinguals, and bilinguals who acquire their L2 past a certain age do not incorporate intra-sentential code-switching in their linguistic system as successfully (as demonstrated in González-Vilbazo 2005). This makes one hesitate to accept the results of Litcofsky and Van Hell (2017), whose subjects were Spanish speakers who began learning English at an average age of 8.1 (SD=6), an age range that suggests that these subjects were a group of bilinguals too heterogenous for a study of intra-sentential code-switching. Others use subjects who learned their L2 in a school environment (Van der Meij et al. 2011) and therefore even less likely to qualify as deep bilinguals. Additionally, we are not even certain that these participants engaged in regular intra-sentential code-switching. The authors of these articles typically ask their participants if they practice code-switching, but they do not report whether participants were interviewed by a confederate of their cohort to check whether they do indeed do fluent intra-sentential code-switching. This is important because the claim "I code-switch" may mean different things to different people.

In this respect, I would like to mention here the intriguing results in Adamou and Shen (2019). In this article, they report on an experiment in which they measured the processing costs of code-switching between Turkish and Romani. In particular, the speakers of this community they investigated commonly use Turkish verbs, with fully fledged Turkish morphology, inserted in Romani speech. Adamou and Shen find that there is no cost in code-switching, provided that the switched verbs are of common usage in the community they studied. Thus, Adamou and Shen (2019) provide evidence that the type of materials and the type of participants one uses significantly alter the measure of cost in code-switching.

For the sake of argument, let's assume that all problems of subjects and stimuli are controlled for and we find that switching does indeed bring about a processing cost. What do the integrationist and separationist hypotheses predict? It seems to me that the separationist hypothesis should predict that initiating code-switching and stopping code-switching should both be costly. That is because initiating code-switching involves activating an additional system that was dormant (even if somewhat co-active) and stopping code-switching involves inhibiting a system that was active. The integrationist hypothesis predicts that stopping code-switching should entail the cost of inhibiting a system but initiating code-switching should not be costly at all, since all it involves is un-inhibiting a section of the system so that all the resources of the system can be used.

A recent article by Blanco-Elorrieta, Emmorey, and Pylkkänen (2018) provides some clue as to how the two predictions can be tested. The focus of their experiment is figuring out whether engaging two systems or disengaging one system is costly – or if both are. In order to disentangle the variables, they study bimodal bilinguals in the act of *code-blending* (see Sections 9.2 and 9.3 for a discussion of code-blending). Bimodal bilinguals can sign and speak either sequentially – thus producing utterances that are reminiscent of code-switching – or simultaneously – what is called code-blending). The MEG evidence shows that going from language+sign to either sign or language recruits brain areas related to executive control. On the other hand, going from only sign or language to both does not. In their own words "the burden of language switching lies in the disengagement from the previous language as opposed to engaging a new language and, in the absence of motor constraints, producing two languages simultaneously is not necessarily more cognitively costly that producing one" (Blanco-Elorrieta et al. 2018).

I think this result is fully consistent with my proposal that the I-language of a bilingual is fully integrated: what is costly is inhibiting part of the system. On the other hand, it is not consistent with the idea that a bilingual person has two systems in their I-language: if you have two systems, engaging both of them should be costly.

8.4 Conclusions

In this chapter, I have discussed three topics at the intersection of syntax and code-switching. In Section 8.1, I discussed the SDH, according to which bilinguals (or at least deep bilinguals) acquires two distinct systems of linguistic competence. I have given pride of place to the main argument that supports SDH, which is based on functional separation – the fact that many bilinguals are able to produce language that is undistinguishable from a monolingual's production. I have shown that the current MDM framework is empirically compatible with functional separation, and therefore that it cannot be used in support of SDH. On the other hand, the SDH is incompatible with the bulk of historical and contact linguistics data, which does show that many bilingual speakers let their languages influence one another, which I believe suggests an integrated competence system.

I have also discussed bilingual co-activation and priming. Both co-activation and priming provide evidence that bilinguals store structures in their discourse models without reference to "language" or to the exponents of the terminals, and this supports the hypothesis of an integrated linguistic competence. Finally, I have shown that Blanco-Elorrieta et al.'s (2018) finding that the cost of code-switching results from disengaging one of the "languages" also supports the integrated hypothesis.

9 Convergent and Divergent Paths

The proposal in these pages was not born in a vacuum. The idea of using DM in the analysis of code-switching has been suggested before. In previous pages I discussed DenDikken's (2011) approach to gender in Esplugisch as well as Bandi-Rao and DenDikken's (2014) analysis of code-switching within the word. I also mentioned how Grimstad, Lohndal, and Åfarli (2014) and Alexiadou, Lohndal, Åfarli, and Grimstad (2015) hit on the idea that the fact that English nouns can be integrated into Norwegian DPs is evidence that realizational morphology is on the right track. Pierantozzi (2008, 2012) studies code-switching within the DP by very young bilingual children using DM notions. Likewise, the leading idea that the linguistic competence of a bilingual should be regarded as an integrated module and not as two separate components or "languages" has been floating around for a few years (Goldrick, Putnam, and Schwartz 2016). I discuss some of the work that intersects with mine more formally in these pages.

I discuss three research projects that have come to the fore in recent years and that have points in common with my project. In Sections 9.1 and 9.2, I discuss two articles that explicitly take DM as the framework of analysis and develop analyses in some detail. In Section 9.1, I discuss the studies on Norwegian American that have been developed by Grimstad and her colleagues. In Section 9.2, I discuss Lillo-Martin, Müller de Quadros, and Pichlet's (2016) approach to *code blending*. Diane Lillo-Martin and her colleagues also argue that code-blending provides direct evidence in favor of a DM architecture. I analyze their arguments and evaluate to what extent they hold. In Section 9.3, I move onto Branchini and Donati's (2016) discussion of code-blending data. Interestingly, they reach the opposite conclusion as Lillo-Martin and colleagues: they argue that code-blending provides evidence against DM and in favor of a lexicalist model. I disagree with this conclusion and argue that Branchini and Donati underestimate the explanatory power of a MDM approach to bilingual grammar. Finally, in Section 9.4 I discuss a "divergent" path, the one taken by Goldrick et al. (2016) toward a soft constraint approach to code-switching.

Reviewing these approaches will give us a deeper understanding of the MDM project in relation to the study of bilingual grammar as well as a more precise understanding of what exactly constitutes evidence in favor or against realizational morphology and/or an integrated I-language model.

9.1 Norwegian American

Norwegian linguists have made a number of recent contributions to the literature on code-switching using corpora data of heritage Norwegian speakers in the USA. Their work has been disseminated in conferences and a few published papers. The speakers they study are second or third generation immigrants from Norway, who can speak Norwegian but "insert" many English words in their speech. We don't have much information about these speakers, in particular regarding family (father/mother), school, literacy, and Norwegian-speaking environment. They seem to be able to speak the language although there are clearly vocabulary gaps, which they fill with English lexemes.

For the present discussion, I focus on Grimstad et al. (2014), which presents the most developed discussion of their approach (but see recent developments in Riksem 2017, Riksem et al. in press, as well as Alexiadou et al. 2015, which adds German/Greek bilingual data to the analysis.) The American Norwegian project is very much ongoing and my remarks here may soon become obsolete.

We are interested in Grimstad et al.'s (2014) argument that a DM (exoskeletal) model of syntax-morphology is superior to a traditional lexicalist model in which words are listed in the lexicon with all their features, including phonological features. Let's see how.

This is the phenomenon Grimstad et al. (2014) are most interested in: the usage of English roots within a Norwegian syntactic structure:

(1) *English*/Norwegian
Jeg ***teach***-a foerste ***grade***-en.
I teach-PAST first grade-DEF.M
'I taught first grade.'

Grimstad et al. 2014

The English verb 'teach' appears with a Norwegian past tense morpheme. The noun 'grade' bears Norwegian morphology that carries information about definiteness, gender, and number. Thus, the English nouns and verbs are fully integrated in a Norwegian morphosyntactic frame.

The tokens of speech that they investigate all involve what we have called "insertionist" code-switching (following Muysken's 2000 terminology). In this corpus, Norwegian is the "main" (or matrix) language to the extent that it is really a Norwegian discourse, while English is a secondary language that provides some lexical roots (as well as category specification, as I shall show). Their empirical question is the following: they never find a structure with a functional exponent in English and a lexical item in English or Norwegian; the spell out of the functional structure is always Norwegian. The question is why.[1]

They address the issue in the verbal and the nominal domain. Here I focus on the nominal domain. Consider the following examples:

(2) *English*/Norwegian

a. *road-* en
DEF.M

b. *fair-* a
DEF.F

c. *field-* et
DEF.N

The examples in (2) show that these speakers of American Norwegian use English lexical items with a Norwegian DP structure, which includes a mark for gender. The analysis they provide for the Norwegian noun phrase is as follows:

(3) D[udef],[u#],[ug] [Def[xdef] [Num[y#] [Gen[zg] [n √]]]]

As you can see, their analytical assumptions are minimally different from mine. In their framework, the head of the structure is a D with unvalued definiteness, number, and gender features. The heads Def, Num, and Gen have the corresponding valued features. By means of probing the heads Def, Num, and Gen, the valued features of these categories are copied onto the feature structure of D. The head *n* has no grammatical properties other than categorization. The English DP is very similar except without a category for gender:

(4) D[udef],[u#] [Def[xdef] [Num[y#] [n √]]]

However, the English DP structure is never projected in this database – in other words, English is never the main or matrix language in any structure. They claim that the reason for this has more to do with communication strategies than formal grammar – this is a piece of American Norwegian, a particular variety of Norwegian.

One more assumption is necessary to close the argument: a DP either has a Norwegian functional structure or an English one, but we do not have an extended D projection with functional heads from different languages. And now we can answer their research question: One can never find an English 'the' in Norwegian American because the feature structure of the DP is always Norwegian. As such, the D terminal node includes a gender feature, and therefore any of the Norwegian exponents, which also include a gender feature, will beat the English one.

This conclusion is, of course, very much in the spirit of this monograph and the possibility of competition among vocabulary items is an exciting idea. However, I have three comments to offer. First, this particular analysis works to the extent that the authors focus on a very circumscribed database. As we know from Chapter 5, there are instances of code-switching in the literature in which none of the languages involved is clearly the main language and when this happens we get code-switching between determiner and noun in a wider variety of environments. Thus, German-Spanish bilinguals accept '*el* brötchen' ('the bun') as easily as 'dem *cuaderno*' ('the notebook') even though the gender structure of German is richer than Spanish. Notice that the *n* and the D in these examples are clearly from different "languages." For instance, *cuaderno* 'notebook' clearly has a Spanish *n*, as shown by the nominal desinence /o/ (see Section 3.2), but the D has a German structure. Thus, mixed structures do exist. It doesn't seem to me that Grimstad et al. (2014) would predict anything in these cases.

A second difficulty arises when the "matrix language" has a poorer feature structure than the "embedded language." Consider our *manguera* example again:

(5) She brought the *manguera*. (=1.2)
hose
Herring et al. 2010
(from the Miami corpus, code-switchingBTP, Bangor)

This example is embedded in a long discourse in English. Thus, English is the matrix language in this sentence, which predicts that the structure of the DP is populated by English features (i.e., no gender or number). This can account for the presence of *the:* the syntactic terminal D is necessarily devoid of gender or number features and the Spanish determiners have too many features. But the word *manguera* itself includes the suffix /a/, which entails that the *n* must include a gender feature (or, in Grimstad et al.'s model, a gender phrase). In particular, there is no reason to assume that *manguera* has lost its internal structure in the same way that *taco* or *tequila*, as words that are fully assimilated in the lexicon of English speakers in the USA, arguably have (see Section 5.3). This means that, once again, we have a *n* from one language and a D from another. In fact, in Chapter 5, I argued that it is possible to have a hybrid structure with a Spanish $n_{[+f]}$ and an English D without an unvalued gender feature. This analysis, if it holds water, seems to contradict Grimstad et al.'s assumption that the morphosyntactic structure must be shaped in the matrix language, an assumption that is necessary for their system to go through.

A second comment is that, since the authors use corpora exclusively for their analysis, we do not know if speakers of American Norwegian would accept an English determiner with a Norwegian or an English noun, particularly if the conversation were set up differently. In other words, we do not really know what the I-language of these speakers really allows and we are not certain that the absence of something like **the roaden* is chance or whether it reveals something about their linguistic system. This should not be taken as a criticism of their project. Grimstad et al. are not trying to provide a description of the Norwegian Americans' I-language; rather, they are seeking to provide empirical evidence for an exoskeletal model of syntax.

Finally, as I am writing these lines, I am not entirely sure that their analysis really provides evidence for DM and against lexicalism, as the authors claim. Lexicalist approaches like MacSwan's and Myers-Scotton's are aware of and integrate into their analyses code-switching data in which a root from one language appears in the morphosyntactic structure of the other while the corresponding mirror image is unacceptable. A clear instance of this sort of work is MacSwan's (1999: 244–250) study of D+NP combinations in Nahuatl/Spanish code-switching, which I discussed in Chapter 5. The contrast with American Norwegian is interesting: determiners in Spanish inflect for gender and number while determiners in Nahuatl do not. The D+NP code-switching combination is acceptable if the determiner is Nahuatl and the noun is Spanish, but not the other way around. This is the opposite of the American Norwegian situation, where the richer determiner wins.

(6) Nahuatl/*Spanish*
Neka *hombre*

MacSwan 1999: 244–245

(7) Nahuatl/*Spanish*
* *Este* tlakatl
'This man'

MacSwan 1999: 244–245

My point in revisiting this Nahuatl/Spanish data is that lexicalist scholars have approached data parallel (or perpendicular) to the Norwegian/English data and have found ways to account for it. Thus, I am not sure it has been demonstrated that the fact that roots of "one language" may appear in the morphosyntactic structure of the other constitutes, as it stands, an argument against lexicalism.

9.2 The Language Synthesis Model and Code-Blending

Hearing persons who grew up in a household where a sign language was used end up being bilingual – even deep bilingual in the sense in which I use this term – in the two modalities. They are called *codas* (there are also *kodas*, who are children codas). When communicating with each other, they may resort to code-switching and, more often, to code-blending, a form of linguistic expression in which ingredients from the oral and from the sign language are used simultaneously. The following are two examples (I follow the convention of representing signs with capitalized words):

(8) Eng/ASL
So they are like LOOK$_{\text{[reciprocal]}}$ and he's like
"ooh, I gotta get that bird."
Lillo-Martin et al. 2016: 739, Emmorey et al. 2008: 47

(9) Dutch/NGT
Dutch: die gaat vallen
NGT: FALL
'That [doll] is going to fall.'
Lillo-Martin et al. 2016: 740, Van den Bogaerde and Baker 2008

(8) is an example of code-switching: the signed word (in American Sign Language) is inserted in the middle of a speech stream. (9) exemplifies code-blending: the sign (in NGT, Dutch Sign Language) doubles the equivalent word in Dutch. Code-blending, as well as k/coda code-switching is of obvious theoretical interest to linguists, hence the recent growth of work in this area. The main question that data like (8) and (9) raises is what kind of linguistic architecture supports these derivations, a question that increases in difficulty as we look at more complex data.

I focus now on Lillo-Martin et al. (2016), an article that presents a model of bilingual grammar and exemplifies its workings with code-blending data. They call their model the *Language Synthesis Model* (henceforth LSM), (see also Koulidobrova 2012 and Lillo-Martin et al. 2010, where some details of the model are developed). As they describe it, the LSM involves a minimalist architecture like MacSwan's (1999) joined to a DM morphology. In the resulting picture, bilinguals share a syntactic engine and items from two lexicons can mingle together in a syntactic derivation. The only restriction to code-switching and code-blending that they recognize is feature matching.

They propose that the LSM be used as the framework to study code-switching and code-blending, as well as other phenomena such as *Transfer* and *Calquing*. Lillo-Martin et al. (2016) is a LAB epistemological paper in which a general framework is presented. As befits the genre, the paper has a programmatic character and details are not developed. As I try to work out the details, it turns out that they are unexpectedly difficult. By pointing this out, I hope the following paragraphs are not seen as an unfair criticism – you can't really criticize someone for not doing what they did not propose to do. Rather, I would like to submit the following discussion as another example that constructing arguments against lexicalism and in favor of some realizational model of grammar is no trivial matter.

On the face of it, the LSM doesn't look too different from the MDM model that I am developing in these pages. There is one point where the two models differ: the VIRs from the two languages do not compete for insertion in the LSM; rather, they are two separate sets and this has consequences for the analysis. Take their analysis of code-switching and analogical agreement, as in the example 'veo las *houses*' (I see the houses) (Lillo-Martin et al. 2016: 728). In their analysis (following Pierantozzi 2012, see Section 5.3), gender is an inherent feature of the noun. What this means is two-fold: the syntactic terminal will have the feature specification N[g]; and the Spanish vocabulary item /casa/ also has a gender feature. The interesting point is that the English /house/ has no gender but, given the subset principle, /house/ can be inserted in a feminine noun terminal. Thus, this analysis presupposes that there is no competition between /house/ and /casa/: if there were competition between /casa/ and /house/, 'la house' would be impossible because the vocabulary item with the richest feature bundle would always win over the vocabulary item with the poorest feature bundle. In any case, their argument is that the Subset Principle explains how the exponent 'house', which has no gender, is able to form part of a syntactic structure that exhibits gender concord. As you may recall, my analysis in Chapter 5 does not require that the bilingual speaker have separate lists of exponents for each of their languages. The possibility that both *las casas* and *las houses* can be generated by the same I-language follows a different set of assumptions, to wit: Crucially, neither the roots nor the exponents have any gender features, these are housed in the functional categorizer *n*. An I-language may contain different flavors of *n*, at least one that has no gender feature and another one that does include gender. The vocabulary items /house/ and /cas-/ can spell out the same root R. The exponent /house/ can collocate with a feminine determiner if it can be selected by $n_{[+f]}$.

Lillo-Martin et al. (2016) also discuss the reverse example: '*the* casas'. In this example, neither the determiner nor the noun terminal bears a gender feature. They claim that insertion of the Spanish vocabulary item, with a feminine feature, is also allowed. But it seems to me that the feature structure of the vocabulary item is too rich to fit into the syntactic terminal, since it has an extra gender feature. The fact that their system allows for both options has led to the criticism that it is unrestricted (Liceras 2016, Putnam, Legendre, and Smolensky 2016). Again, recall that in Chapter 5, I also argued that '*the* casas' is possible because nothing prevents a D head without a gender feature from selecting a *n* with a gender feature. The D without gender necessarily spells out as 'the' ([da]) and the $n_{[+f]}$ spells out as /a/. I also added that the syntactic structure leads to an adaptation of the phonetics.

There are two distinct sections to Lillo-Martin et al. (2016). In the first section they present empirical arguments that, they claim, support the language synthesis model. The second section is the core of their discussion: the code-blending data. In particular, they are interested in exploring the consequences that examples such as (7) may have for our theory of grammar.

As for the empirical evidence, it is hard to reach any conclusions because their discussion is brief and, I would say, programmatic. Essentially, their main point is that in the linguistic expression of very young bimodal bilinguals, one can find vocabulary items from the oral language inserted into a syntactic structure built as in the sign language. For instance, consider word order. There is data in which children use a word order in the oral language that belongs in the sign language. Consider the following example:

(10) Mãe, Laura cabeça bateu.
Mom Laura head hit
'Mom, Laura hit her head.'

Lillo-Martin et al. 2016: 732

This sentence was produced by a very young coda bilingual in Brazilian Portuguese and Brazilian Sign Language (Libras). It looks like a regular Portuguese sentence, except that the word order is OV, which is ungrammatical in Portuguese but grammatical in Libras. Lillo-Martin and colleagues take this sort of example to provide evidence for *syntactic synthesis*, the idea that bilinguals may produce a sentence including ingredients from both their languages, in this case, a syntax brought in from Libras filled with Portuguese vocabulary items. They claim this constitutes evidence for a DM approach to contact phenomena.

Lillo-Martin et al. (2016) do not present a formal analysis of what is actually synthesized in (10), so in what follows I will try my hand at an analysis. It seems to me that all we need to account for (10) is the assumption that the complementizer in sentence (10) is in Libras. The complement T is Portuguese, as revealed by the verbal inflection. As I argued in Chapter 3, the head of the phase decides the word order of the phase constituents (González-Vilbazo and López 2012, 2013). If C is the head, and C is Libras, it follows that the TP must be head final. Since T is Portuguese, we can then conclude that there is overt v-to-T in Portuguese (see Costa 2004). Within these assumptions, we obtain the following structure. The apparent OV order is the result of v-to-T, not because the object is genuinely linearized to the left of the verb:

(11)

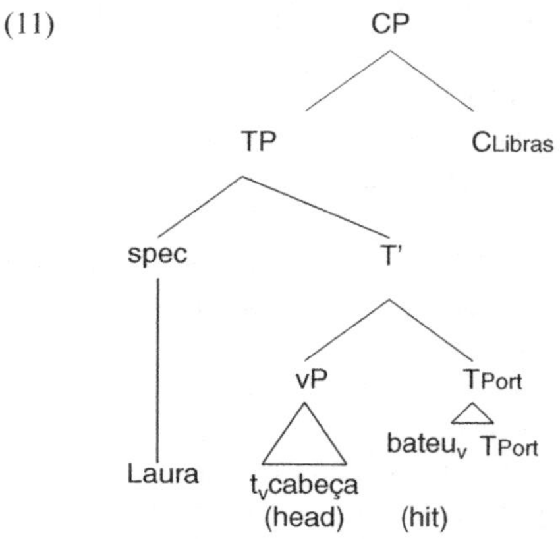

Once the analysis of (8) is fleshed out as in (9), we can ask whether we require DM to account for (8) or whether a lexicalist approach like MacSwan's can take care of it. As far as I can tell, I don't see any difficulty for MacSwan's framework to account for this datum – all that is required is the assumption that C is Libras and C determines the order of the complement. But if I am correct that this is the right analysis of (8), then it follows that this example is consistent with but does not require realizational morphology. Consequently, I am not sure that this data and analysis support language synthesis. A lexicalist could say that what they see is the old-fashioned code-mixing, as instantiated in the speech of very young bilinguals, and that this data is not very different from data that have been available to the community of linguists since at least Volterra and Taeschner (1978).

The other empirical evidence presented in support of LSM is based on wh-dependencies and pro-drop. It is also based on the claim that there is a mixed-match between the syntax and the vocabulary items. Lacking a detailed analysis, it is unclear how strongly they support LSM (see my Section 4.4 where I study calques in light of the 1Lex MDM framework.)

Let's now move on to code-blending and the question of what kind of linguistic architecture can support it. Lillo-Martin et al. (2016: 739–741) present a useful typology of code-blending (borrowed from van den Bogaerde and Baker 2008):

1. Speech based: the utterance is mostly spoken, with occasional concurrent production of signs. They provide example (8) above, repeated here as (12):

(12) Dutch: die gaat vallen
NGT: FALL
'That [doll] is going to fall.'
Lillo-Martin et al. 2016: 740, Van den Bogaerde and Baker 2008

In this example, the coda says (in Dutch) "that is going to fall" while the last word is also signed.

2. Sign-based: the utterance is mostly signed, with some accompanying speech.

(13) NGT: INDEX$_{he}$ COAT BLUE.
Dutch: blauw
'He has a blue coat.'
Lillo-Martin et al. 2016: 740, Van den Bogaerde and Baker 2008

3. Full code-blended: the proposition is fully expressed in both modalities.

(14) NGT: MAMA READ.
Dutch: mama lezen
'Mama (must) read.'
Lillo-Martin et al. 2016: 741, Van den Bogaerde and Baker 2008

4. Mixed code-blended: the proposition can only be reconstructed from constituents in both modalities. An example of the following is an utterance in which a person signed "police shot other people" while she said (in Dutch) "police killed other people." The whole proposition would be something like "the police shot and killed other people" and you need both signs and words to construct it:

(15) NGT: POLICE OTHER PEOPLE SHOT
Dutch: politie andere mensen doomaken
'The police shot other people.'
Lillo-Martin et al. 2016: 741, Van den Bogaerde and Baker 2008

The question Lillo-Martin et al. (2016) address at this point is how to represent the linguistic competence underlying these utterances. For instance, take (15): do we have two separate derivations or just one? If we have two derivations, do they converge on one proposition or two?

Lillo-Martin et al. suggest three options:

Option 1. Code-blending illustrates the expression of two different propositions via two different derivations.

Option 2. Code-blending relies on two derivations for one proposition: the computational system creates two derivations and therefore creates two sentences. Presumably, at the C-I level the two sentences fuse into one proposition.

Option 2. Code-blending uses one derivation to express a single proposition: that is, the sign and oral material all get together in one numeration and mingle in one derivation.

Before I discuss their reasoning, allow me to present my point of view. First of all, we need to recall that we are discussing linguistic competence, not production in real time. We are discussing the properties of well-formed linguistic objects and nothing else. A well-formed linguistic object consists of a syntactic structure, minimally including a root and a categorizing morpheme, which maps successfully onto the two interfaces, the articulatory-perceptual one and the cognitive-intensional one.

From this point of view, options 1 and 3, abstractly considered, pose no problem that I can see for a theory of linguistic competence (although they might be of great interest for theories of linguistic production): given a numeration, Merge creates various work-spaces, which may in the end merge into one, or not. Thus, options 1 and 3 represent the baseline of what anyone would assume: option 1 suggests that there are two derivations and two propositions and option 3 that we have one derivation and one proposition. The examples (12), (13), (14) could be viewed as a natural consequence of the integrated system that I argue for in these pages. At the end of the derivation, a particular root may have more than one spell out – which is a pervasive property among bilinguals, see Chapters 4 and 7: for a Spanish-English bilingual, the root √155 may spell out as /house/ or as /cas-/. Among non-signers, only one vocabulary item may be inserted in a syntactic terminal due to physical limitations imposed by the externalization systems. But a bimodal bilingual has no such constraint and, as a result, both a sign and an oral word may be externalized. As for (15), it is not far-fetched to say that there are indeed two derivations which yield the propositions 'the police shot other people' and 'the police killed other people'. Our mechanisms of pragmatic reasoning allow us to build them into a discourse that says 'the police shot and killed other people'. The fact that both sentences are uttered simultaneously is of no consequence for the theory of linguistic competence.

From the point of view of linguistic theory, it seems to me that only option 2 would present a serious challenge. Our current assumptions say that a particular selection from List 1 – a numeration in Chomsky (1995) – initiates a derivation that yields a propositional meaning. As far as I know, nobody has considered the possibility that two syntactic structures – two work-spaces that do not merge into one – would somehow converge onto one proposition. Option 2 would force us to consider a very non-trivial interface between linguistic computation and semantic interpretation.

Let's now turn to Lillo-Martin's discussion. Lillo-Martin et al. reject option 1: code-blending does not involve the expression of two derivations and two propositions, and the empirical reason that they offer for this conclusion is that what is said and what is signed is *congruent* and therefore we cannot talk about distinct derivations. Likewise, they also discard option 2 because it involves incongruent linguistic production. Finally, they choose option 3: an utterance that includes code-blending is always a single derivation and yields a single proposition.

Branchini and Donati (2016), however, question the assumption that incongruence between sign and speech is rare; in fact, they claim that it is systematic in their database. Moreover, some of the examples that they discuss seem to fall within the scope of option 2, which I claim is the problematic one for linguistic theory. Like Lillo-Martin and her colleagues, they focus their attention on the code-blending of bimodal bilinguals – in their case, bilinguals who speak Italian as well as Italian Sign Language (LIS). However, they reach a conclusion opposed to that of LM: in fact, they argue that the patterns of code-blending they find present evidence against the language synthesis hypothesis and for a lexicalist approach in which lexical items enter the syntactic derivation fully formed. Let's look at the data that led to this conclusion.

9.3 Incongruent Code-Blending

Branchini and Donati (2016) explain that there are important differences between Italian and LIS. First, there is constituent order: While Italian is a head+complement language, LIS is a head final language. Moreover, the position of sentential negation is also different: it is pre-verbal in Italian and post-verbal in LIS. Second, wh-movement is also different: Spec,C branches to the left in Italian but to the right in LIS. These distinct grammatical properties figure prominently in the article. Their argument revolves around the following fact: when bimodal bilinguals use code-blending, they have two choices: accommodate one string to the grammatical requirements of the other or produce them separately. Both are attested in their data and are accepted by their consultants. Thus, they distinguish two types of code-blending:

Type 1 code-blending. The code-blending traces the oral and the sign language on a one-to-one basis. Since the grammatical requirements of these languages are different, the resulting utterance is grammatical in one of the two languages while appearing to be ungrammatical in the other. However, the end result is judged to be acceptable by their bimodal bilinguals. This can be seen in examples (16) and (17). Consider first example (16):

(16)	LIS:	UNCLE	AUNT	REAL	ROME	LIVE
	Ita:	zio	zia	vero	Roma	abita
		uncle	aunt	actually	Rome	live

'My uncle and aunt actually live in Rome.'

Branchini and Donati 2016: 10

The LIS sentence in (16) is a perfectly grammatical sentence. The simultaneous Italian speech is not grammatical in this language, which would require 'Roma' to follow *abita*. Additionally, *abita* 'she/he lives', should agree with the subject in person and number but in (16) it does not, which suggests that the clausal spine does not include Italian functional categories. However, the utterance in (16), in which the Italian words shadow the LIS sentence, is acceptable.

Example (17) is the mirror image of example (16):

(17)	Ita:	Una	bambina	va	allo	zoo.
		A	girl	goes	to.the	zoo
	LIS:	GIRL	GO	ZOO		

'A girl goes to the zoo.'

Branchini and Donati 2016: 10

Here, we have a well-formed Italian sentence. This sentence is shadowed by a string of signs which are not grammatical in LIS because in this language 'zoo' should precede 'go'. But the resulting utterance is acceptable.

Thus, in Type 1 code-blending, Lx follows Ly creating a string that is not grammatical in Lx. This is created with a single numeration (and therefore a single derivation). The most straightforward description of Type 1 code-blending suggests that there is one syntactic derivation but the lexical roots are spelled out twice.

Type 2 code-blending. Both the oral and the visual strings conform grammatical sentences in their respective languages. This can be seen in example (18):

(18) LIS: UNDERSTAND $\overline{\text{NOT}}^{\text{NOT}}$
Ita: Non ho capito.
not have.1 understood
'I don't understand.'

Branchini and Donati 2016: 11

The LIS sentence places the signs in the grammatical word order in this language together with the non-manual markings (the *not* on top of the horizontal line) that are obligatory in this language. Simultaneously, the same speaker/signer produces a grammatical Italian sentence that means exactly the same. Thus, in Type 2 code-blending, Lx and Ly form two independent structures, each grammatical in its own language. This represents two derivations from two separate numerations – in fact, two derivations for one proposition, the option 2 discarded by Lillo-Martin and colleagues.

What is interesting at this point is what the authors found to be unacceptable to adult native speakers of Italian and LIS. In contrast to (19), which received a positive evaluation, examples like (20), (21), and (22) were judged as unacceptable by their consultants:

(19) It: Telefonato chi?
call.ptc who
LIS: $\overline{\text{PHONE WHO}}^{\text{WH}}$

Branchini and Donati 2016: 26

(20) * It: chi telefonato?
who phone.ptc
LIS: $\overline{\text{WHO PHONE}}^{\text{WH}}$

Branchini and Donati 2016: 26

(21) * It: chi telefonato?
who phone.ptc
LIS: $\overline{\text{PHONE WHO}}^{\text{WH}}$

Branchini and Donati 2016: 26

(22) * It: Ha telefonato chi?
aux.3sg call.ptc who

WH
LIS: PHONE WHO

Branchini and Donati 2016: 16–17

Here is a description of examples (19) to (22). If the Italian wh-phrase does not move to the left, the auxiliary must be omitted – this is shown in the contrast between the acceptable (19) and the unacceptable (22). However, if the wh-phrase does move, then the auxiliary is obligatory, regardless of the word order in the LIS sentence, as shown in the unacceptable (20) and (21). More generally: if a sentence is going to be impoverished, it has to follow the word order (word order acts as a proxy to the grammar) of the other language.

According to Branchini and Donati (2016: 18), the unacceptability of (20), (21), and (22) argues against the LSM because the LSM is too unrestrained: "any combination of roots and morphemes belonging to the two languages should be possible, and not only those corresponding to coherent monolingual grammars" (their criticism that the LSM is too unconstrained echoes some of the responses to their target article such as Putnam et al. 2016, Liceras 2016). Consequently, Branchini and Donati (2016) claim, the LSM fails to rule out (20), (21), and (22) and therefore it is not a good characterization of the I-language of bimodal bilinguals.

In Branchini and Donati's view, a lexicalist approach is better positioned to account for the data they present. Why are (20) to (22) ungrammatical? "Its ungrammaticality is explained if what drives the syntactic derivation are complex lexical items already and rigidly endowed with all their formal properties" (2016: 18). The authors do not elaborate on this terse response, and they do not carry out a detailed analysis of (20) to (22). But I think their meaning can be articulated as follows:

Utterance (20) does not conform to the grammar of either language. Since we have the same word order for the LIS and the Italian, it must have been constructed as one derivation. However, the "Italian" should have an overt auxiliary, or the "LIS" should have wh-in-situ. Thus, (20) is not a good sentence in either language.

As for (21): the order of sign and speech are different, so this is the product of two separate derivations, both of which must be grammatical. The LIS derivation is fine but the Italian one is not because it is missing an auxiliary, so the result is out.

As for (22): the common order suggests that there is only one derivation. Since we have wh-in-situ, we may conclude that it is LIS. But if it is a LIS sentence, there is no room for an Italian auxiliary, the numeration could not include it. Likewise, if we conclude this is an Italian sentence, there is no place for wh-in-situ. Either way it is out.

And, how does this argue for lexicalism and against DM? Because the Italian words and the LIS words have independent grammatical requirements that need to be respected. From this Branchini and Donati (2016) conclude that the syntactic terminals do not encapsulate bundles of abstract features but actual lexical items with specific lexical properties.

In the following, I try to convince the reader that the 1Lex/1PF MDM model presented in previous chapters is perfectly capable of addressing the relevant data. The essence of my argument is that Branchini and Donati's assumptions regarding realizational morphology are too sparse. Within the MDM there are tools that allow us to tackle (20) to (22). This is what we need: (i) the assumption that C and T share a number of features, particularly those related to A-dependencies, as was developed within the feature inheritance proposal of Chomsky (2008) (see Section 3.1); and (ii) the PHH, according to which the phase head determines grammatical properties of its complement. With these two assumptions, we can account for Branchini and Donati's data.

Let's start with (20). In (20), wh-movement suggests the presence of an Italian C and precludes the presence of a LIS C. An Italian C should share ϕ-features with its complement T and these features should spell out in the auxiliary. That is, the presence of an Italian C entails the presence of an Italian T. Consequently, a sentence like (20) could never be generated without an auxiliary. The same holds of (21).

In (22), wh-in-situ suggests the presence of a LIS C. LIS does not have obligatory agreement features based on person and number, like Italian, but rather optional agreement based on location (see Branchini and Donati's description). If we assume something like feature inheritance, and if LIS C has no person–number agreement, the presence of these features on the auxiliary becomes mysterious. It follows that (22) is not possible.

To conclude, it seems to me that the fascinating data presented by Branchini and Donati (2016) do not constitute an argument against realizational morphology. I have shown that two independently motivated assumptions based on phase theory and feature inheritance can be recruited to account for it.

Let's summarize what we have learned from these studies on bimodal bilinguals. Lillo-Martin et al. (2016) present a model that they call LSM, which is on the surface identical to the MDM proposal. One difference is that the MDM that I am arguing for in these pages is explicitly a 1Lex and 1PF model while Lillo-Martin and colleagues' is not. Their main contribution, in my view, is that they clearly lay out the challenges that code-blending presents for linguistic theory and propose a reasoning to deal with the data.

Branchini and Donati (2016) also bring to the fore code-blending data that have broad implications for linguistic theory, in this case, incongruent utterances. They argue that code-blending involves the possibility of constructing independent grammatical derivations to yield one proposition, a complex issue for the theory of grammar. They argue that their data support lexicalism against realizational models of grammar but I have shown that the MDM includes tools that allow us to handle their intriguing observations.

The work on bimodal bilingualism will, I am certain, become central to linguistic theory in the coming years because it forces us to rethink basic architectural assumptions. I already mentioned that the connection between syntactic derivation and semantic proposition is going to be affected by the work on code-blending. Let me add one more thing. Embick (2015) codifies our understanding of the morpheme as a pairing of a set of syntactic-semantic features and a set of phonetic features (the Saussurian sign, if you will). Within DM, morphemes in List 1 pair synsem features with a variable Q that is targeted and replaced by a vocabulary item from List 2. As suggested, code-blending suggests that this picture is a simplification: the bundle of synsem features can *simultaneously* be paired with more than one exponent. The Saussurian sign might not be a fundamental property of the language faculty but just a mirage created by the physical constraints of the oral/aural channel.

9.4 Soft Constraints

Consider the following sentence:

(23) Although administration officials **tried** earlier this week **tried** to counter speculation that the president might try to fire Mueller, . . .

Toluse Olorunnipa, Trump lashes out at Top Justice Official, Confirms He's Focus of Probe. Bloomberg.com. June 16, 2017

This sentence includes a repetition of the verb 'tried', in bold. I think I can say with confidence that no English grammarian would conclude from this particular example that the grammar of English allows for repetition of a lexical item. And the reason why is not frequency – this sort of example cannot be so extraordinarily rare in the written press, since I found a couple of examples in the few days in which I looked for them. I bet it is less rare than perfectly grammatical structures like, for example, multiple wh-questions or Raising to Object constructions (Heil 2015 found out Raising to Object is virtually absent from English corpora). Still, we do not regard (23) as being a phenomenon that requires grammatical explanation, rather, it is a simple error. We reach this judgment because native speakers of English unanimously agree that (23) is not a well-formed sentence in English.

Code-switching research, however, does not always abide by the same reasoning. Code-switching corpora occasionally show examples of doubling and Goldrick, Putnam, and Schwartz (2016) have used examples such as (24) as cornerstone for a new theory of code-switching and bilingual grammar. In this example, the lemma GAVE appears twice, once in English and once in Tamil:

(24) English/*Tamil*
They gave me a research grant *kadutaa.*
give.3.PL.PAST
Goldrick et al. 2016: 861 (Sankoff et al. 1990: 93)

Notice that the English verb appears before the object while the Tamil verb appears after the object. This is not chance: English is a VO language while Tamil is OV.

Is there a reason to treat (24) differently from (23)? Earlier work on code-switching tends to say no (Myers-Scotton 1993). Goldrick and colleagues believe there is and provide the following reasons. First, it seems that only heads are doubled, not phrases. Second, the repeated verbs are in different languages. Third, the order VOV does not seem to be random: Tamil is an OV language and English is VO; in (24), the Tamil verb appears after the object while the English verb appears before the object. According to Putnam et al. this is not chance, on the contrary, it reflects a grammatical property of bilingual grammar.

I think the reasoning in Goldrick et al. 2016 should lead us to treat (23) as a grammatical problem too. The location of the verb in (23) is not random, it appears before and after the adjunct because both positions are grammatical for a verb in English. One never finds something like 'tried officials tried to counter speculation' because the English verb never appears before the subject. I take it that the fact that the doubling error in (23) does not violate grammatical principles is not reason enough to consider doubling as a grammatical phenomenon. Further, the same reasoning should apply to (24).

Be that as it may, Goldrick et al. (2016) develop a theory of code-switching based on data such as (24). This is their analysis in a nutshell. Their theory of grammar consists of a system of differently weighted constraints to outputs in the OT tradition. Their goal is to make sure that (25a) and (25b) have higher probability than (25c), while (25d) is extremely unlikely. The tool that ensures this higher probability is the weight of the constraints on their production:

(25) a. They gave me a research grant.
b. They a research grant kadutaa.
c. They gave me a research grant kadutaa.
d. They research grant.

In order to obtain this result, they use the following tools: (i) language-specific grammatical constraints formulated as numerical weighted constraints, (ii) blending of constraints of the two grammars, and (iii) simultaneous co-activation of all constraints. Let's see how.

If we assume that there is a constraint called PARSE that stars structures that randomly ignore lexical items from the input, and if we further assume that PARSE is a "heavy" constraint, it follows that the probability that (25d) be produced is very low. How do we make sure that (25c) has lower probability than (25a) and (25b)? Let's assume that the mental grammars of these bilinguals have two constraints HEAD LAST and HEAD FIRST. HEAD LAST is violated by English VPs in (25a), where the object follows the verb. HEAD FIRST is violated by (25b). But (25c) violates both HEAD FIRST and HEAD LAST. This gives it relatively low probability, which accounts for the fact that examples like (24) are few and far between. (Notice that their model seeks to predict the probability that a form will be produced; it seems that their model is both a model of bilingual I-language and a model of production.)

I presented some discussion of their approach in López (2016). Here I would like to make one additional comment. As suggested around my discussion of (23), I am not certain that the data in (24) is real – or in other words, I am not certain that (24) is more of a grammatical phenomenon than (23) is. I have consulted two Spanish/German bilinguals on sentences equivalent to (24) and they rejected them immediately. As I mentioned above, the fact that data appear in a corpus is no guarantee that the data are actually generated by a grammar and, without some acceptability judgments by native speakers, there is no real way to know. I see no reason why we should derive generalizations from code-switching data that we would never formulate on the basis of monolingual English data.

Moreover, the data that Goldrick et al. (2016) use for their analysis, all of them extracted from published sources, faces other serious problems that make it unusable. There is a notable lack of information on the circumstances regarding the production of blended forms as well as shallow or absent grammatical analyses. Consider the following: notice that in all cases of VOV reported in the literature, the OV language allows for silent objects (Turkish, Tamil, Chinese). This opens the door for an alternative analysis: instead of VOV we might have VO*pro*V. If there is a pause after the O, then we might have a dislocated VP, a less extraordinary phenomenon than it seemed.

On the other hand, doubling of functional categories in code-switching seems to be a real grammatical phenomenon, at least in some cases. Could it be amenable to the sort of analysis that Goldrick et al. (2016) propose? In order to address this question, I turn to Vergara's (2017) analysis of complementizer doubling among Basque-Spanish bilinguals. I choose this one example because it is the only piece of work that I know of that studies doubling in code-switching following experimental protocols that tap the I-language of the subjects.

Spanish is a head initial language and has only one declarative complementizer, *que*. Basque is head final and has an affirmative declarative complementizer /*ela*/ and a negative one /*enik*/. Both Basque complementizers are cliticized to the auxiliary. Vergara (2018) finds that in code-switching contexts in which the matrix clause is in Spanish and the subordinate clause is in Basque, doubling is obligatory for the declarative complementizer and unacceptable for the negative one, as shown in example (26). The contrast between (26a) and (26b) shows that if we code-switch at the C area, both the Spanish and the Basque complementizers are obligatory if the sentence is affirmative. On the other hand, if the Basque complementizer is negative, it cannot be doubled by the Spanish complementizer, as shown in the contrast between (26c) and (26d):

(26) Spanish/*Basque*

a. Pedro cree que *Jon etorri dela*
Pedro believes that Jon arrived AUX.C
'Pedro believes that Jon arrived.'

b. * Pedro cree Jon etorri dela.
Pedro believes Jon arrived AUX.C

c. * Pedro no cree que *Jon etorri denik.*
Pedro not believes that John arrive AUX.C_{NEG}

d. Pedro no cree *Jon etorri denik.*
Pedro not believes John arrive AUX.C_{NEG}
'Pedro does not believe that Jon arrived.'

This is surprising within the Goldrick et al. (2016) framework. If Basque is head final and Spanish head initial, the example (26a) violates both HEAD INITIAL and HEAD FINAL whereas (26b) only violates HEAD INITIAL – but (26a) is good while (26b) is not. With the negative complementizer we get the opposite contrasts. As far as I can tell, (26b,d) violate no constraints: Spanish requires an overt complementizer in declarative sentences but this requirement should be satisfied with /*ela*/ or /*enik*/. But (26b) is unacceptable and (26d) is fine.

Vergara (2018) approaches the surprising contrasts in (26) with an analysis that relies on the distribution of the features Force and Finiteness among the complementizers, following the general framework of assumptions developed in Rizzi (1997). At this point, I don't know if Vergara's approach to duplication in Spanish/Basque code-switching can be generalized to other duplication structures (although, as Deuchar and Biberauer 2016 point out, the feature structure of complementizers varies crosslinguistically considerably). But I would like to use his analysis to extract two morals: (i) duplication of functional categories is not necessarily a shallow phenomenon and it demands detailed linguistic analyses and (ii) accessing the I-language of code-switchers requires some sort of acceptability judgment, corpora data is not enough. I hope we will soon see more examples of experimental work on doubling structures so we can find out if Vergara's sort of analysis is feasible generally.

9.5 Conclusions

In this chapter, I have discussed several approaches to code-switching and/or code-blending that adopt one or both of the following assumptions: (i) an integrated linguistic competence, (ii) a DM approach. We have seen that there have been some interesting explorations but not yet a sustained, coherent proposal. Grimstad et al.'s (2014) analysis of English nouns in Norwegian DPs only works within a very narrow database and cannot be extended to other code-switching pairs that are familiar from the literature. Lillo-Martin et al. (2016) is a programmatic proposal that does not assume an integrated system like the 1Lex/1PF MDM. Branchini and Donati (2016) argue that code-blending provides evidence in favor of lexicalism but, as I argued, they give up on DM too easily. Finally, Goldrick et al. (2016) propose a soft constraint approach to code-switching that seems to be designed for the wrong database. If there is a general conclusion to be drawn, it is that studies of code-switching and bilingual grammar in general are still in their infancy and very soon we are going to see many interesting findings.

10 General Conclusions

The possibility of regarding the I-language of a bilingual as a fully integrated system was discussed in the early approaches to code-switching as a working or default hypothesis. Sankoff and Poplack (1981), in fact, try such a system. As they argue, "code-switching . . . does not entail pauses, hesitations, repetitions, corrections or any other interruption or disruption in the rhythm of speech . . . [it] provides some justification for treating code-switched discourse, at least in parts, as being generated by a single grammar based on the two monolingual ones" (Sankoff and Poplack 1981: 10). Their formal system is couched in a 1970s phrase structure grammar. In such a theory, the Spanish grammar would include a rule like (1.1) while the grammar of English would include (1.2). These rules reflect the fact that adjectives generally follow the noun in Spanish while in English adjectives precede the noun. The lexicon of this bilingual would be the union of both lexicons, as shown in (1.3), (1.4), and (1.5):

(1)
1. NP → D ; N ; A
2. NP → D ; A ; N
3. D → {the, el, la, . . .}
4. A → {white, blanco, . . .}
5. N → {house, casa, . . .}

If the grammar of a bilingual is the union of the two grammars, then both (1.1) and (1.2) should be part of this bilingual person's grammar. This system would yield all the grammatical sentences of English and Spanish but it would also generate a number of undesirable structures like the one in (2):

(2) * the house white

(2) would be generated by applying the rules (1.1), (1.3), (1.4), and (1.5). Thus, Sankoff and Poplack (1981) conclude that a bilingual grammar cannot simply be the union of the two grammars but some additional mechanism – such as tagging the rules for language – should be added. After that, virtually every scholar of bilingualism and code-switching has assumed the commonsense notion that bilinguals do indeed possess two linguistic systems.

Almost twenty-eight years later, our understanding of I-language has advanced considerably. I hope I have shown in these pages that the fact that 'the house white' is ungrammatical for bilingual Spanish speakers does not necessarily lead to the conclusion that bilinguals have a split linguistic competence. Rather, MDM helps us understand that an integrated system can make the necessary distinctions that ensure the attested acceptability judgments.

An important contribution of the MDM is, to my mind, that it helps us abandon the idea that I-languages are count entities and therefore that polyglots have two or more autonomous discrete systems in their head. Individual I-languages are in fact continua of features, like any other natural phenomenon, as shown most dramatically in post-Creole continua. Interestingly, this monograph has also shown that the MDM provides us with tools to study the continuous reality of I-language in a formal, explicit manner.

The bulk of this monograph has been devoted to the presentation of empirical arguments that an integrated MDM is possible and preferable to a split framework. There are some apparently disparate phenomena that can only be formally understood in an integrated model:

(i) **The Mixed Selection Problem**. The apparent cross-linguistic selection of light verbs in code-switching. For example, in Esplugish: the "Spanish" light verb *hacer* 'do, make' selects for a "German" infinitive (Section 4.1). This would not be possible if the bilingual speaker had separate Spanish and German lexicons but is consistent with the assumption of a single lexicon.

(3) Spanish/*German*

Hizo	*nähen*	*das Hemd.*
do.PAST.3	sew.INF	the shirt

'She/he sewed the shirt.'

González-Vilbazo and López 2012: 35

(ii) **The Swahili "Certificate" Problem**. The presence of gender or class assignment on nouns taken from a language that has no gender or class, as was exemplified with Swahili/English code-switching (Section 4.1). I argued that this is unexpected within a 2Lex assumption but perfectly consistent with the MDM, in which the gender and class features are not inherent to a noun but the output of a morphosyntactic structure.

(4) Swahili/*English*

Ø-saa	hi-yo	i-na-*depend*	na
9-time	dem-9	9-pres-depend	with
Ø-certificate	z-ako	z-a	Ø-shule.
10-certificate	10-your	10-with	10-school

'At this time, it depends on the school certificates.'

Myers-Scotton and Jake 2009: 339

(iii) **The Feminization of Beer**. This heading refers to the diachronic process by which new words take on the features of the old words that they displace. This was exemplified with my analysis of Italian *birra* and French *bière*, which became feminine as they displaced the old *cervesia*, which is also feminine. These words were borrowed from Germanic, where *bior (German *bier*) is neuter (Section 4.2).

(iv) **Dependencies**. The presence of cross-linguistic dependencies when the features of the two languages do not match perfectly, as is the case with dislocation dependencies in Spanish/German code-switching (Section 4.3). In the following example, the Spanish clitic *lo* is masculine (or [−f]) and it doubles a neuter German, which is [−f, −m]. This works because of Halle's subset principle, which permits the insertion of an exponent that has only a subset of the features of the syntactic terminal.

(5) *German*/Spanish
Das *Buch,* *Hans* lo hizo *verkaufen.* Spa/*Ger*
DEF.N book Hans CL.ACC.M did sell
'Hans sold the book.'
González-Vilbazo (p.c.)

Generally, the organization of cross-linguistic syntactic dependencies receives a very natural analysis if there are no barriers between the lexicons and the grammars of the bilingual.

(v) **Cantonese hor and English 'give'**. The datum documented by Yip and Matthews (2009) by which their bilingual child use the English word 'give' as an auxiliary to form a passive predicate, mirroring the equivalent structure in Cantonese (Section 4.4). The argument is that if a bilingual has two separate lexicons these sorts of expansions could not happen unless some mysterious channels of communication between the lexicons are bored, while an integrated lexicon makes them almost expected.

(6) I already give the mosquito to bite.
'I have been bitten by a mosquito.'
Yip and Matthews 2009: 385

(vi) **Basque Gender**. Among Basque/Spanish bilinguals, a Basque noun that ends in /a/ can collocate with a Spanish feminine determiner. I argued that gender assignment can depend on a grammatical rule supposedly belonging to the "other language," which leads to the conclusion that the rules of gender assignment are not encapsulated in separate languages (Section 5.2).

(7) *Spanish*/Basque
La makila
The walking-stick.

(vii) **Impossible Genders**. I argued that a 2Lex theory cannot prevent aberrant gender assignments, such as the one in (8):

(8) * *el* *mesa*
the.M table

In a 2Lex theory, the Spanish word *mesa* could be borrowed into the "English" lexicon of the bilingual and be assigned default gender. The 1Lex assumption accounts for the unlikelihood of that happening (Section 5.3).

(viii) **German Determiners**. The unacceptability of (9b) in light of the well-formedness of (9a) was attributed to the contrast of the determiner's feature specification.

(9) *German*/Spanish

a. dem *interruptor*
DEF.M/N.DAT switch(m)

b. ?? der *cuaderno*
DEF.M.NOM notebook(m)

González-Vilbazo 2005:165

(ix) **Clitic Combinations**. The impoverishment rule among Spanish/Catalan bilinguals that affects clitic combinations of the "wrong language" (Section 6.2). I presented this as an argument that the morphology module must be integrated.

(10) Catalan
El Pere [**s'** **ho**] va dir.
the Pere SE 3.NEUT.ACC PAST say.INF
'Pere said it to him/her.'

(x) **Consonant Mutations**. The processing of consonant mutation in English among Welsh/English bilinguals suggests, once again, that a grammatical rule is not specified in the I-language of a bilingual as belonging to one language or the other. Rather, the rule may apply when the conditions of its application are right. (Section 6.3)

(xi) **Constituent Order and Prosodification**, which seem to be independent of the lexical items involved (Section 6.4). This can be most easily seen in our by-now familiar light verb constructions:

(11) Spanish/*German*
Hizo *nähen* *das Hemd.*
do.PAST.3 sew.INF the shirt
'She/he sewed the shirt.'

González-Vilbazo and López 2012: 35

The constituents within the VP are drawn from the German vocabulary, but the word order and the prosody is Spanish, as dictated by the light verb. This shows that even the outer layers of PF cannot be separated into modules corresponding to languages.

Additionally, I have shown that the psycholinguistic work on co-activation, priming and the cost of code-switching is consistent with my integrated model and can also be elegantly reanalyzed in an integrated MDM model. Likewise, I have shown that the integrated MDM model provides insight into lexical acquisition. Thus, I have found many compelling reasons to adopt the integrated model and none to reject it.

A common objection to the integrated approach could be phrased as follows: "bilingual speakers are aware that they have two languages in their head and they can use them independently without mixing them. For instance, my friend Jacques is bilingual in French and Dutch and can speak or write either language without interference. Even his two-year-old daughter knows that she should use French with him and German with her mother. Surely this would not be possible if their two languages were in one system." In Section 8.1, I showed that the assumption of an integrated theory does not conflict with the common observation that (at least some) bilinguals are able to speak in one language or the other without mixing. In particular, I showed that it is possible to formulate a set of VIRs for a bilingual speaker that ensure that the bilingual's competence system can in fact support the production of speech that is undistinguishable from a monolingual person's speech and show no signs that the speaker is also fluent in another language. The ability of speaking in one language or the other without mixing them up can be attributed to mechanisms of production that inhibit those parts of the system that are not in use.

Interestingly, I have found that scholars coming from a different perspective have reached conclusions apparently similar to mine: I am referring to the *translanguaging* project (see Otheguy, Garcia, and Reid 2015 and references therein). The term translanguaging is meant to express the idea that a speaker may choose, in the appropriate environment, to use all of their linguistic resources. Their approach is from the point of view of sociolinguistics and education and their main concern is that schools center their pedagogy around something called "language," understood as a coherent external object (Spanish, English, Portuguese), rather than the reality of individuals' idiolects. It is a worthy effort and my remarks in what follows should not be seen as a fundamental criticism but as remarks that the translanguagers might want to take into consideration.

Translanguaging is defined as "the deployment of a speaker's full linguistic repertoire without regard for watchful adherence to the socially and politically defined boundaries of named (and usually national and state) languages" (Otheguy et al. 2015: 283). It looks like what they call translanguaging is what the rest of us have always called code-switching. According to the translanguaging authors, however, there is an important difference because "the notion of code switching still constitutes a theoretical endorsement of the idea that what the bilingual manipulates, however masterfully, are two separate linguistic systems" (Otheguy et al. 2015: 282). I agree that the literature on code-switching does adopt what I call the separationist assumption and I would even agree that the term itself carries this implication. However, it is not clear to me that we should replace a familiar term whose denotation (if not its definition) is more or less clear to practitioners with a new term whose boundaries are fuzzy.

I can also endorse their view of the bilingual I-language according to which "the mental grammars of bilinguals are structured but unitary collections of features, and the practices of bilinguals are acts of feature selection, not of grammar switch" (Otheguy et al. 2015: 281). Otheguy et al. (2015) explain what this means by means of a culinary metaphor: one can mix in one dish different types of ingredients that one might associate with different national culinary traditions and the end product will not be "Japanese" or "Cuban" and one cannot even say that it is a mix of both – rather, it is a novel product. This is good. Unfortunately, I have not seen in the translanguaging literature any empirical argumentation that the I-language of a bilingual is indeed "a unitary collection of features" or as I put it, an integrated system. As far as I can tell, translanguagers have not carried out the slow, unglamorous digging for evidence work that I have tried to do here. Lacking empirical argumentation, translanguagers open themselves up to the charge that their claims are purely ideological. There is nothing wrong with ideological claims – particularly if the ultimate goal is to shed light on educational practices and move them to a better place – as long as the distinction between ideological and empirical claims is kept clear.

The translanguaging effort has recently been criticized by MacSwan (2017), who argues that his notion that bilinguals have separate lexicons needs to be maintained. He claims that Otheguy et al. (2015) do not correctly separate the notions of I-language and E-language and this leads to conceptual confusion. The confusion is the following: the fact that labeled languages are sociopolitical and not linguistic entities does not lead to the conclusion that individual speakers have fully integrated linguistic systems: The two questions are orthogonal.

I agree with half of MacSwan's criticism. I agree that the awareness that external languages are arbitrary abstractions leads to no conclusion regarding how individual I-languages are organized. The integrated approach cannot be simply asserted or exemplified by means of a metaphor. Rather, it needs to be argued empirically – as I have done in these pages. On the other hand, the second half of MacSwan's criticism seems unfair; it seems to me that Otheguy et al. (2015) are well acquainted with the I-language/E-language distinction; in fact, their focus is in mental grammar, which they understand in a manner that is very close to generativists' I-language (although they deny this).

Be that as it may, it seems that at least some translanguagers have indeed taken the step of assuming that since E-languages have no ontological reality, neither does code-switching. For instance, Makoni and Pennycook (2007) argue extensively that languages (I would say E-languages) are historical inventions and therefore: "The view of language we are suggesting here has serious consequences for many of the treasured icons of liberal-linguistic thought. Not only the notions of language become highly suspect, but so do many related concepts that are premised on the notion of discrete languages, such as language rights, mother tongues, multilingualism or code-switching" (Makoni and Pennycook 2007: 22). This quotation highlights the confusion that MacSwan points out: the acknowledgement that E-languages are indeed political constructs has no bearing on the status of the I-languages of individual speakers. Individual speakers may or may not have separate lexicons for each linguistic sub-system that they speak, regardless of the status of external languages.

Makoni and Pennycook (2007) seem to argue that the adoption of the translanguaging framework entails abandoning the linguistic investigations of code-switching. However, it seems clear to me that the assumption of an integrated system does not leave us scholars off the hook with respect to the empirical facts of code-switching. The fact of the matter is that the I-languages of speakers in contact situations give rise to a number of linguistic forms that constitute empirical puzzles for linguists interested in trying to understand the nature of human language. For instance, almost every piece of data presented in this monograph demands an explanation. If code-switching does not exist, Why is it that Spanish/Basque bilinguals accept *la makila* but not **la etxe?* Why is it that Spanish/German bilinguals like *hacer arbeiten* but do not like **tun trabajar*? Or even more fundamentally, if *hacer* cannot be used as a light verb in monolingual Spanish, how does it become one only in code-switching? The assumption of an integrated system does not make these problems go away; rather, it makes the questions more acute, it limits the sets of possible explanations and analytical tools (always a good thing), and forces us to look at the data with a more potent microscope. Eventually, this effort will lead to new insights into the nature of human language.

And this gives me the segue to finish this monograph with a look to the future. One consequence of this monograph is that code-switching – or translanguaging – is an epiphenomenon. Code-switching is about using one's complete set of linguistic resources in one speech act – not a particularly marked behavior. What we have been calling code-switching should in fact be defined as the avoidance of limiting one's linguistic resources in half. Does this mean that code-switching is (or should be) ended as a focus of linguistic research? Not at all. First, I might be wrong; a lot more research is necessary before the conclusions of this monograph can be regarded as solid. Second, even if this monograph were correct in its entirety (please note my usage of the imperfect subjunctive), there is a wealth of code-switching data available to us that we do not understand yet – and a massive amount of research questions that we are not even able to ask at this point because we don't have reliable data. I believe we have code-switching research *para rato*.

Appendix A: Restrictions on Code-Switching

Code-switching is rule-governed, like any other expression of an individual's I-language. Contrary to naïve opinion, not everything goes – and throughout this monograph we have encountered a number of code-switching instances that bear the asterisk sign, indicating that bilingual speakers of the relevant community reject those structures as ill formed. Thus, the bulk of the formal literature on code-switching attempts at providing general statements that will capture the restrictions on code-switching. But the results do not cease to be controversial. Indeed, as MacSwan (2014) points out, as soon as a proposal is formulated, counterexamples blossom, which has led some people to grow skeptical as to the feasibility of this research agenda. In this appendix, I would like to present my own view on the topic and suggest an alternative path to this research program based on what I think is a more realistic view of human languages.

The most popular approach to code-switching is the one developed by Myers-Scotton and her colleagues (Myers-Scotton 1993, 2002), which utilizes a bespoke collection of assumptions. With respect to its successes and limitations, see the debate between MacSwan (2000, 2014) and Jake et al. (2002). An alternative approach tries to formulate the analysis of code-switching restrictions within a broader theoretical context, the so-called Null Theory (see Woolford 1983, Lipski 1985, Mahootian 1993, MacSwan 1999, among others). These lines are addressed to those interested in this second approach to code-switching restrictions.

The Null Theory comes in two versions. In one version, let's call it *Broad Null Theory*, constraints of UG are used to account for apparent constraints on code-switching. The second version, the *Narrow Null Theory*, seeks to use exclusively grammatical features of the participating languages. Let's start with the Broad Null Theory.

The Broad Null Theory has used the government-binding theory of the 1980s or the hypotheses that arise out of the Minimalist Program to account for stated restrictions on code-switching. For instance, in a very influential article, Belazi, Rubin, and Toribio (1994) argued that code-switching is not possible between two heads such that one functionally selects the other, what they call the *Functional Head Constraint* (FHC). Belazi et al.'s (1994) FHC claimed that it was not possible to code-switch between C and T or between D and N, on the grounds that the *extended projection* of a lexical head could not be split. The notion of extended projection was proposed by Grimshaw (1991): it claimed that a lexical head and the functional heads c-commanding it formed a functional constituent in which every head shared some features, specially category. Thus, the extended projection of a noun included the DP; the extended projection of a verb reached to CP.

The following is an example of C-T code-switching. C comes from Spanish, T comes from English, and the result is ungrammatical, as predicted by the FHC:

(1) Spanish/*English*
* El profesor dijo que *the student had received an A.*
The professor said that
Belazi et al. (1994): 225

But there are counterexamples to the generalization that you cannot code-switch between C and T – some of these counterexamples are sprinkled in the pages of this monograph and will be discussed in some detail below.

MacSwan (2014) presents a good summary of some Broad Null Theory approaches and shows that all of them encounter empirical difficulties. For this reason, scholars have not been able to agree on what restrictions should be applicable or even how we should approach this search for UG-based restrictions. Should we perhaps abandon the notion that a set of universal restrictions on code-switching can be formulated? Certainly, vigorous debate is a crucial feature of any normal science, but it is also important to be able to take one step back and consider whether one's energies should be focused differently.

Why did the Broad Null Theory turn out to be so difficult? In general, broad restrictions that apply to all and any form of code-switching in any language pair *without a deeper analysis of the constituents involved* are going to run into trouble sooner rather than later. Consider the following: in this monograph, I have chosen to divide the clausal spine into four basic categories – C, T, Voice, and v – but we know that the features of each category vary substantially from language to language. The Basque C may have a polarity feature that is absent in the Spanish C; Spanish T has incorporated an aspect feature, absent in English; Greek has a middle voice, absent in English, and so on. In fact, many linguists believe that we should be thinking in terms of fields – the C-field, the T-field, and so on – with multiple categories in each field. According to this view – usually referred to as *cartography* – different languages activate different subsets of features inside each field (see Cinque 1999 and Rizzi 1997, seminal works on cartography). Within the C-field we find that what we call C may house an array of features related to sentence type (declarative, interrogative), mood (realis, irrealis), polarity (negative, positive), finiteness (plus or minus), topic (which can be multiple in some languages or unique in others), focus, or contrast. In other words: the C that we find in one language may have quite different grammatical properties than the C that we find in another language.

Thus, if we find that there is a code-switching restriction between C and TP in one particular language pair, we cannot be certain that we are going to find the same restriction in another language pair because the restriction is, more likely than not, associated with the particular features that are activated in C and T in that pair of languages and not on the C and T labels – if such things as C and T labels exist independently of the features associated with them.

An alternative to the Broad Null Theory is the Narrow Null Theory. It hypothesizes that any form of code-switching is acceptable as long as the grammatical restrictions of the participating languages are respected (see, for instance, MacSwan 2014: 18–26, for a vigorous defense of this idea). The Narrow Null Theory looks sensible on the surface but it is not a trivial idea to apply. For instance, consider MacSwan's example of English/Welsh code-switching. English is SVO while Welsh is VSO. It looks like any form of code-switching within the sentence would violate one of the two grammars? Not so, says MacSwan, the category that determines word order within the sentence is T, which triggers V movement in Welsh but not in English. Therefore, the resulting word order will have to respect the requirements of T: If T is Welsh, we have VSO as a result of V-to-T; if T is English there is no V-to-T and the resulting order is SVO.

The examples presented in MacSwan (2014) are clear enough, but others are harder to tackle. Take Finer's (2014) examples of wh-dependencies in English/Korean code-switching:

(2) English/*Korean*
I wonder he bought *muet* yesterday.
what
Finer 2014: 55

Finer claims that when the wh-phrase is Korean it must stay in situ. This would seem to respect the grammar of Korean. But, does it respect the grammar of English? Mainstream analyses of wh-movement (Pesetsky and Torrego 2001, among many others) take it for granted that the wh-phrase is in a dependency with a C head. If the C head in this example is English, then a requirement of the English language has been violated.

Consider also the examples of Russian/Kazakh code-switching discussed by Auer and Muhamedova (2005). They show that after a Russian complementizer, bilingual speakers may switch to Kazakh, and in this case the Kazakh subordinate clause appears with a fully inflected T. But this contravenes the Kazakh norm, which does not have subordinate finite clauses:

(3) *Russian*/Kazakh

Chasten'ko	*poluchaetsya*	*shto*	aralastïr-a-mïz
often	occur-RFL-3SG	that	mix-PRES.1.PL

'It often occurs that we mix.'

Auer and Muhamedova 2005: 49

Has the Kazakh grammar been violated? If we look only at the subordinate TP, that is clearly the case. However, in Chapter 3, I argued that the grammatical requirements that need to be respected are those of the head of the phase. In this case, C is the head of the phase and decides what shape its complement must have. Since C is Russian, the TP will have a Russian character even if all the terminals bear Kazakh exponents. Thus, it seems that rather than a statement like "the grammars of the languages need to be respected" we should have an alternative: "the grammar of XP, XP a constituent of phase *p*, obeys the requirements of *p*."

Finally, the Narrow Null Theory does not predict the possibility that code-switching gives rise to novel forms that do not belong in either of the participating languages. Consider again the light verb constructions:

(4) Spanish/*German*

Hizo	*nähen*	*das Hemd.*
do.PAST.3	sew.INF	the shirt

'She/he sewed the shirt.' (Cf. Section 4.1)

González-Vilbazo and López 2012: 35

As argued in Chapter 3, the usage of *hacer* 'do' as a light verb is an innovation of Esplugisch speakers; in fact, several variants of light verbs appear in many communities of code-switching bilingual speakers (González-Vilbazo and López 2012, Veenstra and López 2016). Therefore, the light verb in (4) is a violation of the grammar of one of the languages (in this case, Spanish).

Thus, I am not sure that the code-switching restriction research project remains fruitful as long as it is based on broad phrase-structural restrictions or other universal grammatical restrictions such as the Government Restriction (Joshi 1985), the Functional Head Restriction or any other of the proposals listed in MacSwan (2014). But at the same time, the Narrow Null Theory seems too restrictive and hard to apply. I would like to suggest that an alternative based on abstract meta-restrictions like *selection* in combination with detailed analyses of the grammatical features of the language pair involved holds some promise. In other words, I would like to combine features of both the Narrow and the Broad Null Theories.

In the following, I show how selection yields some results in the DP area with the Spanish/Taiwanese data discussed in Bartlett and González-Vilbazo (2013). With selection, and following Bartlett and González-Vilbazo, I mean the most basic notion: X may select Y and may not select Z. A structure in which X is forced to select Z is unacceptable. Notice that this notion of selection is a principle of any syntactic theory one can design.

Bartlett and González-Vilbazo (2013) study acceptable and unacceptable code-switched DPs among Taiwanese/Spanish deep bilinguals. In a nutshell, a Spanish demonstrative cannot select a Taiwanese classifier because classifiers are not a category that Spanish demonstratives can recognize. But a Spanish demonstrative can select a Taiwanese numeral because Spanish demonstratives can recognize numerals. This is shown in (5) and (6):

(5) Spanish/*Taiwanese*
* estos *tai* *cchia*
these CLS car

(6) Spanish/*Taiwanese*
estos *go* *tai* *cchia*
these four CLS car

Bartlett and González-Vilbazo 2013: 68

We can elaborate beyond Bartlett and González-Vilbazo's proposals and integrate their results in the model presented in these pages. We can assume that Taiwanese *go* and Spanish *cuatro* are two alternative spell-outs for the same root for these bilinguals – call it root √#=4. A Spanish determiner selects for any category of type √# and does not care how it ends up being spelled-out.

This analysis is very much language-specific since it depends on features of the languages involved; in particular, Bartlett and González-Vilbazo are not making the false claim that demonstratives cannot select for classifiers, only that demonstratives in Spanish can't. But, at the same time, the notion of selection can be taken to be a meta-restriction that can be deployed in many different contexts.

Let me now explore another example of a restriction that has been around for a while and suggest a possible path toward its resolution. González-Vilbazo (2005) noticed the contrasts in (7) to (12) among his consultants (English glosses and translations are mine). The examples in (7) and (8) suggest that code-switching between an auxiliary and a participle is unacceptable (although if the auxiliary is Spanish and the participle is German the result improves; see González-Vilbazo and Struckmeier 2008 for discussion):

(7) German/*Spanish*
* Du hast es ihm *contado.*
you have.2 it him.DAT told

González-Vilbazo 2005: 88

(8) *Spanish*/German
* *Me* *ha* *dicho* dass Hans *el* *coche* *vendido* hat.
me. DAT has said that Hans the car sold has

González-Vilbazo 2005: 95

Examples (9) to (12) suggest that code-switching between C and TP is also unacceptable, in parallel with the data presented in Belazi et al. (1994). In the grammatical (9) and (11), C and T are in the same language. In (10) the complementizer is Spanish while T is German and in (12) we see the reverse situation.

(9) German/*Spanish*
El Lehrer *dijo* ***que*** *mañana* *no haría* kommen.
The teacher said that tomorrow NEG do.COND come
'The teacher said he would not come tomorrow.'

(10) German/*Spanish*
* Eduardo denkt ***que*** *Elena* *schreibt* *sich im* *Sekretariat.*
Eduardo thinks that Elena registers SELF in.DEF.DAT secretary's
'Eduardo thinks that Elena registers at the secretary's office.'

(11) German/*Spanish*
Juan sabe **dass** ich mit Clara *en el* *zoológico* verabredet **war**.
Juan knows that I with Clara in the zoo dated was
'Juan knows that I made a date with Clara in the zoo.'

(12) German/*Spanish*
* . . ., **dass** er *mañana* *no* ***haría*** kommen.
that he tomorrow NEG do.COND come
' . . . that he would not come tomorrow.'

González-Vilbazo 2005: 68, 77

The data in (7) to (12) have been reproduced with some code-switching pairs (see in particular Belazi et al. 1994 on the C-TP restriction), but not all, as we shall see in a minute.

In order to provide an analysis of (7) to (12), González-Vilbazo (2005) proposes the *Principle of Functional Restriction*, which he formulates as follows (my translation):

(13) *Principle of Functional restriction* (PFR)
a. Let X and Y be functional categories.
b. Let X and Y be members of the extended projection of the same lexical category.
c. Let L1 and L2 be distinct languages.
d. Then: [XP Spec [X' XL1 [YP Spec [Y' YL1/*L2 ZP]]]]

González-Vilbazo 2005: 67

In other words: it is illegal to code-switch between two functional heads that belong in the same extended projection. This PFR ensures that code-switching between C and T and between an auxiliary and its complement are forbidden, thus accounting for (7) to (12).

Notice that the FPR is very close in spirit and in empirical scope to Belazi et al.'s FHC. The main difference is that the FPR only forbids code-switching between two functional categories, not between a functional category and a lexical category. The FHC also forbids code-switching between a functional category and the lexical head that it selects.

Let's pay closer attention to the formulation of the FHC and the FPR: notice that both are restrictions on the languages of the constituents involved. They exhibit an implicit assumption that the I-language of bilingual code-switchers consists of two languages in combination, precisely the assumption that I argued at the onset of this monograph must be abandoned.

The restriction on code-switching between auxiliary and participle is reconceptualized in López, Alexiadou, and Veenstra (2017), using the phase notion (see Section 3.1 for the notion of phase). Their proposal goes as follows. First, they propose the Block Transfer Hypothesis (BTH):

(14) *Block Transfer Hypothesis* (BTH)
The material that is transferred to the interfaces is sent in one fell swoop.

This seems to be a reasonable consequence of phase theory: the phase material is sent to the interfaces in one shot as soon as the next phase head is merged and all unvalued features are valued. López et al. (2017) argue that the restriction against code-switching between an auxiliary and its complement follows from the BTH. The auxiliary and its complement belong in the same phase, as shown in the following diagram:

(15)

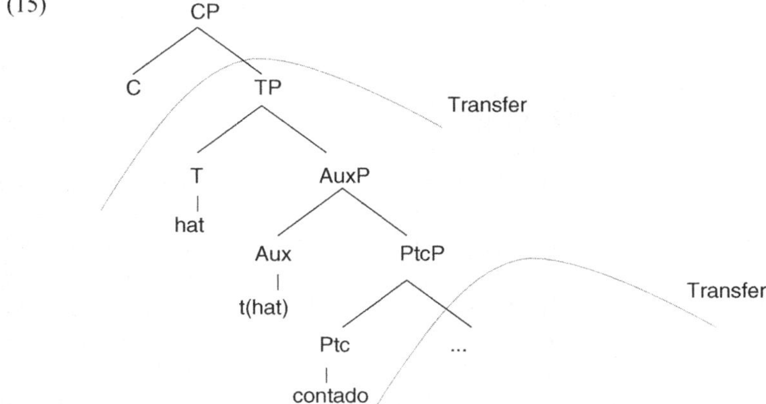

The idea is that if the BTH holds, it should be the case that auxiliary and participle are transferred together to the same PF because if they went to separate PFs, they would violate the BTH. If they are sent to the same PF, it follows that they are "in the same language."

The BTH is not compatible with the conclusions reached in this monograph. Notice that the BTH holds the implicit assumption that bilinguals have two sets of VIRs, one for each PF. But if all VIRs are listed in the same set, nothing prevents inserting vocabulary items from one or the other language as long as they are the best fit for the feature structure of the syntactic terminal – and therefore adopting the BTH does not provide a solution to the original problem. I argued in Section 6.1 that bilingual speakers may have two externalization systems, but this bifurcation only takes place where PF interfaces with the sensorimotor systems. In particular, there is no split competence at any stage in the PF side of the grammar. Therefore, we need to rethink this problem again.

In DM terms, the question of whether the German auxiliary *hat* 'has' can take as a complement the Spanish participle *contado* 'told' reduces to a question of allomorphy: more than one vocabulary item may be inserted in one position and conditions on its feature structure or contextual conditions determine which one goes. As shown in (16), German/Spanish bilinguals have two vocabulary items for the perfect auxiliary, Spanish *haber* (third person pronounced /a/) and German *haben* (third person pronounced as /hat/):

(16)

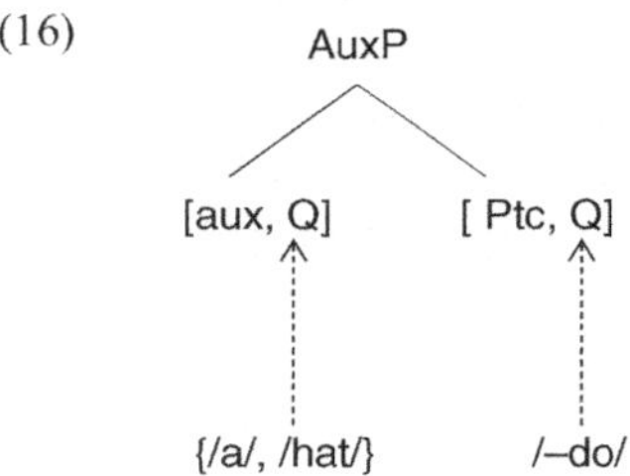

As VI applies from the bottom up, it has already used the Spanish participle form /-do/ to replace Q in the [Ptc,Q] structure. The next step is for either /hat/ or /a/ to replace Q. The grammar necessarily chooses /a/. Why?

I suggest, tentatively, that the reason lies in the feature structure (see Section 4.2). The grammar of perfect aspect in Spanish and German is very different, in terms of word order and prosodic structure (to some extent this can be detected in the examples just cited). If the Spanish aux and the German aux have different feature structures and only the Spanish aux is compatible with the Spanish participle, it follows that the two auxiliaries are not allomorphs and the situation depicted in (16) does not in fact occur – an additional application of the selection meta-restriction. The idea that auxiliaries and participles in

Spanish and German have different properties seems superficially clear – we can detect it in concord and word order. What is not trivial, at least at this point, is what role these differences play in preventing code-switching.

This (admittedly vague) proposal makes a direct prediction: if the two languages involved in code-switching have auxiliaries with the same feature content, code-switching between the auxiliary and the complement should be allowed. In fact, we have some evidence that this is the case. Recall that in Section 4.2 we discussed sentences in Migge (2015) that exemplify precisely this situation in code-switching between two Creole languages:

(17) Sranantongo/*Nengee*

I	kan	*taagi*	en	taki a	tori	dati *mu*	skotu.	Sra/*Nee*
You	can	tell	him	say the	story	that must	end	

Migge 2015: 189

This example shows that code-switching between the modal and the verb is perfectly grammatical, in apparent violation of the PFR as well as the BTH. But let's assume that the choice of one or another auxiliary is a question of allomorphy. Let's further assume that appearances do not deceive and take it as a fact that the grammar of TMA is identical in both languages: TMA and verb have no agreement inflection, word order is the same. If we assume that the feature structure of the auxiliaries in Nengee and Sranantongo must be very similar or identical, it comes as no surprise that auxiliaries from one language can take as a complement a vP in the other (see also Chapter 4, footnote 4).

Let's now turn to the second prediction of the PFR: code-switching between a complementizer and TP is ungrammatical. Notice that in this respect, the PFR and the BTH make different predictions: the BTH should predict that code-switching between C and TP should be acceptable in the general case because C and TP transfer in different phases. As mentioned, the PFR predicts that this type of code-switching should be ungrammatical because C and T are both within the extended projection of the verb.

The data regarding code-switching between C and TP is puzzling. It is indeed documented that this type of code-switching is rejected by consultants who are bilingual in Spanish/German, Spanish/English, and French/Arabic (see in particular Belazi et al. 1994, González-Vilbazo 2005). But this is not always the case. We have seen an example of code-switching between C and TP in Russian/Kazkhan bilinguals, which I repeat here for the reader's convenience:

(18) *Russian*/Kazakh

Chasten'ko	*poluchaetsya*	*shto*	aralastïr-a-mïz
often	occur-rfl-3sg	that	mix-pres.1.pl

'It often occurs that we mix.'

Auer and Muhamedova 2005: 49

Even among the code-switching pairs that Belazi and colleagues and González-Vilbazo describe, the restriction against C-TP code-switching is not absolute. First, it is allowed if there is something in Spec,C (González-Vilbazo and López 2013). In (19), code-switching between the Spanish complementizer *que* and the German T is possible because the position Spec,C is occupied, as represented in (20):

(19) German/*Spanish*
Puesto/ya *que Juan* **ist** spät angekommen . . .
placed/already that Juan is late arrived
'Since Juan arrived late . . . '

(20) [CP puesto [C' que [TP Juan ist spät angekommen]]]

And it is also possible if the subordinate clause is fronted by a wh-phrase (see many examples in Ebert 2014, González-Vilbazo and López 2013):

(21) *English*/Spanish
How many blouses han comprado tus sobrinas *this fall*?
have bought your nieces
Ebert 2014: 102

Thus, it does not seem to me that the PFR holds. But once the PFR is rejected, the unacceptability of sentences like (10) and (12) remains unaccounted for. Again, the example of Spanish/Taiwanese code-switching suggests that a close investigation of the features associated with C and T will be necessary before these puzzles are solved.

Finally, I would like to conclude this section with a few remarks on Alexiadou and Lohndal (2018). In this article, they provide an overview of different strands of data on code-switching within the word and note a number of different asymmetries that have been discussed in the literature. For instance, Esplugisch speakers accept verbs formed on a Spanish root and German morphology but they do not accept the opposite (González-Vilbazo and López 2011: 835):

(22) Spanish/*German*
a. cos-*iren*
sew
b. * näh-*ear*
sew

Their conclusion is that, in the general case, there seems to be an overall requirement that the phonological features of the phase head be respected, and speakers will choose roots and inflectional morphology that best adapt to this condition. But how this condition is fulfilled will vary substantially from one language pair to the next. In (22), for instance, it is the richness of the Spanish *v*, which includes conjugation features, that prevents (22b), as argued in González-Vilbazo and López (2011). Obviously, Alexiadou and Lohndal (2018) is a rich example of the strategy that I propose in these pages.

To conclude this section: A substantial amount of formal work on code-switching tries to account for unacceptable code-switches by hypothesizing universal constraints derived from general properties of the language faculty. It seems that this project is somewhat too ambitious. It is not possible to make broad statements like "code-switching between X and Y is ungrammatical, where X and Y are category labels." On the other hand, it has also been proposed that restrictions on code-switching reduce to restrictions in the grammars of the participating languages, and we have seen that this proposal also has empirical problems. Finally, I have proposed that restrictions on code-switching will emerge from the grammatical properties of the languages involved in a case-by-case basis in tandem with UG-based abstract meta-restrictions.

Appendix B: The Post-Creole Continuum

Since I started this monograph with a discussion of the post-Creole continuum before diving head first into the code-switching data, it seems to me that I cannot quite close it without going back to it and presenting a sketch of the analysis.

In the Introduction, I presented one example of a post-Creole continuum (in (1.3)) and used it as empirical evidence that the I-language of an individual does not consist of compartmentalized units but rather should be regarded as an integrated competence system. Throughout, I also claimed that the MDM model is well suited to formally describe the natural continuum that conforms our I-language. Consequently, the MDM model should also be able to tackle Creole continua. Let's pick the predicate in (1.3) and see how it is made to work. We'll start with the assumption that all of the forms of 'give' that we find in (1.3) are alternative spell-outs of the same root. We see that some spell-outs of 'give' in the past tense require a light verb that carries the past tense morpheme. This past tense can also be spelled out in different ways. I summarize some of the information in (1.3) in the following example:

(1)
a. /gi:/ can be selected by /bɪn/, /dɪ/
b. /gɪ/ can be selected by /bɪn/, /dɪ/, /dɪd/
c. /gɪv/ can be selected by /dɪd/, Ø
d. /geɪv/ can be selected by Ø

On the basis of the generalizations in (1), we can set up the following spell-out rules for [past]:

(2)
1. [past] ⟷ /bɪn/ || ______ {/gi:/, /gɪ/}
2. [past] ⟷ /dɪ/ || ______ {/gi:/, /gɪ/}
3. [past] ⟷ /dɪd/ || ______ {/gɪ/, /gɪv/}
4. [past] ⟷ Ø || ______ {/gɪv/}

The output of the latter rule would then be subject to a readjustment rule that alters the spell out of the root from /gɪv/ to /geɪv/, as in Embick (2015).

The rules in (2) cover only a small set of data and they are certainly simplistic – no doubt the usage of one light verb instead of another triggers other alterations in the clausal structure. Unfortunately, I am not knowledgeable enough to explore these data in depth. The point is simply the following: This sketch shows that a description of Creole continua is intricate, but not indecipherable.

Notes

1 Introduction: Motivating a Unified Linguistic System

1. Throughout this monograph I sometimes use the term "language" in a non-technical manner, as in "Spanish language" or "the bilingual's two languages," etc. Although I don't believe bilinguals have "two languages," I do sometimes use expressions that might look like I sustain the position out of rhetorical expediency. I hope the end result is not too confusing.
2. Parafita, Deuchar, and Fusser (2015) do not find this proportionality – instead, all their subjects gave code-switched sentences the lowest score. I venture that it may be a floor effect due to the type of task.

2 Remarks on Separationist Architectures

1. Myers-Scotton's data on English/Swahili code-switching is based on corpora data enriched with her extensive experience in East Africa. Her consultants typically speak a third language as a native language and acquire English and Swahili via the schooling system and general exposure. Thus, her subjects may not be deep bilinguals as I defined them in the Introduction. However, I believe what Myers-Scotton (1993) describe is quite common in all kinds of bilingual communities.
2. More information on these subjects in Section 9.1.

3 Phases, Distributed Morphology, and Some Contributions from Code-Switching

1. Auer and Muhamedova (2005) provide crucial information regarding the speakers who provide these judgments. They say that in a corpus, when speaking monolingually in Russian, they used default morphology only 7 per cent of the time, which is well within the margin of error for native or near-native speakers. Thus, they probably qualify as deep bilinguals.
2. I adopt the following convention for vocabulary items. Although I represent them with slanted bars / . . . /, I normally use an orthographic representation for the reader's convenience. Sometimes I use an IPA representation if I think it becomes necessary for the discussion.
3. In (35) there is a dotted line with a question mark that goes from List 2 to List 3. This is because I suspect that the actual spell-out of the lexical item may play a role

in the perception of connotations and in idiom interpretation. That is, I am not certain at this point whether a deep Spanish/English bilingual would interpret *patear el cubo* as 'kick the bucket' or whether only the literal meaning is available in their grammar.

4 1Lex in MDM

1. More precisely, the root spells out as 'certif-' and '-icate' is the spell out of $n_{[9/10]}$.
2. *Mutatis mutandis*, this assumption is generally adopted in the psycholinguistics literature (see Kroll and Tokowicz 2001).
3. There is an important challenge to this conclusion: semitic words. As I briefly mentioned in Section 3.3, semitic words are constructed around templates that yield many different exponents with meanings that are both related and idiosyncratic. For instance, the root √pkd yields the verbs 'order', 'be absent', 'deposit' (Kastner 2019: 574). Since semitic roots can embrace a large semantic field in List 3, we do not expect to find among bilingual – e.g., Hebrew/English – speakers roots with two exponents, as we find among Spanish/English or German/Spanish bilinguals. Hampered by my own lack of knowledge, I leave the matter here hoping that future research will clarify the issue.
4. Migge's data comes from a corpus of recordings of conversations. Some of the speakers being recorded are deep bilinguals but others are not (Migge 2015: 186). Thus, I cannot be certain that a sentence like (16) would be pronounced and accepted by a deep bilingual. However, given how tightly interwoven the linguistic materials are, and since we know that only deep bilinguals are good at intrasentential code-switching, I am inclined to assume that this sentence is indeed part of the repertoire of the deep bilingual.
5. In Appendix 1, I go back to this in the context of code-switching between auxiliary and participle in some European languages. The claim in 4.2.2 would lead to the conclusion that unless the auxiliaries of the two languages have exactly the same feature make-up, code-switching should be asymmetric or simply not possible. There is one example that would seem to pose some difficulty to this conclusion. DiSciullo et al. (1986) claim that code-switching between auxiliary and participle is possible among French/Italian bilinguals and show the following example as evidence:

(i) French/*Italian*

No,	parce que	*hanno*	donné	des	cours
no	because	have	given	some	lectures

DiSciullo et al. 1986

Example (i) is cited often, but I am not certain it is a systematic grammatical phenomenon or a simple speech error, and at this point I don't have any information regarding the speaker who produced this sentence.

González-Vilbazo and Struckmeier (2008) argue that there is an asymmetry in Spanish/German code-switching so that code-switching between a Spanish auxiliary and a German participle is possible but code-switching between a German auxiliary and a Spanish participle is not. Giancaspro (2015) and López et al. (2017) argue that it is always ungrammatical in the perfect aspect but grammatical in the progressive. Thus, it seems to be an open issue at this point.

6. *Pace* Harris (1991) and many others who take masculine to be simply the absence of a gender feature: more on this in Section 4.5.
7. Poplack and Dion's (2012) data comes from oral corpora of Quebec French that includes some English material. There is no information regarding the degree of bilingualism of the speakers in the corpora.
8. Backus and Dorleijn (2009) do not provide the actual Dutch verb. I found *opzaleden* in a dictionary.

5 Building the Case for 1Lex: Gender in Code-Switching

1. Munárriz-Ibarrola et al. (2018) present the results of an experiment carried out with different types of Basque/Spanish bilinguals and they did find that many of them used the analogical criterion to choose the gender of the article. They plausibly suggest that language dominance is at play and that Spanish-dominant bilinguals are more likely to use the analogical criterion. For more on this topic, see Parafita Couto et al. (2015).
2. There is some literature that claims that the linguistic environment affects the acceptability of the judgment. Jake et al. (2002) argue that in D+N code-switching the determiner must be in the matrix language. Likewise, Blockzijl, Deuchar, and Parafita Couto (2017) and Parafita and Stadthagen (2019) confirm this tendency: their consultants preferred (i) to (ii):

   (i) Edgar quería estos *shoes*.
   (ii) Edgar quería *these* zapatos.
   Edgar wanted shoes

   However, it seems to me that extracting broad conclusions from these articles might be premature. The sample sentences that they present always involve a direct object adjacent to the verb. Thus, it is hard to say if it is indeed an effect of a matrix language, prosody, or simple adjacency that leads to cliticization – we would need to test sentences in which the direct object is not adjacent or, even better, with a dislocated direct object. I would also like to see if the effect occurs with subject DPs. Additionally, notice that (ii) involves two switches while (i) involves only one, another confounding factor. Lacking a more complete set of evidence and full control of extraneous factors, I remain agnostic with respect to the connection of D+N code-switching and matrix language. See also the experiment reported in Fairchild and Van Hell 2017, where they reported no matrix language effect.
3. Notice that this feature hierarchy is different from what is proposed in Harley and Ritter (2002). These authors lump feminine and masculine together under the value [+animate] and leave neuter in a separate branch as [–animate]. However, as will become clear in the discussion, the Esplugisch data suggests that masculine and neuter share a feature that makes them distinct from feminine.
4. Once again, the VIRs of a bilingual must be somewhat different from those of a monolingual, since a monolingual grammar with only one definiteness feature in their List 1 does not need to specify the contexts of vocabulary insertion for /l-/ and /d-/.
5. In an earlier version of this manuscript that I distributed via Academia, I adopted the assumption that both Spanish D and German D had the same feature structure as

syntactic terminals before spell-out. The separate terminals of Spanish D for gender and number were sprouted during the process of spell-out. As a result, the Spanish and German exponents were allowed to compete. This framework yielded the unacceptability of **der interruptor* 'the switch' correctly but it had two empirical difficulties. The first is that if *el* can compete with a German determiner, one should never get *el brötchen* 'the bun', because *das* would beat *el* any time. In the opposite direction, *los interruptores* 'the switches', which has a specification for gender, would always beat *die interruptores*, which does not. I approached this problem by adopting two optional impoverishment rules. Eventually, I grew disaffected with the ad hoc character of the system and I replaced it with the intuitively more plausible idea that Esplugisch speakers do indeed have two feature structures for D available in their I-language.

6 1PF in MDM

1. Jake et al. (2002) disagree and present a few samples of data, taken from the literature, in which there seems to be word-internal code-switching with complete phonological switch. These data are difficult to evaluate due to lack of information regarding, for example, subjects, specific conditions of production, and so on. In light of the experimental data put forth by Stefanich and Cabrelli (2018), I provisionally put Jake et al.'s (2002) data aside.
2. Akinremi (2016) provides no information as to who her consultants are. I cannot be certain that they are deep bilinguals.

7 Lexical Questions: What Do You Learn When You Learn a Word?

1. Obviously, the works discussed in these pages do not exhaust the number of proposals for the bilingual lexicon that have been proposed in the literature: Athanapoulos (2015) and Williams (2015) provide much more insightful and complete surveys than I can offer in these pages. Rather, the purpose is to exemplify how the MDM 1Lex works and seek possible avenues where scholars of different traditions may find common ground.

8 Psycho-Syntactic Questions: Acquisition, Priming and Co-activation, and a Note on Processing Cost

1. One drawback of Hatzidaki et al. (2010) is that their definition of bilingual is probably much broader than the one that we use here. There is no information in this article regarding the age when the subjects began to learn English (their second language) and there is no measure of their proficiency except their self-report.
2. Pickering and Ferreira (2008) find that an English passive does not prime a German passive. As Pickering and Ferreira note, the word order in both languages is different, where German has the 'by-phrase' before the participle and English has it after the participle. They argue that this order difference prevents priming. I would add that

the auxiliary is also different because passive in German is built around the auxiliary *werden*, which is otherwise glossed as 'become'. In my model, this means that the model in (22) has to be enriched in (22.5) with content regarding the auxiliary involved in the structure. It also means that the Hartsuiker et al.'s (2004) model in (21), in which "passive" is simply a node in the structure, would require a substantial modification. It would be interesting to explore if English passive triggers passive in languages that do not use an auxiliary to form it, as in most non-Indo-European languages. It would also be of interest to see if there could be priming between structures that are only partially similar, for instance, between unaccusative and passive.

3. The bilinguals in these experiments are clearly not deep bilinguals but persons who learned a second language in adulthood. It would be interesting to replicate these experiments with deep bilinguals. My own guess is that deeper exposure to the second language should favor priming.

9 Convergent and Divergent Paths

1. However, in Alexiadou et al. (2015) they do show examples of an English determiner taking a Norwegian noun phrase as complement:

(i) *English*/Norwegian
the engst eung-en
only child-DEF

(ii) *the* by
city

References

Acquaviva, Paolo. 2009. Roots and lexicality in Distributed Morphology. *York Papers in Linguistics Series* 2: 1–21.

Adamou, Evangelia and Xingjia R. Shen. 2019. There are no language switching costs when codeswitching is frequent. *International Journal of Bilingualism* 23(1): 53–70.

Adger, David, and Jennifer Smith. 2010. Variation in agreement: A lexical feature-based approach. *Lingua* 120: 1109–1134.

Aikhenvald, Alexandra. 2006. Grammars in contact: A cross-linguistic perspective. In Alexandra Aikhenvald and Robert M. W. Dixon (eds.), *Areal Grammars in Contact: A Crosslinguistic Typology*. Oxford: Oxford University Press, pp. 1–66.

Akinremi, Ihuoma. 2016. Phonological adaptation and morphosyntactic integration in Igbo-English insertional codeswitching. *Journal of Universal Language* 17(1): 53–79.

Alexiadou, Artemis, and Terje Lohndal. 2017. On the division of labor between roots and functional structure. In Roberta D'Alessandro, Irene Franco, and Angel Gallego (eds.), *The Verbal Domain*. Oxford University Press, pp. 85–104.

Alexiadou, Artemis, and Terje Lohndal. 2018. Units of language mixing: A cross-linguistic perspective. *Frontiers in Psychology* 19, Article 1719.

Alexiadou, Artemis, and Gereon Müller. 2008. Class features as probes. In Asaf Bachrach and Andrew Nevins (eds.), *Inflectional Identity*. Oxford University Press, pp. 101–155.

Alexiadou, Artemis, Terje Lohndal, Tor Åfarli, and Maren Berg Grimstad. 2015. Language mixing: A Distributed Morphology approach. In Thuy Bui and Denis Ozildiz (eds.), *Proceedings of NELS*. Amherst, MA: GLSA Publications, pp. 25–38.

Amaral, Luiz, and Tom Roeper. 2014. Multiple grammars and second language representation. *Second Language Research* 30(1): 3–36.

Ameel, E., B. Malt, G. Storms, and S. Sloman. 2005. How bilinguals solve the naming problem. *Journal of Memory and Language* 53: 60–80.

Arad, Maya. 2003. Locality constraints on the interpretation of roots: The case of Hebrew denominal verbs. *Natural Language and Linguistic Theory* 21: 737–778.

Arregi, Karlos, and Andrew Nevins. 2012. *Morphotactics: Basque Auxiliaries and the Structure of Spellout*. Studies in Natural Language and Linguistic Theory 86. Dordrecht: Springer.

Athanasopoulos, Panos. 2009. Cognitive representation of colour in bilinguals: The case of Greek blues. *Bilingualism: Language and Cognition* 12: 83–95.

Athanasopoulos, Panos. 2015. Conceptual Representation in bilinguals. In John Schwieter (ed.), *The Cambridge Handbook of Bilingual Processing*. Cambridge University Press, pp. 275–292.

Athanasopoulos, Panos, B. Dering, A. Wigget, J. Kuipers, and G. Thierry. 2010. Perceptual shift in bilingualism: Brain potentials reveal plasticity in pre-attentive colour perception. *Cognition* 116: 437–443.

Auer, Peter, and R. Muhamedova. 2005. "Embedded language" and "matrix language" in insertional language mixing: Some problematic cases. *Rivista di Linguistica* 17: 35–54.

Backus, Ad, and Margreet Dorleijn. 2009. Loan translations versus code-switching. In Barbara Bullock and Jacqueline Toribio (eds.), *The Cambridge Handbook of Linguistic Code-Switching*. Cambridge University Press, pp. 75–94.

Badiola, Lucía, Rodrigo Delgado, Ariane Sande, and Sara Stefanich. 2018. Code switching attitudes and their effects on acceptability judgment tasks. *Linguistic Approaches to Bilingualism* 8(1): 5–24.

Badiola, Lucía, and Ariane Sande. 2018. Gender assignment in Basque mixed Determiner Phrases: A study of Gernika Basque. In Luis López (ed.), *Code-switching: Experimental Answers to Theoretical Questions*. Amsterdam: John Benjamins, pp. 15–38.

Bandi-Rao, Shoba, and Marcel DenDikken. 2014. Light switches: On v as a pivot in code-switching, and the nature of the ban on word-internal switches. In Jeff MacSwan (ed.), *Grammatical Theory and Bilingual Code-switching*. Cambridge, MA: MIT Press, pp. 161–184.

Bangor Miami Corpus. http://bangortalk.org.uk/speakers.php?c=miami.

Bartlett, Laura, and Kay González-Vilbazo. 2013. The structure of the Taiwanese DP in Taiwanese-Spanish bilinguals: Evidence from code-switching. *Journal of East Asian Linguistics* 22: 65–99.

Basnight-Brown, D. M., and J. Altarriba. 2007. Differences in semantic and translation priming across languages: The role of language direction and language dominance. *Memory & Cognition* 35, 953–965.

Belazi, Hedi, Ed Rubin, and Jacqueline A. Toribio. 1994. Code switching and X-bar theory: The functional head constraint. *Linguistic Inquiry* 25(2): 221–237.

Bell, R. T. 1976. *Sociolinguistics: Goals, Approaches and Problems*. London: Batsford.

Bittner, Maria, and Ken Hale. 1996. The structural determination of case and agreement. *Linguistic Inquiry* 27: 1–68.

Blanco-Elorrieta, Esti, Karen Emmorey, and Liina Pylkkänen. 2018. Language switching decomposed through MEG and evidence from bimodal bilinguals. *PNAS*.

Blokzijl, Jeffrey, Margaret Deuchar, and Maria Carmbe Parafita Couto. 2017. Determiner asymmetry in mixed nominal constructions: The role of grammatical factors in data from Miami and Nicaragua. *Languages* 2(4). doi:10.3390/languages2040020.

Bonet, Eulàlia. 1995. Feature structure of Romance clitics. *Natural Language and Linguistic Theory* 13: 607–647.

Borer, Hagit. 2013. *Taking Form*. Oxford University Press.

Boutonnet, Bastien, Panos Athanasopoulos, and Guillaume Thierry. 2012. Unconscious effects of grammatical gender during object categorisation. *Brain Research* 1479: 72–79.

Branchini, Chiara, and Caterina Donati. 2016. Assessing lexicalism through bimodal eyes. *Glossa* 1(1), Article 48: 1–30.

Branigan, Holly, and Martin J. Pickering. Forthcoming. An experimental approach to linguistic representation. *Behavioral and Brain Sciences*.

Brysbaert, Marc, and Wouter Duyk. 2010. Is it time to leave behind the Revised Hierarchical Model of bilingual language processing after fifteen years of service? *Bilingualism: Language and Cognition* 13(3): 359–371.

Büring, Daniel, and R. Gutiérrez-Bravo. 2001. Focus related word order variation without the NSR: A prosody-based crosslinguistic analysis. In James McCloskey (ed.), *SASC 3: Syntax and Semantics at Santa Cruz*. Santa Cruz: Linguistics Research Center, University of California.

Campbell, Alistair. 1962. *Old English Grammar*. Revised edition. Oxford University Press.

Cantone, Katja. 2007. *Code Switching in Bilingual Children*. Studies in Theoretical Psycholinguistics 37. Dordrecht: Springer.

Cantone, Katja, and Natascha Müller. 2008. *Un nase* or *una nase*? What gender marking within switched DPs reveals about the architecture of the bilingual language faculty. *Lingua* 118: 810–826.

Carstens, Vicki. 1991. DP Structure in KiSwahili. PhD dissertation, University of California, Los Angeles.

Carstens, Vicki. 2000. Concord in minimalist theory. *Linguistic Inquiry* 31(2): 319–355.

Chomsky, Noam. 1995. *The Minimalist Program*. Cambridge, MA: MIT Press.

Chomsky, Noam. 2000. Minimalist inquiries: The framework. In Roger Martin, David Michaels and Juan Uriagereka (eds.), *Step by Step: Essays on Minimalist Syntax in Honor of Howard Lasnik*. Cambridge, MA: MIT Press, pp. 89–155.

Chomsky, Noam. 2001. Derivation by phase. In Michael Kenstowicz (ed.), *Ken Hale: A Life in Language*. Cambridge, MA: MIT Press, pp. 1–52.

Chomsky, Noam. 2007. Approaching UG from below. In Uli Sauerland and Hans Martin Gärtner (eds.), *Interfaces + Recursion = Language?* Berlin: Mouton de Gruyter, pp. 1–31.

Chomsky, Noam. 2008. On phases. In R. Freidin, C. P. Otero and M. L. Zubizarreta (eds.), *Foundational Issues in Linguistic Theory*. Cambridge, MA: MIT Press, pp. 133–66.

Cinque, Guglielmo. 1999. *Adverbs and Functional Heads*. Cambridge, MA: MIT Press.

Citko, Barbara. 2014. *Phase Theory: An Introduction*. Cambridge University Press.

Clegg, Jens. 2006. Lone English-origin nouns in the Spanish of New Mexico: A variationist analysis of phonological and morphological adaptation. PhD dissertation, University of New Mexico.

Cocchi, Gloria, and Cristina Pierantozzi. 2012. Nominal gender agreement outside the DP domain in code-switching. *Lingue e Linguaggio* 16(1): 35–62.

Collins, Chris, and Philip Branigan. 1997. Quotative inversion. *Natural Language and Linguistic Theory* 15: 1–41.

Costa, João. 2004. *Subject Positions and Interfaces: The Case of European Portuguese*. Berlin: Mouton de Gruyter.

De Houwer, Anneke. 1990. *The Acquisition of Two Languages from Birth: A Case Study*. Cambridge University Press.

De Houwer, Anneke. 2005. Early bilingual acquisition. In Judith Kroll and Annette de Groot (eds.), *Handbook of Bilingualism*. Oxford University Press, pp. 30–48.

Delgado, Rodrigo. 2018. The familiar and the strange: Gender assignment in Spanish/English mixed DPs. In Luis López (ed.), *Code-Switching: Experimental Answers to Theoretical Questions*. Amsterdam: John Benjamins, pp. 39–62.

Delgado, Rodrigo. 2019. The *mesa*: The phonetics of English/Spanish code-switched determiner phrases. Poster presented at *Bilingualism in the Hispanic and Lusophone Worlds*, Leiden University, January 10.

DenDikken, Marcel. 2011. The distributed morphology of code-switching. Paper presented at UIC Bilingualism Forum.

Deuchar, Margaret, and Teresa Biberauer. 2016. Doubling: An error or an illusion. *Bilingualism: Language and Cognition* 19(5): 881–882.

Deuchar, Margaret, and Jonathan Stammers. 2016. English-origin verbs in Welsh: Adjudicating between two theoretical approaches. *Languages* 1, 7.

Dijkstra, Ton. 2005. Bilingual visual word recognition and lexical access. In Judith Kroll and Annette de Groot (eds.), *Handbook of Bilingualism*. Oxford University Press, pp. 179–201.

DiSciullo, A.-M., Peter Muysken and R. Singh. 1986. Government and code-switching. *Journal of Linguistics* 22: 1–24.

Ebert, Shane. 2014. The morphosyntax of wh-questions: Evidence from Spanish-English code-switching. PhD dissertation, University of Illinois in Chicago. https://hip.uic.edu/research-groups/brl/our-research/.

Ebert, Shane, and Bradley Hoot. 2018. That-trace effects in Spanish-English code-switching. In Luis López (ed.), *Code-Switching: Experimental Answers to Theoretical Questions*. Amsterdam: John Benjamins, pp. 101–146.

Eichler, Nadine, Veronika Jansen, and Natascha Müller. 2013. Gender acquisition in bilingual children: French-German, Italian-German, Spanish-German and Italian-French. *International Journal of Bilingualism* 17: 550–572.

Embick, David. 2010. *Localism versus Globalism in Morphology and Phonology*. Cambridge, MA: MIT Press.

Embick, David. 2015. *The Morpheme*. Berlin: Mouton de Gruyter.

Embick, David, and Rolph Noyer. 2001. Movement operations after syntax. *Linguistic Inquiry* 32(4): 555–595.

Embick, David, and Rolph Noyer. 2007. Distributed morphology and the syntax/morphology interface. In *The Oxford Handbook of Linguistic Interfaces*. Oxford University Press, pp. 289–324.

Emmorey, K., H. B. Borinstein, R. Thompson, and T. H. Gollan. 2008. Bimodal bilingualism. *Bilingualism: Language and Cognition* 11(1): 43–61.

Estomba, Diego. 2016. El género sintáctico y la proyección functional del nombre. MA Thesis, Universidad del Comahue.

Evans, Vyvyan. 2015. What's in a concept? Analog versus parametric concepts in LCCM theory. In Eric Margolis and Stephen Laurence (eds.), *The Conceptual Mind: New Directions in the Study of Concepts*. Cambridge, MA: MIT Press, pp. 251–290.

Fairchild, Sarah, and Janet Van Hell. 2017. Determiner-noun code-switching in Spanish heritage speakers. *Bilingualism: Language and Cognition* 20(1): 150–161.

Fernández Fuertes, Raquel, Juana M. Liceras, and Anahí Alba de la Fuente. 2016. Beyond the subject DP versus the subject pronoun divide in agreement switches. In Christina Tortorra, Marcel de Dikken, Ignacio Montoya, and Teresa O'Neill (eds.),

Romance Linguistics 2013: Selected papers from the 43rd Linguistic Symposium of Romance Languages. Amsterdam: John Benjamins, pp. 79–91.

Finer, Daniel. 2014. Movement triggers and relativization in Korean-English Code Switching. In Jeff MacSwan (ed.), *Grammatical Theory and Bilingual Code-Switching*. Cambridge, MA: MIT Press, pp. 37–62.

Frascarelli, Mara. 2007. Subjects, topics and the interpretation of referential pro. *Natural Language and Linguistic Theory* 25: 691–734.

Fukui, Naoki, and Mamoru Saito. 1998. Order in phrase structure and movement. *Linguistic Inquiry* 29(3): 439–474.

Genesee, Fred, Elena Nicoladis, and Johanne Paradis. 1995. Language differentiation in bilingual development. *Journal of Child Language* 22: 611–631.

Giancaspro, David. 2015. Code-switching at the auxiliary-VP boundary. *Linguistic Approaches to Bilingualism* 5(3): 379–407.

Goddard, C., and A. Wierzbicka. 2014. *Words and Meanings: Lexical Semantics across Domains, Languages and Cultures*. Oxford and New York: Oxford University Press.

Goldrick, Matt, Michael Putnam, and Linda Schwartz. 2016. Coactivation in bilingual grammars: A computational account of code mixing. *Bilingualism: Language and Cognition* 19: 857–876.

González-Vilbazo, Kay. 2005. Die Syntax des Code-Switching. PhD dissertation, Universität zu Köln.

González-Vilbazo, Kay, and Luis López. 2011. Some properties of light verbs in codeswitching. *Lingua* 121, 832–850.

González-Vilbazo, Kay, and Luis López. 2012. Little v and parametric variation. *Natural Language & Linguistic Theory* 30(1): 33–77.

González-Vilbazo, Kay, and Luis López. 2013. *Phase Switching*. Unpublished manuscript, University of Illinois in Chicago. https://uic.academia.edu/LuisLopez.

González-Vilbazo, Kay, and Volker Struckmeier. 2008. Asymmetrien im Code-Switching: Eine DM-Lösung zur Partizipselektion. In Guido Mensching and Eva Remberger (eds.), *Romanistische Sprachwissenschaft: minimalistisch*. Tübingen: G. Narr Verlag, pp. 83–102.

Grimshaw, Jane. 1991. Extended Projection. Brandeis University manuscript.

Grimstad, Maren Berg, Terje Lohndal, and Tor A. Åfarli. 2014. Language mixing and exoskeletal theory: A case study of word-internal mixing in American Norwegian. *Nordlyd* 41(2): 213–237, special issue on Features edited by Martin Krämer, Sandra Ronai, and Peter Svenonius. University of Tromsø – The Arctic University of Norway. http://septentrio.uit.no/index.php/nordlyd.

Grosjean, F. 1982. *Life with Two Languages: An Introduction to Bilingualism*. Cambridge, MA: Harvard University Press.

Gullberg, Marianne, Peter Indefrey, and Pieter Muysken. 2009. Research techniques for the study of code-switching. In Barbara Bullock and Jacqueline Toribio (eds.), *The Cambridge Handbook of Linguistic Code-Switching*. Cambridge University Press, pp. 21–39.

Halle, M. 1997. Distributed morphology: Impoverishment and fission. In Benjamin Bruening, Y. Kang, and Martha Jo McGinnis (eds.), *Papers at the Interface. MIT Working Papers in Linguistics 30*, pp. 425–449.

Halle, Morris, and Alec Marantz. 1993. *Distributed Morphology and the Pieces of Inflection*. In Ken Hale and S. Jay Keyser (eds.), *The View from Building 20*. Cambridge, MA: MIT Press, pp. 111–176.

Halle, Morris, and Alec Marantz. 1994. Some key features of distributed morphology. *MIT Working Papers in Linguistics* 21: 275–288.

Hannahs, S. J. 2013. *The Phonology of Welsh*. Oxford University Press.

Harley, Heidi. 2014. On the identity of roots. *Theoretical Linguistics* 40(3/4): 225–276.

Harley, Heidi, and Rolph Noyer. 2000. Formal versus encyclopedic properties of vocabulary: Evidence from nominalizations. In Bert Peeters (ed.), *The Lexicon-Encyclopedia Interface*. Amsterdam: Elsevier Press, pp. 349–374.

Harley, Heidi, and Elizabeth Ritter. 2002. Person and number in pronouns: A feature geometric analysis. *Language* 78: 482–526.

Harris, Jim. 1991. The exponence of gender in Spanish. *Linguistic Inquiry* 22: 27–62.

Hartsuiker, Robert, Martin J. Pickering, and Eline Veltkamp. 2004. Is syntax separate or shared between languages? *Psychological Science* 15: 409–415.

Hatzidaki, A., H. P. Branigan, and J. Pickering. 2010. Co-activation of syntax in bilingual language production. *Cognitive Psychology* 62(2): 123–150.

Heil, Jeanne. 2015. Infinitivals at the end state: Evidence for L2 acquisition of English non-finite complementation. Unpublished dissertation, University of Illinois in Chicago.

Herring, Jon Russell, Margaret Deuchar, M. Carmen Parafita, and Mónica Moro. 2010. "*I saw the* madre." Evaluating predictions about codeswitched determiner-noun sequences using Spanish-English and Welsh-English data. *International Journal of Bilingual Education and Bilingualism* 13(5): 553–573.

Hoot, Bradley, and Luis López. 2012. The I-language of bilinguals. Paper presented at Bilingualism Research Forum, University of Illinois in Chicago, October 5.

Hualde, José Ignacio, and Jon Ortiz de Urbina. 2003. *A Grammar of Basque*. Berlin: Mouton de Gruyter.

Hulk, Aafke, and Natascha Müller. 2000. Bilingual first language acquisition at the interface between syntax and pragmatics. *Bilingualism: Language and Cognition* 4: 227–244.

Jake, Janice, Carol Myers-Scotton, and S. Gross. 2002. How to make a minimalist approach to codeswitching work: Adding the matrix language. *Bilingualism, Language and Cognition* 5: 61–91.

Jarvis, Scott, and Aneta Pavlenko. 2008. *Crosslinguistic Influence in Language and Cognition*. New York: Routledge.

Joshi, Aravind. 1985. Processing sentences with intrasentential code-switching. In David Dowty, Laurie Karttunen, and Arnold Zwicky (eds.), *Natural Language Parsing: Psychologica, Computational and Theoretical Perspectives*. Cambridge, UK: Cambridge University Press, pp. 206–250.

Kamp, Hans, and Uwe Reyle. 1993. *From Discourse to Logic: Introduction to Modeltheoretic Semantics of Natural Language, Formal Logci and Discourse Representation Theory*. Springer: Dordrecht.

Kastner, Itamar. 2019. Templatic morphology as an emergent property. *Natural Language and Linguistic Theory* 37: 571–619.

Kato, Mary. 2003. Child L2 acquisition: An insider account. In Natascha Müller (ed.), *(In)vulnerable Domains in Multilingualism*, Amsterdam/Philadelphia: John Benjamins, pp. 271–293.

Kayne, Richard. 1993. *The Antisymmetry of Syntax*. Cambridge, MA: MIT Press.

Kihm, A. 2005. Noun class, gender, and the lexicon-syntax-morphology interfaces: A comparative study of Niger-Congo and Romance languages. In Guglielmo Cinque and Richard Kayne (eds.), *Comparative Syntax*. Oxford University Press, pp. 459–512.

Klassen, Rachel, and Juana M. Liceras. 2017. The representation of gender in the mind of Spanish-English bilinguals: Insights from code-switched adjectival predicates. *Borealis: An International Journal or Hispanic Linguistics* 6: 77–96.

Koeneman, Olaf, and Hedde Zeijlstra. 2017. *Introducing Syntax*. Cambridge University Press.

Köppe, Regina. 1996. Language differentiation in bilingual children: The development of grammatical and pragmatic competence. *Linguistics* 34: 927–954.

Koronkiewicz, Bryan. 2014. Pronoun categorization: Evidence from Spanish-English code-switching. PhD dissertation, University of Illinois in Chicago. https://hip.uic.edu/research-groups/brl/our-research/.

Koulidobrova, Helena. 2012. When the Quiet Surfaces: "Transfer" of Argument Omission in the Speech of ASL-English Bilinguals. PhD dissertation, University of Connecticut.

Kramer, Ruth. 2015. *The Morphosyntax of Gender*. Oxford University Press.

Kroll, Judith F., Paola E. Dussias, Kinsey Bice, and Lauren Perrotti. 2015. Bilingualism, mind, and brain. *Annual Review of Linguistics* 1: 377–394.

Kroll, Judith F., and E. Stewart. 1994. Category interference in translation and picture naming: Evidence for asymmetric connections between bilingual memory representations. *Journal of Memory and Language* 33: 149–174.

Kroll, Judith F., and Natasha Tokowicz. 2001. The development of conceptual representation for words in a second language. In J. Nicol (ed.), *One Mind, Two Languages: Bilingual Language Processing*. Explaining Linguistics 2. Malden, MA: Blackwell, pp. 49–71.

Kroll, Judith F., and Natasha Tokowicz. 2005. *Models of Bilingual Representation and Processing: Looking Back and to the Future*. In Judith Kroll and A. M. B. De Groot (eds.), *Handbook of Bilingualism: Psycholinguistic Approaches*. Oxford University Press, pp. 531–553.

Kroll, Judith F., Janette van Hell, Natasha Tokowicz, and D. W. Green. 2010. The Revised Hierarchical Model: A critical review and assessment. *Bilingualism: Language and Cognition* 13: 373–381.

kučerová, Ivona. 2018. ϕ-features at the syntax-semantics interface: evidence from nominal inflection. *Linguistic Inquiry* 49(4): 813–45.

Laka, Itziar. 1990. The Syntax of Negation. PhD dissertation, MIT.

Levin, Beth, and Martha Rappaport-Hovav. 2005. *Argument Structure*. Cambridge University Press.

Liceras, Juana M. 2016. Linguistic theory and the synthesis model: Beyond feature matching restrictions. *Linguistic Approaches to Bilingualism* 6: 776–781.

Liceras, Juana M., Raquel Fernández Fuertes, and Rachel Klassen. 2016. Language dominance and language nativeness. The view from English-Spanish codeswitching. In Rosa Guzzardo, Catherine Mazak, and M.Carmen Parafita Couto (eds.), *Spanish-English Codeswitching in the Caribbean and the US*. Amsterdam/Philadelphia: John Benjamins, pp. 107–138.

Liceras, Juana M., Raquel Fernández Fuertes, S. Perales, and K. T. Spradlin. 2008. Gender and gender agreement in bilingual native and non-native grammars: A view from child and adult functional-lexical mixings. *Lingua* 118: 827–851.

Lillo-Martin, Diane, Ronice Müller de Quadros, and Deborah Chen Pichlet. 2016. The development of bimodal bilingualism. *Linguistic Approaches to Bilingualism*. 6: 776–781.

Lillo-Martin, Diane, Ronice Müller de Quadros, Helen Koulidobrova, and Deborah Chen Pichler. 2010. Bimodal Bilingual Cross-Language Influence in Unexpected Domains. Proceedings of GALA.

Lipski, John. 1985. *Linguistic Aspects of Spanish-English Language Switching*. Tempe: Center for Latin American Studies, Arizona State University.

Litcofsky, Kaitlyn, and Janet Van Hell. 2017. Switching direction affects switching costs: Behavioral, ERP and time-frequency analyses of intra-sentential code-switching. *Neuropsychologia* 97: 112–139.

Lohndal, Terje. 2014. *Phrase Structure and Argument Structure*. Oxford University Press.

López, Luis. 2007. *Locality and the Architecture of Syntactic Dependencies*. London: Palgrave.

López, Luis. 2009. Ranking the linear correspondence axiom. *Linguistic Inquiry* 40(2), 239–276.

López, Luis. 2016. Questions on data and input to GEN. *Bilingualism, Language and Cognition* 19: 889–890. doi:10.1017/S1366728916000079.

López, Luis. 2019. *Case, concord and the origins of default*. University of Illinois in Chicago, manuscript. Academia.edu

López, Luis, Artemis Alexiadou, and Tonjes Veenstra. 2017. Code switching by phase. *Languages 2*(3): 9. doi:10.3390/languages2030009

Luque, Alicia, Nethaum Mizyed, and Kara Morgan-Short. 2018. Event-related potentials reveal evidence for syntactic co-activation in bilingual language processing. In Luis López (ed.), *Code-Switching: Experimental Answers to Theoretical Questions*. Amsterdam: John Benjamins, pp. 175–192.

MacSwan, Jeff. 1999. *A Minimalist Approach to Intrasentential Code Switching*. New York: Garland Press.

MacSwan, Jeff. 2000. The architecture of the bilingual language faculty: evidence from intrasentential code switching. *Bilingualism, Language and Cognition* 3(1): 37–54.

MacSwan, Jeff. 2005. Code-switching and generative grammar: A critique of the MLF model and some remarks on "modified minimalism." *Bilingualism, Language and Cognition* 8(1): 1–22.

MacSwan, Jeff. 2014. Programs and proposals in codeswitching research. In Jeff MacSwan (ed.), *Grammatical Theory and Bilingual Codeswitching*. Cambridge, MA: MIT Press, pp. 1–34.

MacSwan, Jeff. 2017. A multilingual perspective on translanguaging. *American Educational Research Journal* 54: 167–201.

MacSwan, Jeff, and Sonia Colina. 2014. Some consequences of language design: Codeswitching and the PF interface. In Jeff MacSwan (ed.), *Grammatical Theory and Bilingual Codeswitching*. Cambridge, MA: MIT Press, pp. 185–210.

Mahootian, Shahrzad. 1993. A null theory of code-switching. PhD dissertation, Northwestern University.

Mahootian, Shahrzad, and Beatrice Santorini. 1996. Code switching and the complement/adjunct distinction. *Linguistic Inquiry* 27(3): 464–479.

Makoni, Sinfree, and Alistair Pennycook. 2007. Disinventing and reconstituting languages. In Sinfree Makoni and Alistair Pennycook (eds.), *Disinventing and Reconstituting Languages*. Clevedon, UK: Multilingual Matters, pp. 1–41.

Malt, Barbara C., Silvia Gennari, Mutsumi Imai, Eef Ameel, Noburo Saji, and Asifa Majid. 2015. Where are the concepts? What words can and can't reveal. In Eric Margolis and Stephen Laurence (eds.), *The Conceptual Mind*. Cambridge, MA: MIT Press, pp. 291–326.

Marantz, Alec. 1997. No escape from syntax: Don't try morphological analysis in the privacy of your own lexicon. In Alexis Dimitradis et al. (eds.), *Proceedings of the 21st Penn Linguistics Colloquium*. Philadelphia: University of Pennsylvania. Upenn Working Papers in Linguistics, pp. 221–225.

Meisel, Jürgen. 2011. Bilingual language acquisition and theories of diachronic change: Bilingualism as cause and effect of grammatical change. *Bilingualism: Language and Cognition* 14: 121–145.

Meisel, Jürgen. 2012. Remarks on the acquisition of Basque-Spanish bilingualism. *International Journal of Bilingualism* 17: 392–399.

Migge, Bettina. 2015. The role of discursive information in analyzing multilingual practices. In Kofi Yakpo and Gerald Stell (eds.), *Code-Switching Between Structural and Sociolinguistic Perspectives*. Berlin: Mouton de Gruyter, pp. 185–206.

Montrul, Silvina. 2004. *The Acquisition of Spanish: Morphosyntactic Development in Monolingual and Bilingual L1 Acquisition and in Adult L2 Acquisition*. [Series on Language Acquisition and Language Disorders]. Amsterdam: John Benjamins.

Moro Quintanilla, Mónica. 2014. The semantic interpretation and syntactic distribution of determiner phrases in Spanish-English codeswitching. In J. MacSwan (ed.), *Grammatical Theory and Bilingual Codeswitching*. Cambridge, MA: MIT Press, pp. 213–226.

Munárriz-Ibarrola, Amaia, Varun de Castro-Arrazola, Maria Carmen Parafita Couto, and María José Ezeizabarrena. 2018. Gender in Spanish-Basque mixed DPs: Evidence from a "forced" elicitation task. Paper presented at the Bilingualism Research Forum, University of Illinois in Chicago, October 12.

Muntendam, Antje. 2013. On the nature of cross-linguistic transfer: A case study of Andean Spanish. *Bilingualism: Language and Cognition* 16(1): 111–131.

Muysken, Pieter. 2000. *Bilingual Speech*. Cambridge University Press.

Muysken, Pieter. 2012. Spanish affixes in the Quechua languages: A multidimensional perspective. *Lingua* 122: 481–493.

Myers-Scotton, Carol. 1993. *Duelling Languages*. Oxford: Clarendon Press.

Myers-Scotton, Carol. 2002. *Contact Linguistics*. Oxford: Oxford University Press.

Myers-Scotton, Carol, and Janice Jake. 2009. A universal model of code-switching and bilingual language processing and production. In Barbara Bullock and Jacqueline Toribio (eds.), *The Cambridge Handbook of Linguistic Code-Switching*. Cambridge University Press, pp. 336–357.

Nas, G. 1983. Visual word recognition in bilinguals: Evidence for a cooperation between visual and sound based codes during access to a common lexical store. *Journal of Verbal Learning and Verbal Behavior* 22: 526–534.

Oltra-Massuet, Olga. 1999. On the constituent structure of Catalan verbs. In Karlos Arregi, Benjamin Bruening, Cornelia Krause, and Vivian Lin (eds.), *Papers on Morphology and Syntax, MITWPL 33*. Cambridge, MA: Department of Linguistics and Philosophy, MIT, pp. 279–322.

Oltra-Massuet, Olga, and Karlos Arregi. 2005. Stress by structure in Spanish. *Linguistic Inquiry* 36(1), 43–84.

Otheguy, Ricardo. 1993. A reconsideration of the notion of loan translation in the analysis of U.S. Spanish. In A. Roca and J. Lipski (eds.), *Spanish in the United States: Linguistic contact and diversity*. Mouton de Gruyter: New York, pp. 21–45.

Otheguy, Ricardo. 2007. La filología y el unicornio: el verdadero referente del vocablo *Spanglish* y su función como adjudicador de posiciones de poder en la población de origen hispano en los EEUU. In Enric Serra (ed.), *La incidencia del contexto en los discursos*. LynX, Annexa 14, pp. 5–19.

Otheguy, Ricardo, and Naomi Lapidus. 2003. An adaptive approach to noun gender in New York contact Spanish. In Rafael Núñez-Cedeño, Luis López, and Richard Cameron (eds.), *A Romance Perspective on Language Knowledge and Use*. Amsterdam: John Benjamins, pp. 209–229.

Otheguy, Ricardo, Ofelia García, and Wallis Reid. 2015. Clarifying translanguaging and deconstructing named languages: A perspective from linguistics. *Applied Linguistics Review* 6: 281–307.

Paradis, Michel. 2007. The neurofunctional components of the bilingual cognitive system. In Istvan Kecskes and Liliana Albertazzi (eds.), *Cognitive Aspects of Bilingualism*. Dordrecht: Springer, pp. 3–28.

Parafita, Carmen, Margaret Deuchar and Marika Fusser. 2015. How do Welsh-English bilinguals deal with conflict? Adjective-noun order resolution. In G. Stell and K. Yakpo (eds.), *Code-switching at the crossroads between structural and socio-linguistic perspectives*. Mouton de Gruyter, pp. 65–84.

Parafita Couto M. C., A. Munarriz, I. Epelde, M. Deuchar, and B. Oyharçabal. 2015. Gender conflict resolution in Basque-Spanish mixed DPs. *Bilingualism: Language and Cognition* 18(2): 304–323.

Parafita Couto, Carmen, and Marianne Gullberg. 2017. Code-switching within the noun phrase: Evidence from three corpora. *International Journal of Bilingualism*. 23(2), pp. 695–714.

Parafita Couto, Carmen, and Hans Stadthagen. 2019. El book or the libro? Insights from acceptability judgments into determiner/noun code-switches. *International Journal of Bilingualism* 23(1), 349–360.

Pavlenko, Aneta. 2009. Conceptual representation in the bilingual lexicon and second language vocabulary learning. In Aneta Pavlenko (ed.), *The Bilingual Mental Lexicon: Interdisciplinary Approaches*. Bristol: Multilingual Matters, pp. 125–160.

Pavlenko, Aneta, and B. Malt. 2011. Kitchen Russian: Crosslinguistic differences and first language object naming by Russian-English bilinguals. *Bilingualism: Language and Cognition* 14: 19–45.

Pesetsky, David, and Esther Torrego. 2001. T-to-C movement: Causes and consequences. In Michael Kenstowicz (ed.), *Ken Hale: A Life in Language*. Cambridge, MA: MIT Press, pp. 355–426.

Pfau, Roland. 2009. *Grammar as Processor: A Distributed Morphology Account of Spontaneous Speech Errors*. Amsterdam: John Benjamins.

Pfau, Roland. 2016. Switching, blending and slipping. *Linguistic Approaches to Bilingualism* 6: 802–807.

Picallo, Carme. 2008. Gender and number in Romance. *Lingue e Linguaggio* 7: 47–66.

Pickering, Martin and Holly Branigan. 1998. The representation of verbs: Evidence from syntactic priming in language production. *Journal of Memory and Language* 39: 633–651.

Pickering, Martin J., and Victor S. Ferreira. 2008. "Structural priming: A critical review." *Psychological Bulletin* 134(3): 427–459.

Pierantozzi, Cristina. 2008. La relazione di accordo nel DP misto nel bilinguismo infantile precoce. PhD dissertation, University of Urbino.

Pierantozzi, Cristina. 2012. Agreement within the early mixed DP: What mixed agreement can tell us about the bilingual language faculty. In Kurt Braunmüller and Christoph Gabriel (eds.), *Multilingual Individuals and Multilingual Societies*. Amsterdam/Philadelphia: John Benjamins, pp. 137–152.

Poplack, Shana. 1980. "Sometimes I'll start a sentence in Spanish y termino en Español": Toward a typology of code-switching. *Linguistics* 18: 581–618.

Poplack, Shana. 1981. The syntactic structure and social function of code-switching. In R. Durán (ed.), *Latino Language and Communicative Behavior*. Norwood, NJ: Ablex, pp. 169–184.

Poplack, Shana, and Nathalie Dion. 2012. Myths and facts about loanword development. *Language Variation and Change* 24: 279–315.

Poplack, Shana, and Marjory Meechan. 1998. How languages fit together in codemixing. *International Journal of Bilingualism* 2(2): 127–138.

Preminger, Omer. 2014. *Agreement and Its Failures*. Cambridge, MA: MIT Press.

Purmohammad, M. 2015. Grammatical encoding in bilingual language production: A focus on code-switching. *Frontiers in Psychology*, 6, 1797. doi:10.3389/fpsyg.2015.01797.

Putnam, Michael T., Geraldine Legendre, and Paul Smolensky. 2016. How constrained is language mixing in bi- and uni-modal production? *Linguistic Approaches to Bilingualism* 6: 812–816.

Radford, Andrew, Tanja Kupisch, Regina Köppe, and Gabriele Azzaro. 2007. Concord, convergence and accommodation in bilingual children. *Bilingualism: Language and Cognition* 10: 239–256.

Ramchand, Gillian. 2008. *Verb Meaning and the Lexicon*. Cambridge University Press.

Richards, Norvin. 2016. *Contiguity Theory*. Cambridge, MA: MIT Press.

Riksem, Brita. 2017. Language mixing in American Norwegian noun phrases. Dissertation, Norwegian University for Science and Technology, Trodheim, Norway.

Riksem, Brita, Maren Grimstad, Terie Lohndal, and Tor Afarli (2019) Language mixing within verbs and nouns in American Norwegian. *Journal of Comparative Germanic Linguistics* 22: 189–209.

Rizzi, Luigi. 1982. *Issues in Italian Syntax*. Dordrecht: Foris.

Rizzi, Luigi. 1997. The fine structure of the left periphery. In Liliane Haegeman (ed.), *Elements of Grammar*. Dordrecht: Kluwer, pp. 281–337.

Roca, Iggy. 1989. The organisation of grammatical gender. *Transactions of the Philological Society* 87(1): 1–32.

Roeper, Tom. 1999. Universal bilingualism. *Bilingualism: Language and Cognition* 2: 169–186.

Saab, Andrés. 2008. Hacia una teoría de la identidad parcial en la ellipsis. PhD dissertation, University of Buenos Aires.

Sánchez, Liliana. 2003. *Quechua-Spanish Bilingualism: Interference and Convergence in Functional Categories*. Amsterdam: John Benjamins.

Sandalo, Filomena, and Hubert Truckenbrodt. 2002. Some notes on phonological phrasing in Brazilian Portuguese. In Aniko Csirmaz, Zhiqiang Li, Andrew Nevins, Olga Vaysman, and Michael Wagner (eds.), *MITWPL 42: Phonological Answers (and Their Corresponding Questions)*. Cambridge, MA: MIT Working Papers in Linguistics, pp. 285–310.

Sande, Ariane. 2018. C plus T is a necessary condition for pro-drop: Evidence from code-switching. Unpublished PhD dissertation, University of Illinois in Chicago. https://lcsl.uic.edu/hispanic-italian/research-groups/bilingualism-research-laboratory/research.

Sankoff, David, and Shana Poplack. 1981. A formal grammar for code-switching. *Papers in Linguistics* 14: 3–45.

Sankoff, David, Shana Poplack, and Swathi Vanniarajan. 1990. The case of the nonce loan in Tamil. *Language Variation and Change* 2: 71–101.

Sanoudaki, Eirini, and Guillaume Thierry. 2014. Juggling two grammars. In Enlli Mon Thomas and Ineke Mennen (eds.), *Advances in the Study of Bilingualism*. Bristol, UK: Multilingual Matters, pp. 216–232.

Schoonbaert, S., W. Duyck, M. Brysbaert, and R. J. Hartsuiker. 2009. Semantic and translation priming from a first language to a second and back: Making sense of the findings. *Memory & Cognition* 37: 569–586.

Selkirk, Elisabeth. 1995. Sentence prosody: Intonation, stress and phrasing. In John Goldsmith (ed.), *The Handbook of Phonological Theory*. Oxford: Blackwell, pp. 550–569.

Selkirk, Elisabeth, and Koichi Tateishi. 1991. Syntax and downstep in Japanese. In Carol Georgopoulos and Roberta Ishihara (eds.), *Interdisciplinary Approaches to Language: Essays in Honor of S.-Y. Kuroda*. Dordrecht, Kluwer, pp. 519–544.

Serratrice, Ludovica. 2016. Cross-linguistic influence, cross-linguistic priming and the nature of shared syntactic structures. *Linguistic Approaches to Bilingualism* 6: 822–827.

Shim, Ji Young. 2016. Mixed verbs in code-switching: The syntax of light verbs. *Languages* 1(8): 1–31.

Siloni, Tal, Julia Horvath, Hadar Klunover, and Ken Wexler. 2018. Idiom storage and the lexicon. *Journal of Linguistics* 54: 189–215.

Silva-Corvalán, Carmen. 2001. *Sociolinguistics and Pragmatics of Spanish*. Cambridge University Press.

Sprouse, Jon, and Diogo Almeida. 2018. Setting the empirical record straight: Acceptability judgments appear to be reliable, robust and replicable. *Behavioral and Brain Sciences* 40: 43–44.

Stadthagen, Hans, Luis López, Maria Carmen Parafita Couto, and Jorge Párraga. 2018. Using two-alternative forced choice tasks and Thurstone's law of comparative judgments for code-switching research. *Linguistic Approaches to Bilingualism* 8(1): 67–97.

Stefanich, Sara. 2019. A morphophonological account of Spanish/English word-internal code-switching. Unpublished PhD dissertation, University of Illinois in

Chicago. https://lcsl.uic.edu/hispanic-italian/research-groups/bilingualism-research-laboratory/research.

Stefanich, Sara, and Jennifer Cabrelli. 2018. Phonological factors of Spanish/English word internal code-switching. In Luis López (ed.), *Code-Switching: Experimental Answers to Theoretical Questions*. Amsterdam: John Benjamins, pp. 193–220.

Thierry, Guillaume, and Y. J. Wu. 2007. Brain potentials reveal unconscious translation during foreign language comprehension. *Proceedings of the National Academy of Sciences of the United States of America* 104: 12530–12535.

Toribio, Almeida Jacqueline. 2001. On the emergence of bilingual code-switching competence. *Bilingualism: Language and Cognition* 4(3): 203–231.

Valdés-Kroff, Jorge. 2016. Mixed NPs in Spanish-English bilingual speech. In Rosa E. Guzzardo Tamargo, Catherine M. Mazak, and M. Carmen Parafita Couto (eds.), *Spanish-English Code Switching in the Caribbean and the US*. Amsterdam: John Benjamins, pp. 281–319.

van den Bogaerde, B., and A. E. Baker. 2008. Bimodal language acquisition in kodas. In M. Bishop and S. L. Hicks (eds.), *HEARING, MOTHER FATHER DEAF: Hearing People in Deaf Families*. Washington, DC: Gallaudet University Press, pp. 99–131.

Van der Meij, Maartje, Fernando Cuetos, Manuel Carreiras, and Horacio Barber. 2011. Electrophysiological correlates of language switching in second language learners. *Psychophysiology* 48: 44–54.

Van Hell, Janet, Kaitlyn Litcofsky, and Caitlin Ting. 2015. Intra-sentential code-switching: Cognitive and neural approaches. In John Schwieter (ed.), *The Cambridge Handbook of Bilingual Processing*. Cambridge University Press, pp. 459–482.

Vaughan-Evans, Awel, Jan R. Kuipers, Guillaume Thierry, and Manon W. Jones. 2014. Anomalous transfer of syntax between languages. *The Journal of Cognitive Neuroscience* 34(24): 8333–8335.

Veenstra, Tonjes, and Luis López, 2016. Little v and cross-linguistic variation: Evidence from Code-Switching and Suriname Creoles. In Ermenegildo Bidese, Federica Cognola, and Manuela Caterina Moroni (eds.), *Theoretical Approaches to Linguistic Variation* [LA 234], Amsterdam/ Philadelphia: John Benjamins, pp. 317–336.

Vergara, Daniel. 2017. A Minimalist Analysis of Spanish Negative Concord. Unpublished PhD dissertation, University of Illinois in Chicago.

Vergara, Daniel. 2018. Basque complementizers under the microscope: A Spanish/Basque code-switching approach. In Luis López (ed.), *Code-Switching: Experimental Answers to Theoretical Questions*. Amsterdam: John Benjamins, pp. 221–254.

Vergara, Daniel and Luis López. 2017. Obliteration after Vocabulary Insertion. In K. Bellamy, M. Child, P. González, A. Muntendam, and M. C. Parafita Couto (eds.), *Multidisciplinary Approaches to Bilingualism in the Hispanic and Lusophone World*. Amsterdam: John Benjamins, pp. 261–282.

Volterra, Virginia, and Traute Taeschner. 1978. The acquisition and development of language by bilingual children. *Journal of Child Language* 5: 311–326.

White, Lydia. 2003. *Second Language Acquisition and Universal Grammar*. Cambridge University Press.

Williams, John. 2015. The bilingual lexicon. In John Taylor (ed.), *The Oxford Handbook of the Word*. Oxford University Press pp. 493–507.

Woolford, Ellen. 1983. Bilingual code-switching and syntactic theory. *Linguistic Inquiry* 14(3): 520–536.

Yip, Virginia, and Stephen Mathews. 2000. Syntactic transfer in a Cantonese-English bilingual child. *Bilingualism: Language and Cognition* 3(3): 193–208.

Yip, Virginia, and Stephen Matthews. 2009. Contact-induced grammaticalization. *Studies in Language* 33(2): 366–395.

Zentella, Ana Celia. 1997. *Growing up Bilingual*. Oxford: Blackwell.

Zwart, Jan-W. 2011. *The Syntax of Dutch*. Cambridge University Press.

Index